T0286224

Artificial Intelligence: Concepts, Techniques and Applications

Artificial Intelligence: Concepts, Techniques and Applications

Alexis Keller

Artificial Intelligence: Concepts, Techniques and Applications
Alexis Keller
ISBN: 978-1-63989-062-0 (Hardback)

Published by States Academic Press,
109 South 5th Street,
Brooklyn, NY 11249, USA

Cataloging-in-Publication Data

Artificial intelligence : concepts, techniques and applications / Alexis Keller.
p. cm.
Includes bibliographical references and index.
ISBN 978-1-63989-062-0
1. Artificial intelligence. 2. Fifth generation computers. 3. Neural computers.
I. Keller, Alexis.
Q335 .A78 2022
006.3--dc23

For more information regarding States Academic Press and its products, please visit the publisher's website www.statesacademicpress.com

Table of Contents

Preface

The ability of a digital computer to perform complex tasks which are associated with humans is termed as artificial intelligence. It is a multi-disciplinary field which employs the principles of computer science, information engineering, psychology, mathematics, philosophy and linguistics. The primary goals of research in artificial intelligence are knowledge representation, reasoning, learning, planning, perception, and the ability to move and manipulate objects. It uses statistical approaches and computational modeling methods to achieve its long term goal of general intelligence. Artificial intelligence can be divided into machine learning, deep learning, natural language processing and robotics. It finds extensive application in the fields of military simulation, delivery and distribution networks, strategic game systems and self-driving cars. The topics included in this book on artificial intelligence are of utmost significance and bound to provide incredible insights to readers. Different approaches, evaluations and methodologies on artificial intelligence have been included herein. This book is an essential guide for both academicians and those who wish to pursue this discipline further.

A foreword of all Chapters of the book is provided below:

Chapter 1 - Artificial intelligence is the ability demonstrated by machines to perform tasks successfully by simulating human intelligence. Knowledge representation and reasoning play an important role in artificial intelligence as they help represent information in a form understandable by a machine to solve complex tasks. Such machines are called intelligent agents. This chapter closely examines artificial intelligence and its related aspects to provide an extensive understanding of the subject; **Chapter 2 -** While all intelligent agents possessing artificial intelligence show a similarity in the way they mimic human intelligence to complete tasks, they can be differentiated into various categories based on their limits and capabilities. Artificial narrow intelligence, artificial general intelligence, artificial strong intelligence, reactive machines, united machines, self-aware machines, etc. are all different types of artificial intelligence which are covered in this chapter; **Chapter 3 -** Machine Learning can be defined as an application of artificial intelligence that provides machine systems the ability to automatically learn and improve from experience. According to this concept a computer program can learn and adapt to new data without human intervention given the right set of algorithms. This chapter has been carefully written to provide an easy understanding of machine learning and its related concepts; **Chapter 4 -** Natural language processing is a component of artificial intelligence that helps computer understand, interpret and manipulate human language in either a speech or text form. Born out of the necessity to fill the gap between human communication and computer understanding, natural language processing employs various methods like parsing and machine translation. The topics elaborated in this chapter will help the reader gain a better perspective of natural language processing and its techniques; **Chapter 5 -** Artificial intelligence finds diverse applications in the present world. The healthcare sector is a major beneficiary of the user of artificial intelligence. Even in other fields like robotics, virtual reality, optical character recognition or game theory, artificial intelligence is being employed for the benefit of mankind. This chapter delves into the applications of artificial intelligence to provide a better understanding.

I would like to thank the entire editorial team who made sincere efforts for this book and my family who supported me in my efforts of working on this book. I take this opportunity to thank all those who have been a guiding force throughout my life.

Alexis Keller

1

Understanding Artificial Intelligence

Artificial intelligence is the ability demonstrated by machines to perform tasks successfully by simulating human intelligence. Knowledge representation and reasoning play an important role in artificial intelligence as they help represent information in a form understandable by a machine to solve complex tasks. Such machines are called intelligent agents. This chapter closely examines artificial intelligence and its related aspects to provide an extensive understanding of the subject.

Artificial intelligence (AI) refers to the simulation of human intelligence in machines that are programmed to think like humans and mimic their actions. The term may also be applied to any machine that exhibits traits associated with a human mind such as learning and problem-solving. The ideal characteristic of artificial intelligence is its ability to rationalize and take actions that have the best chance of achieving a specific goal.

Artificial intelligence is based on the principle that human intelligence can be defined in a way that a machine can easily mimic it and execute tasks, from the most simple to those that are even more complex. The goals of artificial intelligence include learning, reasoning, and perception.

As technology advances, previous benchmarks that defined artificial intelligence become outdated. For example, machines that calculate basic functions or recognize text through optimal character recognition are no longer considered to embody artificial intelligence, since this function is now taken for granted as an inherent computer function. AI is continuously evolving to benefit many different industries. Machines are wired using a cross-disciplinary approach based in mathematics, computer science, linguistics, psychology, and more.

Algorithms often play a very important part in the structure of artificial intelligence, where simple algorithms are used in simple applications, while more complex ones help frame strong artificial intelligence.

Applications of Artificial Intelligence

The applications for artificial intelligence are endless. The technology can be applied to many different sectors and industries. AI is being tested and used in the healthcare industry for dosing drugs and different treatment in patients, and for surgical procedures in the operating room.

Other examples of machines with artificial intelligence include computers that play chess and self-driving cars. Each of these machines must weigh the consequences of any action they take, as each action will impact the end result. In chess, the end result is winning the game. For self-driving cars, the computer system must account for all external data and compute it to act in a way that prevents a collision.

Artificial intelligence also has applications in the financial industry, where it is used to detect and flag activity in banking and finance such as unusual debit card usage and large account deposits—all of which help a bank's fraud department. Applications for AI are also being used to help streamline and make trading easier. This is done by making supply, demand, and pricing of securities easier to estimate.

Categorization of Artificial Intelligence

Artificial intelligence can be divided into two different categories: weak and strong. Weak artificial intelligence embodies a system designed to carry out one particular job. Weak AI systems include video games such as the chess example from above and personal assistants such as Amazon's Alexa and Apple's Siri. You ask the assistant a question, it answers it for you.

Strong artificial intelligence systems are systems that carry on the tasks considered to be human-like. These tend to be more complex and complicated systems. They are programmed to handle situations in which they may be required to problem solve without having a person intervene. These kinds of systems can be found in applications like self-driving cars or in hospital operating rooms.

Special Considerations

- Since its beginning, artificial intelligence has come under scrutiny from scientists and the public alike. One common theme is the idea that machines will become so highly developed that humans will not be able to keep up and they will take off on their own, redesigning themselves at an exponential rate.
- Another is that machines can hack into people's privacy and even be weaponized. Other arguments debate the ethics of artificial intelligence and whether intelligent systems such as robots should be treated with the same rights as humans.
- Self-driving cars have been fairly controversial as their machines tend to be designed for the lowest possible risk and the least casualties. If presented with a scenario of colliding with one person or another at the same time, these cars would calculate the option that would cause the least amount of damage.
- Another contentious issue many people have with artificial intelligence is how it may affect human employment. With many industries looking to automate certain jobs through the use of intelligent machinery, there is a concern that people would be pushed out of the workforce. Self-driving cars may remove the need for taxis and car-share programs, while manufacturers may easily replace human labor with machines, making people's skills more obsolete.

Knowledge Representation

A knowledge representation is most fundamentally a surrogate, a substitute for the thing itself that is used to enable an entity to determine consequences by thinking rather than acting, that is, by reasoning about the world rather than taking action in it.

Second, it is a set of ontological commitments, that is, an answer to the question, In what terms should we think about the world?

Third, it is a fragmentary theory of intelligent reasoning expressed in terms of three components:

- The representation's fundamental conception of intelligent reasoning.
- The set of inferences that the representation sanctions.
- The set of inferences that it recommends.

Fourth, it is a medium for pragmatically efficient computation, that is, the computational environment in which thinking is accomplished. One contribution to this pragmatic efficiency is supplied by the guidance that a representation provides for organizing information to facilitate making the recommended inferences.

Fifth, it is a medium of human expression, that is, a language in which we say things about the world.

Understanding the roles and acknowledging their diversity has several useful consequences. First, each role requires something slightly different from a representation; each accordingly leads to an interesting and different set of properties that we want a representation to have.

Second, we believe the roles provide a framework that is useful for characterizing a wide variety of representations. We suggest that the fundamental mind set of a representation can be captured by understanding how it views each of the roles and that doing so reveals essential similarities and differences.

Third, we believe that some previous disagreements about representation are usefully disentangled when all five roles are given appropriate consideration. We demonstrate the clarification by revisiting and dissecting the early arguments concerning frames and logic.

Finally, we believe that viewing representations in this way has consequences for both research and practice. For research, this view provides one direct answer to a question of fundamental significance in the field. It also suggests adopting a broad perspective on what's important about a representation, and it makes the case that one significant part of the representation endeavor—capturing and representing the richness of the natural world—is receiving insufficient attention. We believe that this view can also improve practice by reminding practitioners about the inspirations that are the important sources of power for a variety of representations. Perhaps the most fundamental question about the concept of knowledge representation is, What is it? We believe that the answer is best understood in terms of the five fundamental roles that it plays.

Role: A Knowledge Representation is a Surrogate

Any intelligent entity that wants to reason about its world encounters an important, inescapable fact: Reasoning is a process that goes on internally, but most things it wants to reason about exist only externally. A program (or person) engaged in planning the assembly of a bicycle, for example, might have to reason about entities such as wheels, chains, sprockets, and handle bars, but such things exist only in the external world.

This unavoidable dichotomy is a fundamental rationale and role for a representation: It functions as a surrogate inside the reasoner, a stand-in for the things that exist in the world. Operations on and with representations substitute for operations on the real thing, that is, substitute for direct interaction with the world. In this view, reasoning itself is, in part, a surrogate for action in the world when we cannot or do not (yet) want to take that action.

Viewing representations as surrogates leads naturally to two important questions. The first question about any surrogate is its intended identity: What is it a surrogate for? There must be some form of correspondence specified between the surrogate and its intended referent in the world; the correspondence is the semantics for the representation.

The second question is fidelity: How close is the surrogate to the real thing? What attributes of the original does it capture and make explicit, and which does it omit? Perfect fidelity is, in general, impossible, both in practice and in principle. It is impossible in principle because anything other than the thing itself is necessarily different from the thing itself (in location if nothing else). Put the other way around, the only completely accurate representation of an object is the object itself. All other representations are inaccurate; they inevitably contain simplifying assumptions and, possibly, artifacts.

Two minor elaborations extend this view of representations as surrogates. First, it appears to serve equally well for intangible objects as well as tangible objects such as gear wheels: Representations function as surrogates for abstract notions such as actions, processes, beliefs, causality, and categories, allowing them to be described inside an entity so it can reason about them. Second, formal objects can of course exist inside the machine with perfect fidelity: Mathematical entities, for example, can be captured exactly, precisely because they are formal objects. Because almost any reasoning task will encounter the need to deal with natural objects (that is, those encountered in the real world) as well as formal objects, imperfect surrogates are pragmatically inevitable.

Two important consequences follow from the inevitability of imperfect surrogates. One consequence is that in describing the natural world, we must inevitably lie, by omission at least. At a minimum, we must omit some of the effectively limitless complexity of the natural world; in addition, our descriptions can introduce artifacts not present in the world.

The second and more important consequence is that all sufficiently broad-based reasoning about the natural world must eventually reach conclusions that are incorrect, independent of the reasoning process used and independent of the representation employed. Sound reasoning cannot save us: If the world model is somehow wrong (and it must be), some conclusions will be incorrect, no matter how carefully drawn. A better representation cannot save us: All representations are imperfect, and any imperfection can be a source of error.

The significance of the error can, of course, vary; indeed, much of the art of selecting a good representation is in finding one that minimizes (or perhaps even eliminates) error for the specific task at hand. But the unavoidable imperfection of surrogates means that we can supply at least one guarantee for any entity reasoning in any fashion about the natural world: If it reasons long enough and broadly enough, it is guaranteed to err.

Thus, drawing only sound inferences does not free reasoning from error; it can only ensure that inference is not the source of the error. Given that broad-based reasoning is inevitably wrong, the step from sound inference to other models of inference is thus not a move from total accuracy to error, but is instead a question of balancing the possibility of one more source of error against the gains (for example, efficiency) it might offer.

We do not suggest that unsound reasoning ought to be embraced casually, but we do claim that given the inevitability of error, even with sound reasoning, it makes sense to pragmatically evaluate the relative costs and benefits that come from using both sound and unsound reasoning methods.

Role

A Knowledge Representation is a Set of Ontological Commitments

If, as we argue, all representations are imperfect approximations to reality, each approximation attending to some things and ignoring others, then in selecting any representation, we are in the very same act unavoidably making a set of decisions about how and what to see in the world. That is, selecting a representation means making a set of ontological commitments. The commitments are, in effect, a strong pair of glasses that determine what we can see, bringing some part of the world into sharp focus at the expense of blurring other parts.

These commitments and their focusing blurring effect are not an incidental side effect of a representation choice; they are of the essence: A knowledge representation is a set of ontological commitments. It is unavoidably so because of the inevitable imperfections of representations. It is usefully so because judicious selection of commitments provides the opportunity to focus attention on aspects of the world that we believe to be relevant.

The focusing effect is an essential part of what a representation offers because the complexity of the natural world is overwhelming. We (and our reasoning machines) need guidance in deciding what in the world to attend to and what to ignore. The glasses supplied by a representation can provide this guidance: In telling us what and how to see, they allow us to cope with what would otherwise be untenable complexity and detail. Hence, the ontological commitment made by a representation can be one of its most important contributions.

There is a long history of work attempting to build good ontologies for a variety of task domains, including early work on ontology for liquids, the lumped element model widely used in representing electronic circuits as well as ontologies for time, belief, and even programming itself. Each of these ontologies offers a way to see some part of the world.

The lumped-element model, for example, suggests that we think of circuits in terms of components with connections between them, with signals flowing instantaneously along the connections. This view is useful, but it is not the only possible one. A different ontology arises if we need to attend to the electrodynamics in the device: Here, signals propagate at finite speed, and an object (such as a resistor) that was previously viewed as a single component with an input-output behavior might now have to be thought of as an extended medium through which an electromagnetic wave flows.

Ontologies can, of course, be written down in a wide variety of languages and notations (for exam-ple, logic, Lisp); the essential information is not the form of this language but the content, that is, the set of concepts offered as a way of thinking about the world. Simply put, the important part is notions such as connections and components, and not whether we choose to write them as predi-cates or Lisp constructs.

The commitment we make by selecting one or another ontology can produce a sharply different view of the task at hand. Consider the difference that arises in selecting the lumped element view of a circuit rather than the electrodynamic view of the same device. As a second example, medical diagnosis viewed in terms of rules (for example, MYCIN) looks substantially different from the same task viewed in terms of frames (for example, INTERNIST). Where MYCIN sees the medical world as made up of empirical associations connecting symptom to disease, INTERNIST sees a set of prototypes, in particular prototypical diseases that are to be matched against the case at hand.

Commitment Begins with the Earliest Choices

The INTERNIST example also demonstrates that there is significant and unavoidable ontological commitment even at the level of the familiar representation technologies. Logic, rules, frames, and so on, embody a viewpoint on the kinds of things that are important in the world. Logic, for example, involves a (fairly minimal) commitment to viewing the world in terms of individual entities and relations between them. Rule-based systems view the world in terms of attribute object-value triples and the rules of plausible inference that connect them, while frames have us thinking in terms of prototypical objects.

Thus, each of these representation technologies supplies its own view of what is important to attend to, and each suggests, conversely, that anything not easily seen in these terms may be ignored. This suggestion is, of course, not guaranteed to be correct because anything ignored can later prove to be relevant. But the task is hopeless in principle—every representation ignores something about the world; hence, the best we can do is start with a good guess. The existing representation technologies supply one set of guesses about what to attend to and what to ignore. Thus, selecting any of them involves a degree of ontological commitment: The selection will have a significant impact on our perception of, and approach to, the task and on our perception of the world being modeled.

The Commitments Accumulate in Layers

The ontological commitment of a representation thus begins at the level of the representation technologies and accumulates from there. Additional layers of commitment are made as we put the technology to work. The use of frame like structures in INTERNIST illustrates. At the most fundamental level, the decision to view diagnosis in terms of frames suggests thinking in terms of prototypes, defaults, and a taxonomic hierarchy. But what are the prototypes of, and how will the taxonomy be organized? An early description of the system shows how these questions were answered in the task at hand, supplying the second layer of commitment.

The knowledge base underlying the INTERNIST system is composed of two basic types of elements: disease entities and manifestations. It also contains a hierarchy of disease categories, organized primarily around the concept of organ systems, having at the top level such categories as "liver disease," "kidney disease," etc.

Thus, the prototypes are intended to capture prototypical diseases (for example, a classic case of a disease), and they will be organized in a taxonomy indexed around organ systems. This set of choices is sensible and intuitive, but clearly, it is not the only way to apply frames to the task; hence, it is another layer of ontological commitment.

At the third (and, in this case, final) layer, this set of choices is instantiated: Which diseases will be included, and in which branches of the hierarchy will they appear? Ontological questions that arise even at this level can be fundamental. Consider, for example, determining which of the following are to be considered diseases (that is, abnormal states requiring cure): alcoholism, homosexuality, and chronic fatigue syndrome. The ontological commitment here is sufficiently obvious and sufficiently important that it is often a subject of debate in the field itself, independent of building automated reasoners.

Similar sorts of decisions have to be made with all the representation technologies because each of them supplies only a first order guess about how to see the world: They offer a way of seeing but don't indicate how to instantiate this view. Frames suggest prototypes and taxonomies but do not tell us which things to select as prototypes, and rules suggest thinking in terms of plausible inferences but don't tell us which plausible inferences to attend to. Similarly, logic tells us to view the world in terms of individuals and relations but does not specify which individuals and relations to use. Thus, commitment to a particular view of the world starts with the choice of a representation technology and accumulates as subsequent choices are made about how to see the world in these terms.

A Knowledge Representation is not a Data Structure

Note that at each layer, even the first (for example, selecting rules or frames), the choices being made are about representation, not data structures. Part of what makes a language representational is that it carries meaning; that is, there is a correspondence between its constructs and things in the external world. In turn, this correspondence carries with it a constraint.

A semantic net, for example, is a representation, but a graph is a data structure. They are different kinds of entity, even though one is invariably used to implement the other, precisely because the net has (should have) a semantics. This semantics will be manifest in part because it constrains the network topology: A network purporting to describe family memberships as we know them cannot have a cycle in its parent links, but graphs (that is, data structures) are, of course, under no such constraint and can have arbitrary cycles. Although every representation must be implemented in the machine by some data structure, the representational property is in the correspondence to something in the world and in the constraint that correspondence imposes.

A Knowledge Representation is a Fragmentary Theory of Intelligent Reasoning

The third role for a representation is as a fragmentary theory of intelligent reasoning. This role comes about because the initial conception of a representation is typically motivated by some insight indicating how people reason intelligently or by some belief about what it means to reason intelligently at all.

The theory is fragmentary in two distinct senses:

- The representation typically incorporates only part of the insight or belief that motivated it.
- This insight or belief is, in turn, only a part of the complex and multifaceted phenomenon of intelligent reasoning.

A representation's theory of intelligent reasoning is often implicit but can be made more evident by examining its three components:

- The representation's fundamental conception of intelligent inference.
- The set of inferences that the representation sanctions.
- The set of inferences that it recommends.

Where the sanctioned inferences indicate what can be inferred at all, the recommended inferences are concerned with what should be inferred. (Guidance is needed because the set of sanctioned inferences is typically far too large to be used indiscriminately.) Where the ontology we examined earlier tells us how to see, the recommended inferences suggest how to reason.

These components can also be seen as the representation's answers to three corresponding fundamental questions:

- What does it mean to reason intelligently?
- What can we infer from what we know?
- What should we infer from what we know? Answers to these questions are at the heart of a representation's spirit and mind set; knowing its position on these issues tells us a great deal about it.

What is Intelligent Reasoning?

What are the essential, defining properties of intelligent reasoning? As a consequence of the relative youth of AI as a discipline, insights about the nature of intelligent reasoning have often come from work in other fields. Five fields—mathematical logic, psychology, biology, statistics, and economics—have provided the inspiration for five distinguishable notions of what constitutes intelligent reasoning.

One view, historically derived from mathematical logic, makes the assumption that intelligent reasoning is some variety of formal calculation, typically deduction; the modern exemplars of this view in AI are the logicists. A second view, rooted in psychology, sees reasoning as a characteristic human behavior and has given rise to both the extensive work on human problem solving and the large collection of knowledge-based systems.

A third approach, loosely rooted in biology, takes the view that the key to reasoning is the architecture of the machinery that accomplishes it; hence, reasoning is a characteristic stimulus-response behavior that emerges from the parallel interconnection of a large collection of very simple processors. Researchers working on several varieties of connectionism are the current descendants of this line of work. A fourth approach, derived from probability theory, adds to logic the notion of uncertainty, yielding a view in which reasoning intelligently means obeying the axioms of probability theory. A fifth view, from economics, adds the further ingredient of values and preferences, leading to a view of intelligent reasoning that is defined by adherence to the tenets of utility theory.

Table: Views of Intelligent Reasoning and Their Intellectual Origins.

Mathematical Logic	Psychology	Biology	Statistics	Economics
Aristotle				
Descartes				
Boole	James		Laplace	Bentham
				Pareto
Frege			Bernoullii	Friedman
Peano				
	Hebb	Lashley	Bayes	

Goedel	Bruner	Rosen-blatt		
Post	Miller	Ashby	Tversky	Von Neumann
Church	Newell	Lettvin	Kahneman	Simon
Turing	Simon	McCull-och, Pitts		Raiffa
Davis		Heubel, Weisel		
Putnam				
Robinson				
Logic PROLOG	SOAR KBS, Frames	Connec-tionism	Casual Networks	Rational Agents

Briefly exploring the historical development of the first two of these views (the logical and the psychological) illustrates the different conceptions they have of the fundamental nature of intelligent reasoning and demonstrates the deep-seated differences in mind set that arise as a consequence.

Consider first the tradition that surrounds mathematical logic as a view of intelligent reasoning. This view has its historical origins in Aristotle's efforts to accumulate and catalog the syllogisms in an attempt to determine what should be taken as a convincing argument. The line continues with René Descartes, whose analytic geometry showed that Euclid's work, apparently concerned with the stuff of pure thought (lines of zero width, perfect circles of the sorts only the gods could make), could, in fact, be married to algebra, a form of calculation, something mere mortals can do.

By the time of Gottfried Wilhelm von Leibnitz in the seventeenth century, the agenda was specific and telling: He sought nothing less than a calculus of thought, one that would permit the resolution of all human disagreement with the simple invocation, "Let us compute." By this time, there was a clear and concrete belief that as Euclid's once godlike and unreachable geometry could be captured with algebra, so some (or perhaps any) variety of that ephemeral stuff called thought might be captured in calculation, specifically, logical deduction.

In the nineteenth century, G. Boole provided the basis for propositional calculus in his "Laws of Thought"; later work by G. Frege and G. Peano provided additional foundation for the modern form of predicate calculus. Work by M. Davis, H. Putnam, and G. Robinson in the twentieth century provides the final steps in sufficiently mechanizing deduction to enable the first automated theorem provers. The modern offspring of this line of intellectual development include the many efforts that use first-order logic as a representation and some variety of deduction as the reasoning engine as well as the large body of work with the explicit agenda of making logical reasoning computational, exemplified by PROLOG.

This line of development clearly illustrates how approaches to representation are founded on and embed a view of the nature of intelligent reasoning. There is here, for example, the historical development of the underlying premise that reasoning intelligently means reasoning logically; anything else is a mistake or an aberration. Allied with this premise is the belief that logically, in turn, means first-order logic, typically, sound deduction. By simple transitivity, these two theories collapse into one key part of the view of intelligent reasoning underlying logic: Reasoning intelligently means reasoning in the fashion defined by first-order logic. A second important part of the view is the allied belief that intelligent reasoning is a process that can be captured in a formal description, particularly a formal description that is both precise and concise.

But very different views of the nature of intelligent reasoning are also possible. One distinctly different view is embedded in the part of AI that is influenced by the psychological tradition. This tradition broke through the stimulus-response view demanded by behaviorism and suggested instead that human problem-solving behavior could usefully be viewed in terms of goals, plans, and other complex mental structures. Modern manifestations include work on SOAR as a general mechanism for producing intelligent reasoning and knowledge-based systems as a means of capturing human expert reasoning.

Comparing these two traditions reveals significant differences and illustrates the consequences of adopting one or the other view of intelligent reasoning. In the logicist tradition intelligent reasoning is taken to be a form of calculation, typically, deduction in first-order logic, while the tradition based in psychology takes as the defining characteristic of intelligent reasoning that it is a particular variety of human behavior. In the logicist view, the object of interest is, thus, a construct definable in formal terms through mathematics, while for those influenced by the psychological tradition, it is an empirical phenomenon from the natural world. Thus, there are two very different assumptions here about the essential nature of the fundamental phenomenon to be captured.

A second contrast arises in considering the character of the answers each seeks. The logicist view has traditionally sought compact and precise characterizations of intelligence, looking for the kind of characterizations encountered in mathematics (and at times in physics). By contrast, the psychological tradition suggests that intelligence is not only a natural phenomenon, it is also an inherently complex natural phenomenon: As human anatomy and physiology are inherently complex systems resulting from a long process of evolution, so perhaps is intelligence. As such, intelligence may be a large and fundamentally ad hoc collection of mechanisms and phenomena, one that complete and concise descriptions might not be possible for.

Several useful consequences result from understanding the different positions on this fundamental question that are taken by each tradition. First, it demonstrates that selecting any of the modern offspring of these traditions—that is, any of the representation technologies shown at the bottom of the table—means choosing more than a representation. In the same act, we are also selecting a conception of the fundamental nature of intelligent reasoning.

Second, these conceptions differ in important ways: There are fundamental differences in the conception of the phenomenon we are trying to capture. The different conceptions in turn mean there are deep-seated differences in the character and the goals of the various research efforts that are trying to create intelligent programs. Simply put, different conceptions of the nature of intelligent reasoning lead to different goals, definitions of success, and different artifacts being created.

Finally, these differences are rarely articulated. In turn, this lack of articulation leads to arguments that may be phrased in terms of issues such as representation choice (for example, the virtues of sound reasoning in first-order predicate calculus versus the difficult-to-characterize inferences produced by frame-based systems) when the real issues are, we believe, the different conceptions of the fundamental nature of intelligence. Understanding the different positions assists in analyzing and sorting out the issues appropriately.

Which Inferences are Sanctioned?

The second component of a representation's theory of intelligent reasoning is its set of sanctioned inferences, that is, a selected set of inferences that are deemed appropriate conclusions to draw from the information available. The classic definition is supplied by traditional formal logic, where the only sanctioned inferences are sound inferences (those encompassed by logical entailment, in which every model for the axiom set is also a model for the conclusion). This answer has a number of important benefits, including being intuitively satisfying (a sound argument never introduces error), explicit (so we know precisely what we're talking about), precise enough that it can be the subject of formal proofs, and old enough that we have accumulated a significant body of experience with it.

Logic has also explored several varieties of unsound inference, including circumscription and abduction. This exploration has typically been guided by the requirement that there be "a well-motivated model-theoretic justification", such as the minimal model criterion of circumscription. This requirement maintains a fundamental component of the logicist approach: Although it is willing to arrive at conclusions that are true in some subset of the models (rather than true in every model), the set of sanctioned inferences is still conceived of in model-theoretic terms and is specified precisely in these terms.

Other representations have explored other definitions: probabilistic reasoning systems sanction the inferences specified by probability theory, while work on rational agents relies on concepts from the theory of economic rationality.

Among the common knowledge representation technologies, rule-based systems capture guesses of the sort that a human expert makes, guesses that are not necessarily either sound or true in any model. A frame-based representation encourages jumping to possibly incorrect conclusions based on good matches, expectations, or defaults. Both of these representations share the psychological tradition of defining the set of sanctioned inferences with reference to the behavior of the human expert rather than reference to an abstract formal model.

As these examples show, different approaches to representation specify sanctioned inferences in ways that differ in both content and form. Where the specification for logic, for example, is expressed in terms of model theory and is mathematically precise, other representations provide answers phrased in other terms, often with considerably less precision. Frames theory, for example, offers a definition phrased in terms of human behavior and is specified only approximately.

The differences in both content and style in turn have their origin in the different conceptions of intelligent reasoning that were explored previously. Phrasing the definition in terms of human behavior is appropriate for frames because the theory conceives of intelligent reasoning as a characteristic form of human behavior. In attempting to describe this behavior, the theory is faced with the task of characterizing a complex empirical phenomenon that can be captured only roughly at the moment and that might never be specifiable with mathematical precision, hence the appropriateness of an approximate answer.

For frames theory then, the specification of sanctioned inferences is both informal and empirical, as an unavoidable consequence of its conception of intelligence. The work (and other work like it) is neither sloppy nor causally lacking in precision; the underlying conception of intelligent reasoning dictates a different approach to the task, a different set of terms in which to express the answer, and a different focus for the answer.

For frames theory then, the specification of sanctioned inferences is both informal and empirical, as an unavoidable consequence of its conception of intelligence. The work (and other work like it) is neither sloppy nor causally lacking in precision; the underlying conception of intelligent reasoning dictates a different approach to the task, a different set of terms in which to express the answer, and a different focus for the answer.

The broader point here is to acknowledge the legitimacy of a variety of approaches to specifying sanctioned inferences: Model theory might be familiar and powerful, but even for formal systems, it is not the only possible language. More broadly still, formal definitions are not the only terms in which the answer can be specified. The choice of appropriate vocabulary and the degree of formality depends, in turn, on the basic conception of intelligent behaviour.

Which Inferences are Recommended?

While sanctioned inferences tell us what conclusions we are permitted to make, this set is invariably very large and, hence, provides insufficient constraint. Any automated system attempting to reason, guided only by knowing what inferences are sanctioned, and soon finds itself overwhelmed by choices. Hence, we need more than an indication of which inferences we can legally make; we also need some indication of which inferences are appropriate to make, that is, intelligent. This indication is supplied by the set of recommended inferences. Note that the need for a specification of recommended inferences means that in specifying a representation, we also need to say something about how to reason intelligently. Representation and reasoning are inextricably and usefully intertwined: A knowledge representation is a theory of intelligent reasoning.

This theory often results from observation of human behavior. Minsky's original exposition of frame theory, for example, offers a clear example of a set of recommended inferences inspired by observing human behavior. Consider the following statement from Minsky's abstract to his original frames paper:

> "This is a partial theory of thinking. Whenever one encounters a new situation (or makes a substantial change in one's viewpoint), he selects from memory a structure called a frame; a remembered framework to be adapted to fit reality by changing details as necessary".

The first sentence illustrates the intertwining of reasoning and representation: This topic is about knowledge representation, but it announces at the outset that it is also a theory of thinking. In turn, this theory arose from an insight about human intelligent reasoning, namely, how people might manage to make the sort of simple common sense inferences that appear difficult to capture in programs. The theory singles out a particular set of inferences to recommend, namely, reasoning in the style of anticipatory matching.

Similar characterizations of recommended inferences can be given for most other representation technologies. Semantic nets in their original form, for example, recommend bidirectional propagation through the net, inspired by the interconnected character of word definitions and the part of human intelligence manifested in the ability of people to find connections between apparently disparate concepts. The rules in knowledge based systems recommend plausible inferences, inspired by the observation of human expert reasoning. By contrast, logic has traditionally taken a minimalist stance on this issue. The representation itself offers only a theory of sanctioned inferences, seeking to remain silent on the question of which inferences to recommend.

The silence on this issue is motivated by a desire for generality in the inference machinery and a declarative (that is, use-dependent) form for the language, both fundamental goals of the logicist approach: "Logicists strive to make the inference process as uniform and domain independent as possible and to represent all knowledge (even the knowledge about how to use knowledge) declaratively".

But a representation with these goals cannot single out any particular set of inferences to recommend for two reasons. First, if the inference process is to be general and uniform (that is, work on all problems and work in the same way), it must be neutral about which inferences to recommend; any particular subset of inferences it attempted to single out might be appropriate in one situation but fatally bad in another because no inference strategy (unit preference, set of support, and so on) is universally appropriate. Second, if statements in the language are to be declarative, they must express a fact without any indication of how to reason with it (use-free expression is a defining characteristic of a declarative representation). Hence, the inference engine can't recommend any inferences (or it loses its generality and uniformity), and the statements of fact in the language cannot recommend any inferences (because by embedding such information, they lose their declarative character). Thus, the desire for generality and use-free expression prevents the representation itself from selecting inferences to recommend. But if the representation itself cannot make the recommendation, the user must because the alternative—unguided search—is untenable.

Requiring the user to select inferences is, in part, a deliberate virtue of the logicist approach: Preventing the representation from selecting inferences and, hence, requiring the user to do so offers the opportunity for this information to be represented explicitly rather than embedded implicitly in the machinery of the representation (as, for example, in rule-based systems or PROLOG).

One difficulty with this admirable goal arises in trying to provide the user with the tools to express the strategies and guide the system. Three approaches are commonly used: have the user tell the system what to do, have the user lead it into doing the right thing, and build in special-purpose inference strategies. By telling the system what to do, we mean that the user must recommend a set of inferences by writing statements in the same (declarative) language used to express facts about the world. By leading the system into doing the right thing, we mean that the user must carefully select the axioms, theorems, and lemmas supplied to the system. The presence of a lemma, for example, is not simply a fact the system should know; it also provides a way of abbreviating a long chain of deductions into a single step, in effect allowing the system to take a large step in a certain direction (namely, the direction in which the lemma takes us). By carefully selecting facts and lemmas, the user can indirectly recommend a particular set of inferences. By special-purpose inference strategies, we mean building specific control strategies directly into the theorem prover. This approach can offer significant speedup and a pragmatically useful level of computational efficiency.

Each of these approaches has both benefits and drawbacks. Expressing reasoning strategies in first-order logic is in keeping with the spirit of the logicist approach, namely, explicit representation of knowledge in a uniform, declarative representation. But this approach is often problematic in practice: a language designed to express facts declaratively is not necessarily good for expressing the imperative information characteristic of a reasoning strategy.

Careful selection of lemmas is, at best, an indirect encoding of the guidance information to be supplied. Finally, special-purpose deduction mechanisms are powerful but embed the reasoning strategy both invisibly and procedurally, defeating the original goals of domain-independent inference and explicit, declarative representation.

On the negative side, the task of guiding the system is left to the user, with no conceptual assistance offered, and the practices that result at times defeat some of the key goals that motivated the approach at the outset.

A Knowledge Representation is a Medium for Efficient Computation

From a purely mechanistic view, reasoning in machines (and, perhaps, in people) is a computational process. Simply put, to use a representation, we must compute with it. As a result, questions about computational efficiency are inevitably central to the notion of representation.

This fact has long been recognized, at least implicitly, by representation designers: Along with their specification of a set of recommended inferences, representations typically offer a set of ideas about how to organize information in ways that facilitate making these inferences.

The notion of triggers and procedural attachment in frames is not so much a statement about what procedures to write (the theory is rather vague here) as it is a description of a useful way to organize information, for example (paraphrasing the previous quotation), attach to each frame information about how to use the frame and what to do if expectations are not confirmed. Similarly, organizing frames into taxonomic hierarchies both suggests taxonomic reasoning and facilitates its execution (as in structured inheritance networks).

Other representations provide similar guidance. Traditional semantic nets facilitate bidirectional propagation by the simple expedient of providing an appropriate set of links, while rule-based systems facilitate plausible inferences by supplying indexes from goals to rules whose conclusion matches (backward chaining) and from facts to rules whose premise matches (forward chaining).

While the issue of efficient use of representations has been addressed by representation designers, in the larger sense, the field appears to have been historically ambivalent in its reaction. Early recognition of the notion of heuristic adequacy demonstrates that early on, researchers appreciated the significance of the computational properties of a representation, but the tone of much subsequent work in logic suggested that epistemology (knowledge content) alone mattered and defined computational efficiency out of the agenda. Of course, epistemology does matter, and it can be useful to study it without the potentially distracting concerns about speed. But eventually, we must compute with our representations; hence efficiency must be part of the agenda.

The pendulum later swung sharply over to what we might call the computational imperative view. Some work in this vein offered representation languages whose design was strongly driven by the desire to provide not only efficiency but also guaranteed efficiency. The result appears to be a language of significant speed but restricted power.

Either end of this spectrum seems problematic: We ignore computational considerations at our peril, but we can also be overly concerned with them, producing representations that are fast but inadequate for real use.

A Knowledge Representation is a Medium of Human Expression

Finally, knowledge representations are also the means by which we express things about the world, the medium of expression and communication in which we tell the machine (and perhaps one another) about the world. This role for representations is inevitable as long as we need to tell the machine (or other people) about the world and as long as we do so by creating and communicating representations. Thus, the fifth role for knowledge representations is as a medium of expression and communication for our use.

In turn, this role presents two important sets of questions. One set is familiar: How well does the representation function as a medium of expression? How general is it? How precise? Does it provide expressive adequacy? and so on.

An important question that is discussed less often is, How well does it function as a medium of communication? That is, how easy is it for us to talk or think in this language? What kinds of things are easily said in the language, and what kinds of things are so difficult that they are pragmatically impossible?

Note that the questions here are of the form, How easy is it? rather than, Can we? This language is one that we must use; so, things that are possible in principle are useful but insufficient; the real question is one of pragmatic utility. If the representation makes things possible but not easy, then as real users we might never know whether we misunderstood the representation and just do not know how to use it or whether it truly cannot express some things that we would like to say. A representation is the language in which we communicate; hence, we must be able to speak it without heroic effort.

Types of Knowledge

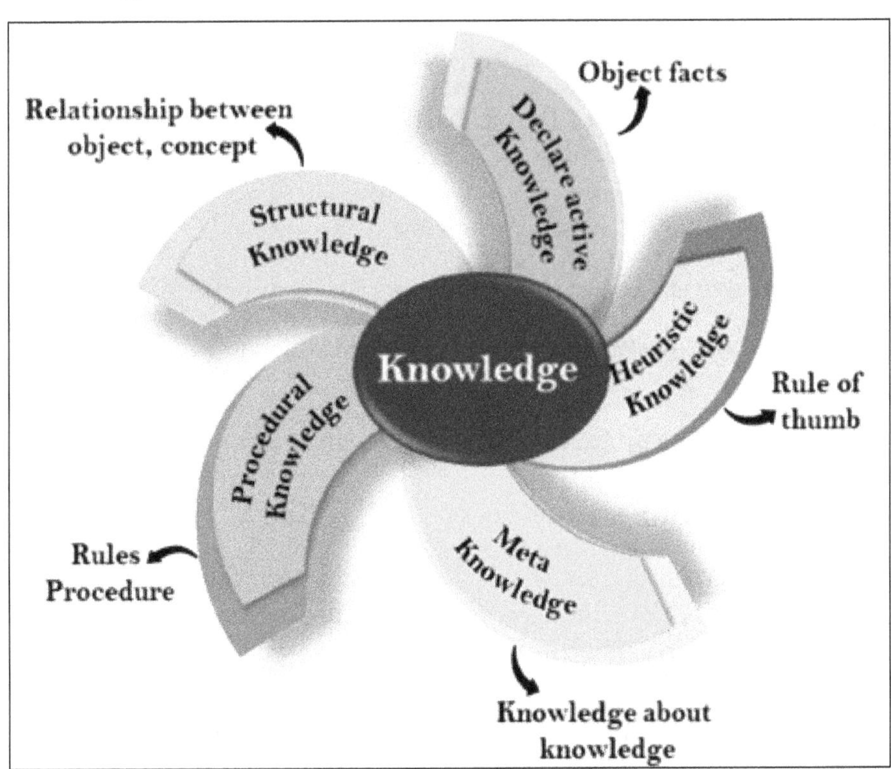

Following are the various types of knowledge:

Declarative Knowledge

- Declarative knowledge is to know about something.
- It includes concepts, facts, and objects.
- It is also called descriptive knowledge and expressed in declarative sentences.
- It is simpler than procedural language.

Procedural Knowledge

- It is also known as imperative knowledge.
- Procedural knowledge is a type of knowledge which is responsible for knowing how to do something.
- It can be directly applied to any task.
- It includes rules, strategies, procedures, agendas, etc.
- Procedural knowledge depends on the task on which it can be applied.

Meta-knowledge

- Knowledge about the other types of knowledge is called Meta-knowledge.

Heuristic Knowledge

- Heuristic knowledge is representing knowledge of some experts in a filed or subject.
- Heuristic knowledge is rules of thumb based on previous experiences, awareness of approaches, and which are good to work but not guaranteed.

Structural Knowledge

- Structural knowledge is basic knowledge to problem-solving.
- It describes relationships between various concepts such as kind of, part of, and grouping of something.
- It describes the relationship that exists between concepts or objects.

The Relation between Knowledge and Intelligence

Knowledge of real-worlds plays a vital role in intelligence and same for creating artificial intelligence. Knowledge plays an important role in demonstrating intelligent behavior in AI agents. An agent is only able to accurately act on some input when he has some knowledge or experience about that input. Let's suppose if you met some person who is speaking in a language which you don't know, then how you will able to act on that. The same thing applies to the intelligent behavior of the agents.

There is one decision maker which act by sensing the environment and using knowledge. But if the knowledge part will not present then, it cannot display intelligent behavior.

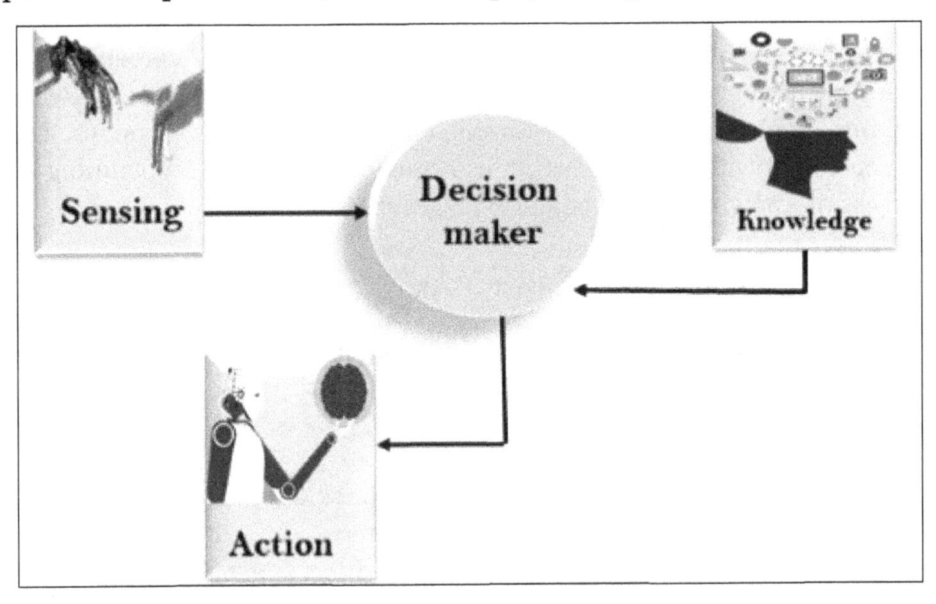

AI knowledge Cycle

An Artificial intelligence system has the following components for displaying intelligent behavior:

- Perception,
- Learning,
- Knowledge Representation and Reasoning,
- Planning,
- Execution.

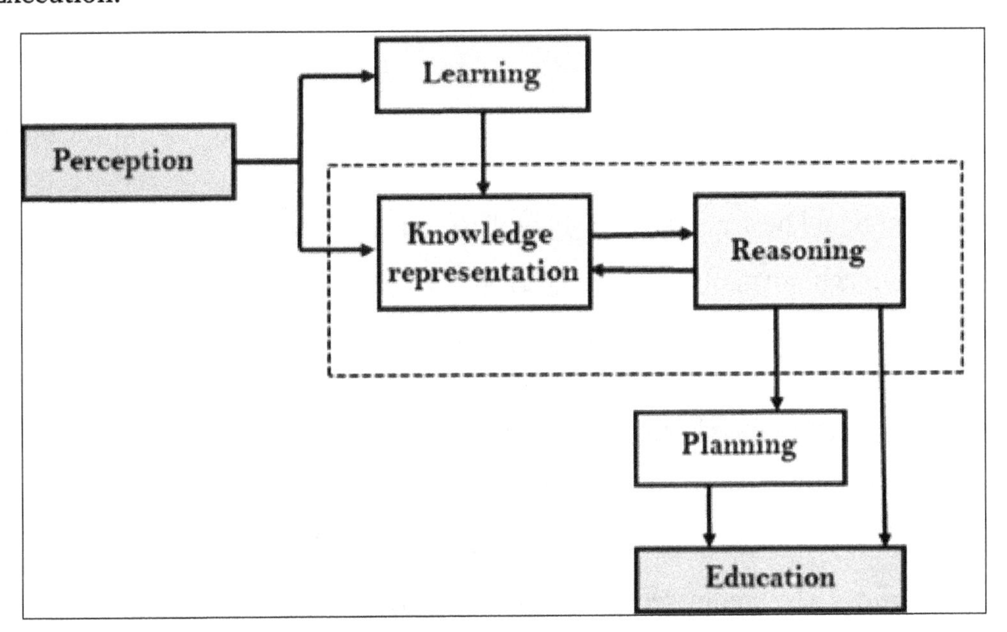

The above diagram is showing how an AI system can interact with the real world and what components help it to show intelligence. AI system has Perception component by which it retrieves information from its environment. It can be visual, audio or another form of sensory input. The learning component is responsible for learning from data captured by Perception comportment. In the complete cycle, the main components are knowledge representation and Reasoning. These two components are involved in showing the intelligence in machine-like humans. These two components are independent with each other but also coupled together. The planning and execution depend on analysis of Knowledge representation and reasoning.

Approaches to Knowledge Representation

There are mainly four approaches to knowledge representation, which are given below:

Simple Relational Knowledge

- It is the simplest way of storing facts which uses the relational method, and each fact about a set of the object is set out systematically in columns.
- This approach of knowledge representation is famous in database systems where the relationship between different entities is represented.
- This approach has little opportunity for inference.

Example: The following is the simple relational knowledge representation.

Player	Weight	Age
Player1	65	23
Player2	58	18
Player3	75	24

Inheritable Knowledge

- In the inheritable knowledge approach, all data must be stored into a hierarchy of classes.
- All classes should be arranged in a generalized form or a hierarchal manner.
- In this approach, we apply inheritance property.
- Elements inherit values from other members of a class.
- This approach contains inheritable knowledge which shows a relation between instance and class, and it is called instance relation.
- Every individual frame can represent the collection of attributes and its value.
- In this approach, objects and values are represented in Boxed nodes.
- We use Arrows which point from objects to their values.

Example:

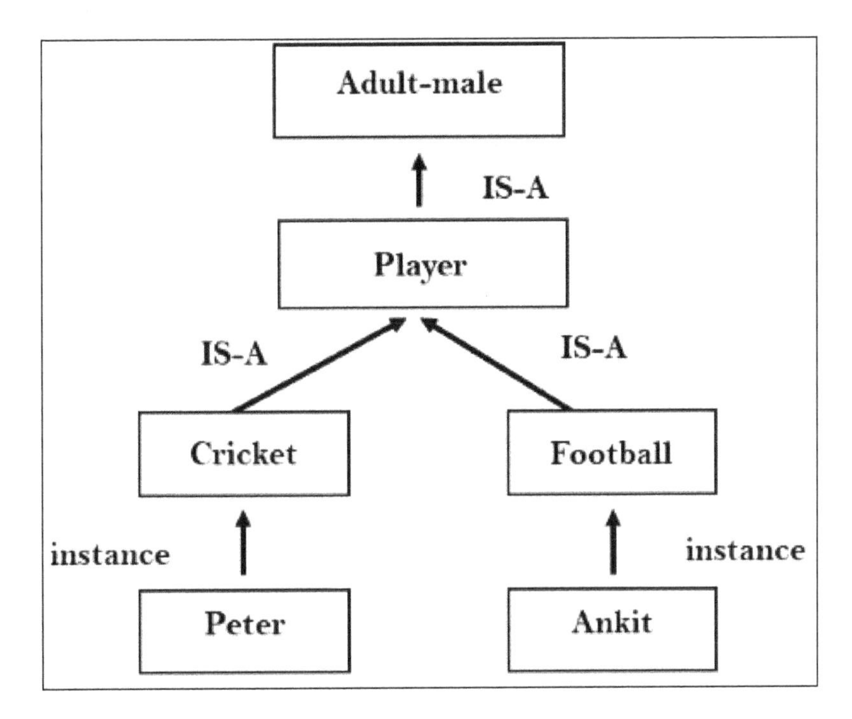

Inferential Knowledge

- Inferential knowledge approach represents knowledge in the form of formal logics.
- This approach can be used to derive more facts.
- It guaranteed correctness.
- Example: Let's suppose there are two statements:
    - Marcus is a man.
    - All men are mortal.
    - Then it can represent.

  man(Marcus)

  $\forall x$ = man (x) $\longrightarrow$ mortal (x)s

Procedural Knowledge

- Procedural knowledge approach uses small programs and codes which describes how to do specific things, and how to proceed.
- In this approach, one important rule is used which is If-Then rule.
- In this knowledge, we can use various coding languages such as LISP language and Prolog language.
- We can easily represent heuristic or domain-specific knowledge using this approach.

- But it is not necessary that we can represent all cases in this approach.

Requirements for Knowledge Representation System

A good knowledge representation system must possess the following properties:

- Representational Accuracy: KR system should have the ability to represent all kind of required knowledge.
- Inferential Adequacy: KR system should have ability to manipulate the representational structures to produce new knowledge corresponding to existing structure.
- Inferential Efficiency: The ability to direct the inferential knowledge mechanism into the most productive directions by storing appropriate guides.
- Acquisitional efficiency: The ability to acquire the new knowledge easily using automatic methods.

Reasoning

The reasoning is the mental process of deriving logical conclusion and making predictions from available knowledge, facts, and beliefs. Or we can say, "Reasoning is a way to infer facts from existing data." It is a general process of thinking rationally, to find valid conclusions. In artificial intelligence, the reasoning is essential so that the machine can also think rationally as a human brain, and can perform like a human.

Types of Reasoning

In artificial intelligence, reasoning can be divided into the following categories:

- Deductive reasoning.
- Inductive reasoning.
- Abductive reasoning.
- Common Sense Reasoning.
- Monotonic Reasoning.
- Non-monotonic Reasoning.

Deductive Reasoning

- Deductive reasoning is deducing new information from logically related known information. It is the form of valid reasoning, which means the argument's conclusion must be true when the premises are true.
- Deductive reasoning is a type of propositional logic in AI, and it requires various rules and facts. It is sometimes referred to as top-down reasoning, and contradictory to inductive reasoning.

- In deductive reasoning, the truth of the premises guarantees the truth of the conclusion.
- Deductive reasoning mostly starts from the general premises to the specific conclusion.
    - Example:
        - Premise-1: All the human eats veggies.
        - Premise-2: Suresh is human.
        - Conclusion: Suresh eats veggies.

The general process of deductive reasoning:

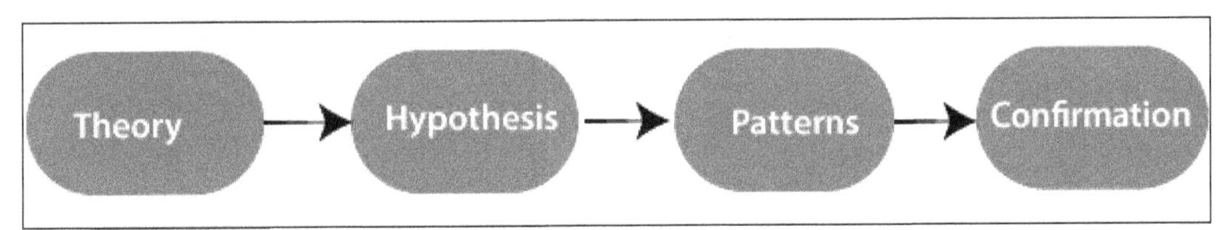

Inductive Reasoning

- Inductive reasoning is a form of reasoning to arrive at a conclusion using limited sets of facts by the process of generalization. It starts with the series of specific facts or data and reaches to a general statement or conclusion.
- Inductive reasoning is a type of propositional logic, which is also known as cause-effect reasoning or bottom-up reasoning.
- In inductive reasoning, we use historical data or various premises to generate a generic rule, for which premises support the conclusion.
- In inductive reasoning, premises provide probable supports to the conclusion, so the truth of premises does not guarantee the truth of the conclusion.
    - Example:
        - Premise: All of the pigeons we have seen in the zoo are white.
        - Conclusion: Therefore, we can expect all the pigeons to be white.

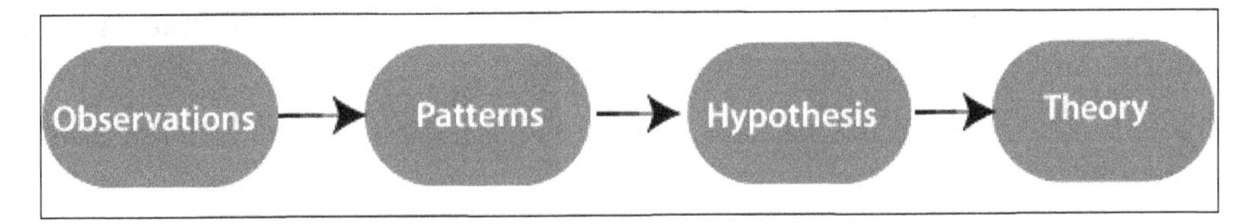

Abductive Reasoning

- Abductive reasoning is a form of logical reasoning which starts with single or multiple observations then seeks to find the most likely explanation or conclusion for the observation.

- Abductive reasoning is an extension of deductive reasoning, but in abductive reasoning, the premises do not guarantee the conclusion.

Example:

- Implication: Cricket ground is wet if it is raining.
- Axiom: Cricket ground is wet.

Conclusion it is raining.

Common Sense Reasoning

- Common sense reasoning is an informal form of reasoning, which can be gained through experiences.
- Common Sense reasoning simulates the human ability to make presumptions about events which occurs on every day.
- It relies on good judgment rather than exact logic and operates on heuristic knowledge and heuristic rules.

Example:

- One person can be at one place at a time.
- If I put my hand in a fire, then it will burn.

The above two statements are the examples of common sense reasoning which a human mind can easily understand and assume.

Monotonic Reasoning

- In monotonic reasoning, once the conclusion is taken, then it will remain the same even if we add some other information to existing information in our knowledge base. In monotonic reasoning, adding knowledge does not decrease the set of prepositions that can be derived.
- To solve monotonic problems, we can derive the valid conclusion from the available facts only, and it will not be affected by new facts.
- Monotonic reasoning is not useful for the real-time systems, as in real time, facts get changed, so we cannot use monotonic reasoning.
- Monotonic reasoning is used in conventional reasoning systems, and a logic-based system is monotonic.
- Any theorem proving is an example of monotonic reasoning.

Example:

- Earth revolves around the Sun.

It is a true fact, and it cannot be changed even if we add another sentence in knowledge base like, “The moon revolves around the earth” Or “Earth is not round,” etc.

Advantages of Monotonic Reasoning

- In monotonic reasoning, each old proof will always remain valid.
- If we deduce some facts from available facts, then it will remain valid for always.

Disadvantages of Monotonic Reasoning

- We cannot represent the real world scenarios using Monotonic reasoning.
- Hypothesis knowledge cannot be expressed with monotonic reasoning, which means facts should be true.
- Since we can only derive conclusions from the old proofs, so new knowledge from the real world cannot be added.

Non-monotonic Reasoning

- In Non-monotonic reasoning, some conclusions may be invalidated if we add some more information to our knowledge base.
- Logic will be said as non-monotonic if some conclusions can be invalidated by adding more knowledge into our knowledge base.
- Non-monotonic reasoning deals with incomplete and uncertain models.
- "Human perceptions for various things in daily life, "is a general example of non-monotonic reasoning.

Example: Let suppose the knowledge base contains the following knowledge:

- Birds can fly.
- Penguins cannot fly.
- Pitty is a bird.

So from the above sentences, we can conclude that Pitty can fly.

However, if we add one another sentence into knowledge base "Pitty is a penguin", which concludes "Pitty cannot fly", so it invalidates the above conclusion.

Advantages of Non-monotonic Reasoning

- For real-world systems such as Robot navigation, we can use non-monotonic reasoning.
- In Non-monotonic reasoning, we can choose probabilistic facts or can make assumptions.

Disadvantages of Non-monotonic Reasoning

- In non-monotonic reasoning, the old facts may be invalidated by adding new sentences.
- It cannot be used for theorem proving.

Intelligent Agents

An AI agent can have mental properties like knowledge, belief, intention, etc. A rational agent might be anything which makes decisions, as an individual, firm, machine, or software.

It acts with the simplest outcome after considering past and current percepts (agent's perceptual inputs at a given instance). Intelligent agents are often described schematically as an abstract functional system almost like a computer virus. Researchers like Russell & Norvig consider goal-directed behaviour to be the essence of intelligence; a normative agent is often labelled with a term borrowed from economics, "rational agent". During this rational-action paradigm, an AI possesses an indoor "model" of its environment. This model encapsulates all the agent's beliefs about the planet. In this agent has some "objective function" that encapsulates all the AI's goals that are required. Such an agent is meant to make and execute whatever plan will, upon completion, maximise the arithmetic mean of the target function.

A reinforcement learning agent can have a "reward function" that permits the programmers to shape the AI's desired behaviour, and an evolutionary algorithm's behaviour is formed by a "fitness function of AI". An abstract is the descriptions of intelligent agents that are sometimes called abstract intelligent agents (AIA) because it is difficult to differentiate them from their real-world implementations as computer systems, biological systems, or organisations. Some autonomous intelligent agents are designed to function within the absence of human intervention.

Types of Artificial Intelligence Agents

Agents are often grouped into five classes supported their degree of perceived intelligence and capability. of these agents can improve their performance and generate better action over time. These are given below:

- Simple Reflex Agent.
- Model-Based Reflex Agent.
- Goal-Based Agents.
- Utility-Based Agent.
- Learning Agent.

Simple Reflex Agent

These agents take decisions supported the present percepts and ignore the remainder of the percept history. These agents only achieve a fully observable environment. The Simple reflex agent doesn't consider any a part of percepts history during their decision and action process. This agent works on Condition-action rule, which suggests it maps the present state to action. like an area Cleaner agent, it works as long as there's dirt within the room.

Problems for the straightforward reflex agent design approach:

- They have very limited intelligence.

- They do not know non-perceptual parts of the present state.
- Mostly too big to get and to store.
- Not adaptive to changes within the environment.

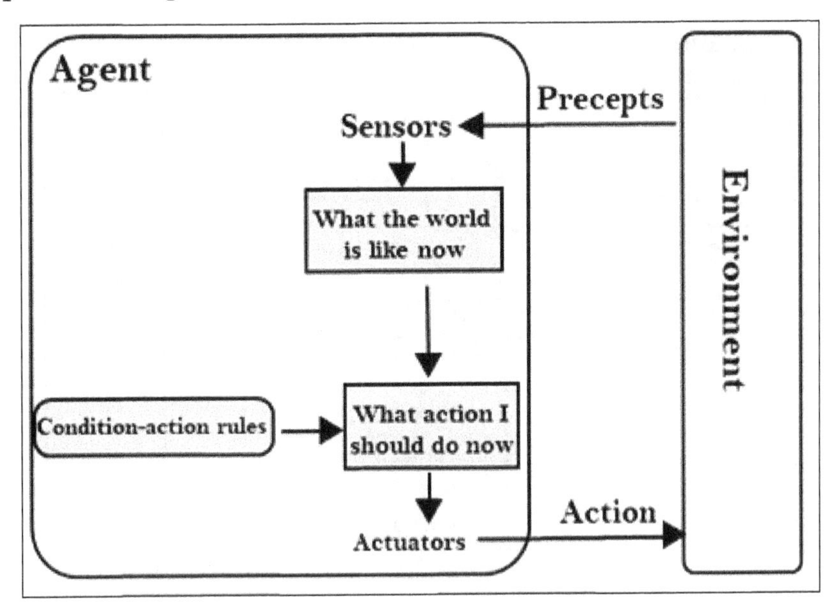

Model-Based Reflex Agent: This agent can add a partially observable environment, and track things. A model-based agent has two important factors:

- Model: It's knowledge about "how things happen within the world," so it's called a Model-based agent.
- Internal State: It's a representation of the present state-based on percept history.

These agents have the model, "which is knowledge of the world" and supported the model they perform actions. Updating the agent state requires information about how the planet evolves and how the agent's action affects the planet.

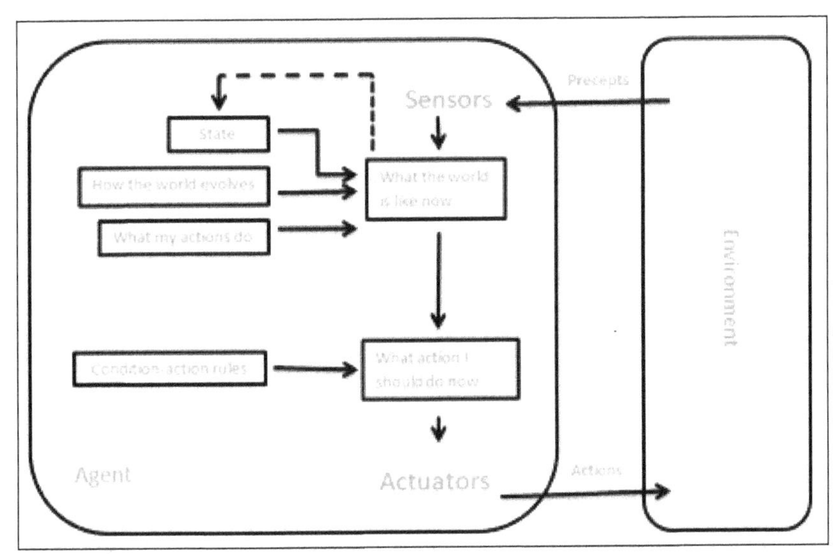

Goal-Based Agent

The knowledge of the present state environment isn't always sufficient to make a decision for an agent to what to try. The agent must know its goal which describes desirable situations. Goal-based agents are very important as they are used to expand the capabilities of the model-based agent by having the "goal" information.

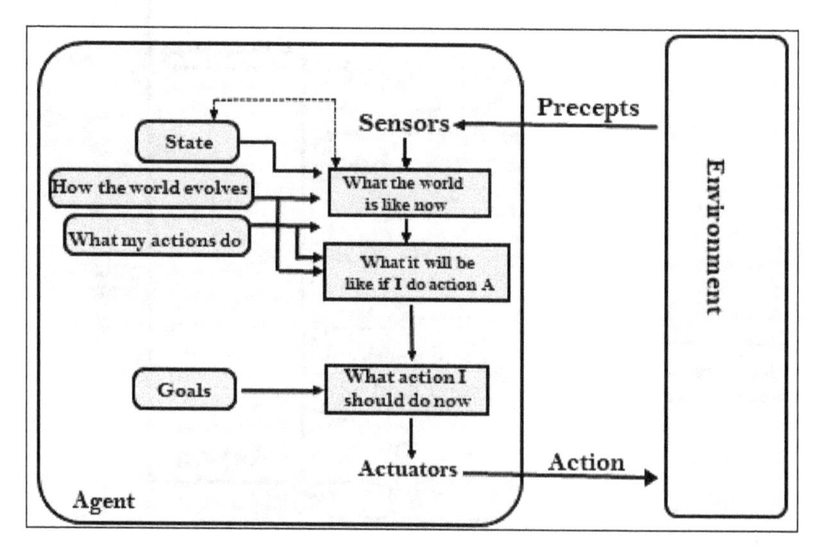

They choose an action, in order that they will achieve the goal. These agents may need to consider an extended sequence of possible actions before deciding whether the goal is achieved or not. Such considerations of various scenario are called searching and planning, which makes an agent proactive.

Utility-based Agents

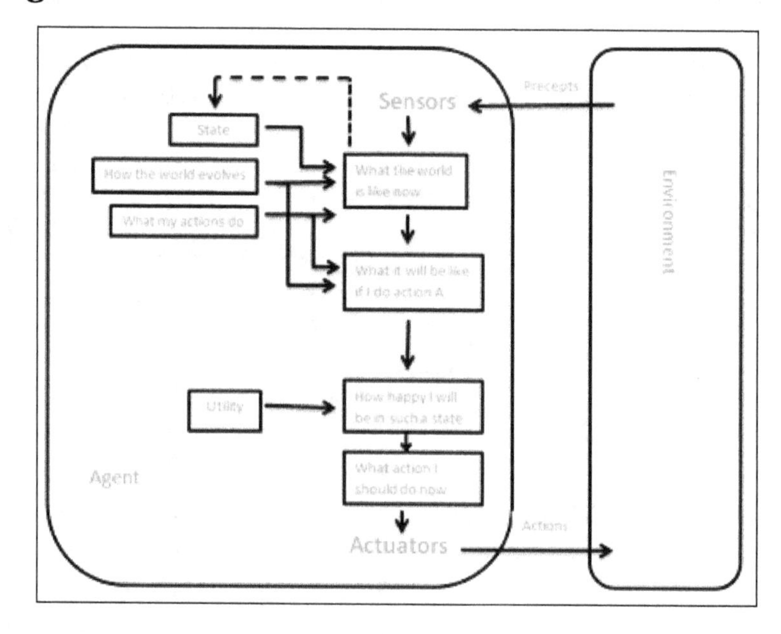

These agents are almost like the goal-based agent but provide an additional component of utility measurement which makes them different by providing a measure of success at a given state.

Utility-based agent act based not only goals but also the simplest thanks to achieving the goal. The Utility-based agent is beneficial when there are multiple possible alternatives, and an agent has got to prefer to perform the simplest action. The utility function maps each state to a true number to see how efficiently each action achieves the goals.

Learning Agents

A learning agent in AI is that the sort of agent which may learn from its past experiences, or it's learning capabilities. It starts to act with basic knowledge then ready to act and adapt automatically through learning. A learning agent has the main four conceptual components that are: Learning element: it's liable for making improvements by learning from the environment.

- Critic: Learning element takes feedback from critic which describes how well the agent is doing for a hard and fast performance standard.
- Performance Element: It's liable for selecting external action.
- Problem Generator: This component is liable for suggesting actions which will cause new and informative experiences.

Hence, learning agents can learn, analyse performance, and appearance for brand spanking new ways to enhance the performance.

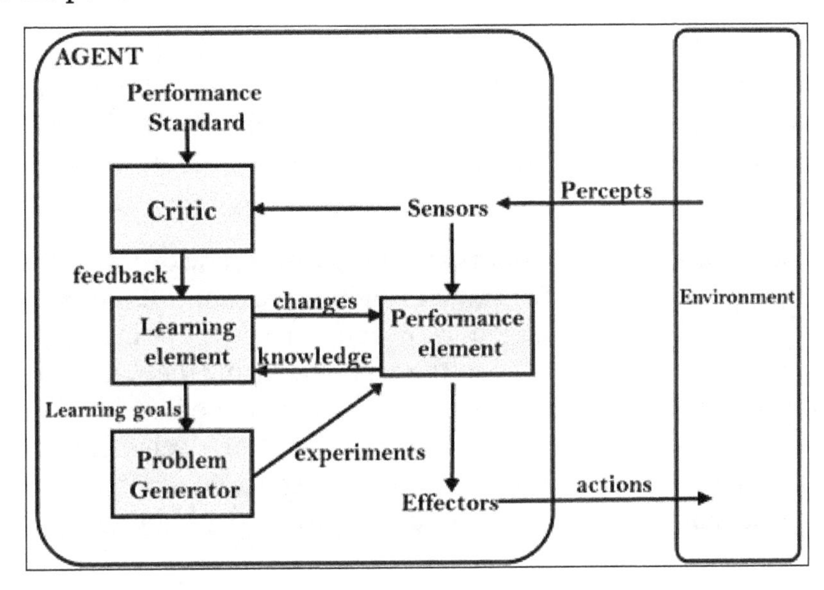

Structure of Artificial Intelligence Agent

The task of AI is to style an agent program which implements the agent function. The structure of an intelligent agent may be a combination of architecture and agent program. It is often viewed as Agent = Architecture + Agent programme.

Following are the most three terms involved within the structure of an AI agent:

- Architecture: It is a machinery that an AI agent executes on and is very useful.
- Agent Function: Agent function is employed to map a percept to an action.

- $f: P^* \rightarrow A$
- Agent Programme: It is an implementation of agent function in which agent function plays a vital role. An agent program executes on the physical architecture to supply function f.

PEAS Representation

It may be a sort of model on which an AI agent works upon. once we define an AI agent or rational agent, then we will group its properties under PEAS representation model. It's made from four words:

- P: Performance measure.
- E: Environment.
- A: Actuators.
- S: Sensors.

Performance measure is that the objective for the success of an agent's behaviour.

Taxonomy of Agents

There is no consensus on the way to classify agents. This is often because there's no agreed-upon taxonomy of agents. With this in mind, allow us to begin to classify the various sorts of agents, using some suggestions from the sector of agent theory. Charles Petrie, Stan Franklin, Art Glaesser and other agent theorists, suggest that we offer an operational definition. So we'll attempt to describe the agent's basic components and specify what the agent seeks to accomplish.

Environment (this must be a dynamic description, that is, an outline of a state of affairs that changes over time as real-life situations do). Sensing capabilities (this depends on the sensor equipment; it determines the type of knowledge the agent is capable of receiving as input). Actions (this would be a change within the environment caused by the agent, requiring the agent to update its model of the planet, which successively may cause the agent to vary its immediate intention). Desires (these are the general policies or goals of the agent). Action Selection Architecture (the agent decides what to due next by consulting both its internal state, the state of the planet, and its current goal; then it uses decision-making procedures to pick an action).

Intelligent agents are applied as automated online assistants, where they function to perceive the requirements of consumers to perform individualised customer service. Such an agent may contain a dialogue system, an avatar, also an expert system to supply specific expertise to the user. they will even be wont to optimise the coordination of human groups online.

- To acquaint the peruser with the thought of an operator and specialist based frameworks.
- To help the peruser with perceiving the space qualities that show the fittingness of an operator based arrangement.
- To present the elemental application regions wherein operator innovation has been effectively sent so far.

- To acknowledge the principle obstructions that dwell the tactic of the operator framework designer, lastly.

Rationality

Rationality is nothing but status of being reasonable, sensible, and having good sense of judgment. It is concerned with expected actions and results depending upon what the agent has perceived. Performing actions with the aim of obtaining useful information is an important part of rationality.

What is Ideal Rational Agent?

An ideal rational agent is the one, which is capable of doing expected actions to maximize its performance measure, on the basis of:

- Its percept sequence.
- Its built-in knowledge base.

Rationality of an agent depends on the following:

- The performance measures, which determine the degree of success.
- Agent's Percept Sequence till now.
- The agent's prior knowledge about the environment.
- The actions that the agent can carry out.

A rational agent always performs right action, where the right action means the action that causes the agent to be most successful in the given percept sequence. The problem the agent solves is characterized by Performance Measure, Environment, Actuators, and Sensors (PEAS).

The Structure of Intelligent Agents

Agent's structure can be viewed as:

- Agent = Architecture + Agent Program.
- Architecture = The machinery that an agent executes on.
- Agent Program = An implementation of an agent function.

Simple Reflex Agents

- They choose actions only based on the current percept.
- They are rational only if a correct decision is made only on the basis of current precept.
- Their environment is completely observable.

Condition-Action Rule – It is a rule that maps a state (condition) to an action.

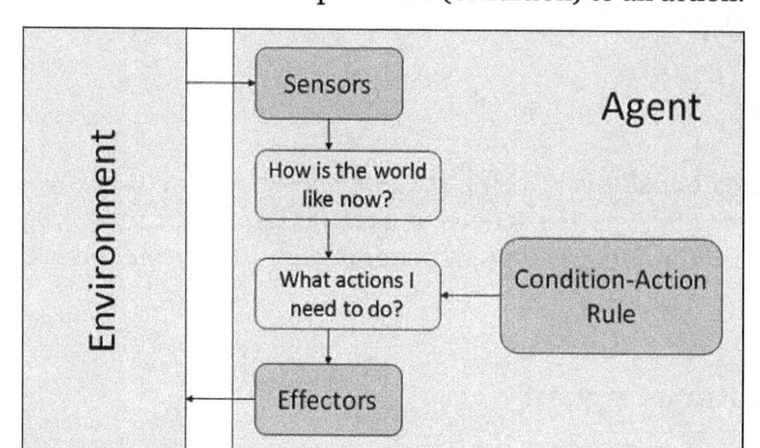

Model Based Reflex Agents

They use a model of the world to choose their actions. They maintain an internal state.

- Model – Knowledge about "how the things happen in the world".
- Internal State – It is a representation of unobserved aspects of current state depending on percept history.
- Updating the state requires the information about:
    - How the world evolves.
    - How the agent's actions affect the world.

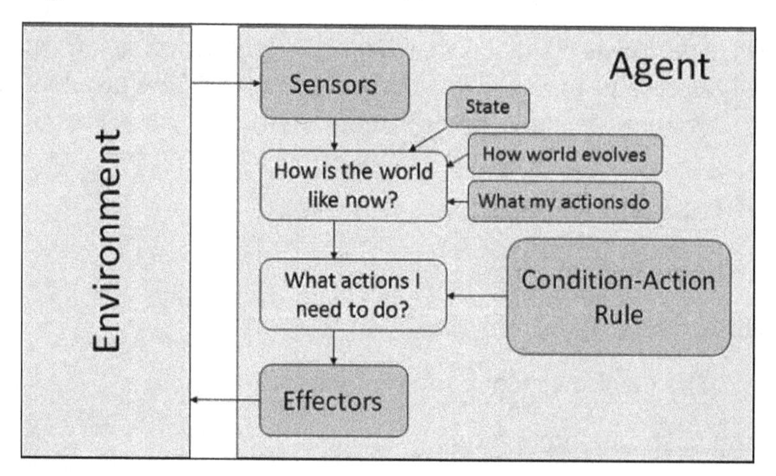

Goal Based Agents

They choose their actions in order to achieve goals. Goal-based approach is more flexible than reflex agent since the knowledge supporting a decision is explicitly modeled, thereby allowing for modifications.

- Goal – It is the description of desirable situations.

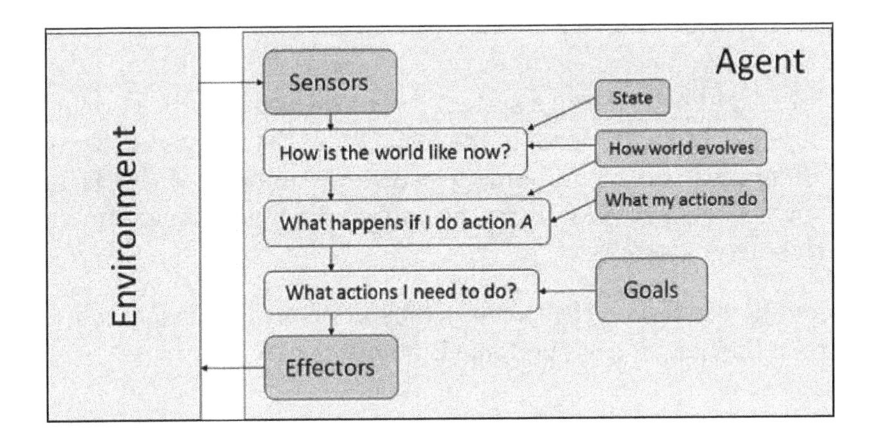

Utility Based Agents

They choose actions based on a preference (utility) for each state.

Goals are inadequate when:

- There are conflicting goals, out of which only few can be achieved.
- Goals have some uncertainty of being achieved and you need to weigh likelihood of success against the importance of a goal.

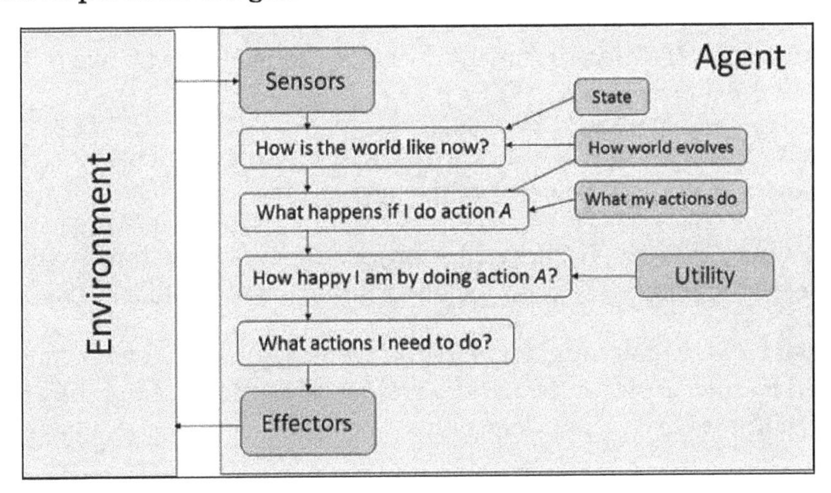

The Nature of Environments

Some programs operate in the entirely artificial environment confined to keyboard input, database, computer file systems and character output on a screen. In contrast, some software agents (software robots or softbots) exist in rich, unlimited softbots domains. The simulator has a very detailed, complex environment. The software agent needs to choose from a long array of actions in real time. A softbot designed to scan the online preferences of the customer and show interesting items to the customer works in the real as well as an artificial environment.

The most famous artificial environment is the Turing Test environment, in which one real and other artificial agents are tested on equal ground. This is a very challenging environment as it is highly difficult for a software agent to perform as well as a human.

Turing Test

The success of an intelligent behavior of a system can be measured with Turing Test. Two persons and a machine to be evaluated participate in the test. Out of the two persons, one plays the role of the tester. Each of them sits in different rooms. The tester is unaware of who is machine and who is a human. He interrogates the questions by typing and sending them to both intelligences, to which he receives typed responses.

This test aims at fooling the tester. If the tester fails to determine machine's response from the human response, then the machine is said to be intelligent.

Properties of Environment

The environment has multifold properties:

- Discrete / Continuous – If there are a limited number of distinct, clearly defined, states of the environment, the environment is discrete (For example, chess); otherwise it is continuous (For example, driving).
- Observable / Partially Observable – If it is possible to determine the complete state of the environment at each time point from the percepts it is observable; otherwise it is only partially observable.
- Static / Dynamic – If the environment does not change while an agent is acting, then it is static; otherwise it is dynamic.
- Single agent / Multiple agents – the environment may contain other agents which may be of the same or different kind as that of the agent.
- Accessible / Inaccessible – If the agent's sensory apparatus can have access to the complete state of the environment, and then the environment is accessible to that agent.
- Deterministic / Non-deterministic – If the next state of the environment is completely determined by the current state and the actions of the agent, then the environment is deterministic; otherwise it is non-deterministic.
- Episodic / Non-episodic – In an episodic environment, each episode consists of the agent perceiving and then acting. The quality of its action depends just on the episode itself. Subsequent episodes do not depend on the actions in the previous episodes. Episodic environments are much simpler because the agent does not need to think ahead.

Computational Intelligence

Computational intelligence (C.I.) is a set of nature-inspired computational methodologies and approaches to address complex real-world problems to which mathematical or traditional modeling can be useless for a few reasons: the processes might be too complex for mathematical reasoning, it might contain some uncertainties during the process, or the process might simply be stochastic in nature.

Computational intelligence techniques and their applications are fast-growing with attention & tremendous effort by researchers over the years. It brings together many different aspects of the current research on intelligence technologies such as neural networks, support vector machines, fuzzy logic and evolutionary computation, and covers a wide range of applications from pattern recognition and system modelling, to intelligent control problems and biomedical applications. It would interesting to study theoretical foundations which have been carried and also both theoretical & practical applications. Computational intelligence could be used to obtain the solutions in scientific and commercial application areas.

Scientific problem solving stems from the acquisition of knowledge from a specific environment, the manipulation of such knowledge, and the intervention in the real world with the manipulated knowledge. The more exhaustive and better structured the knowledge base, the more it emulates a scientific advancements and therefore the easier the solution is to explore more scientific problems with adequate interpretations. As its history proves, computational intelligence is not just about robots. It is also about understanding the nature of intelligent thought and action using computers as experimental devices.

Computers have been used for better understanding and interpretation of process behavior based on the available information to obtain input-output mapping and decision making. The utilization of expert (operator) knowledge, ability to use imprecise, uncertain information, integration of knowledge over multiple disciplines, automated machine learning inspired from nature (neuroscience, genetics, behavioral science), development of models for optimizing the system performance satisfying the inherent system/process constraints. CI is something in which Intelligence is built in computer programs. The first clear definition of Computational Intelligence was introduced by Bezdek in 1994: a system is called computationally intelligent if it deals with low-level data such as numerical data, has a pattern-recognition component and does not use knowledge in the AI sense, and additionally when it begins to exhibit computational adaptively, fault tolerance, speed approaching human-like turnaround and error rates that approximate human performance. According to Bezdek, Computational Intelligence is a subset of Artificial Intelligence. The artificial one based on hard computing techniques and the computational one based on soft computing method, which enables adaptation to many situations.

Artificial Intelligence and Computational Intelligence seek a similar long-term goal: reach general intelligence, which is the intelligence of a machine that could perform any intellectual task that a human being can; there's a clear difference between them. According to Bezdek, Computational Intelligence is a subset of Artificial Intelligence.

There are two types of machine intelligence:

- The artificial one based on hard computing techniques.
- The computational one based on soft computing methods, which enable adaptation to many situations.

The main applications of Computational Intelligence include computer science, engineering, data analysis and biomedicine. In the following we try to classify the application areas and analyse where and how of using C.I. This broadly covers Evolutionary computing, Fuzzy computing, neuro-computing and soft computing. Computational Intelligence is thus a way of performing like human beings. Indeed, the characteristic of "intelligence" is usually attributed to humans. More recently, many products and items also claim to be "intelligent", an attribute which is directly linked to the reasoning and decision making.

Technologies

Basically Computational intelligence techniques include artificial Intelligence (AI) techniques [artificial Neural Networks (ANNs), fuzzy Logic (FL), support Vector Machines (SVM), Self Organizing Maps (SOM) (unsupervised)] ; genetic Algorithms (GA), genetic Programming (GP) and swarm Intelligence or particles swarm optimization (PSO).

CI also makes use of ANN consisting of multi-layer Perceptron concept (MLP), radial Basis Function (RBF), and probabilistic Neural Networks (PNN). Also fuzzy Logic & ANN techniques makes use of adaptive neuro-fuzzy inference system (ANFIS).

The ANN structure consists of an input layer, hidden Layer (s), Output layer, number of nodes in each layer and functions and their parameters.

The steps of fuzzy logic approach are Fuzzification using membership functions (MFs)-input, generation of rule base, aggregation and De-fuzzification using MFs –output. The input-output of membership functions need number, type, parameters and a rule base. The Neuro-fuzzy system combines the procedures of fuzzy logic (FL) and ANNs. This actually starts with an initial FL structure. Further the Neuro fuzzy system also uses ANN for adapting the FL (MF) parameters and the rule base to the training data.

The Genetic algorithms contain the steps:

- Construction of genome (individual).
- Generation of initial population (group of individuals).
- Evaluation of individuals.
- Selection of individuals based on criteria.
- Generation of new individuals (Mutation, Crossover).
- Repetition of the process - generation, evaluation, selection.
- Termination of the process based on max generation no. and/or performance criteria.

Sometimes we may use combinations where in we Combine advantages of GA and other classifiers, GA and ANN, GA and ANFIS, GA and SVM, automatic selection of classifier structure and parameters, Selection of most important system features from a pool, Selection of most important sensors (in the context of on-line condition monitoring and diagnostics)- sensor fusion. In fact automatic selection of classifier structure and parameters consist of ANNs -Number of neurons in hidden layer, ANFIS - Number of MFs and their parameters and SVM parameters.

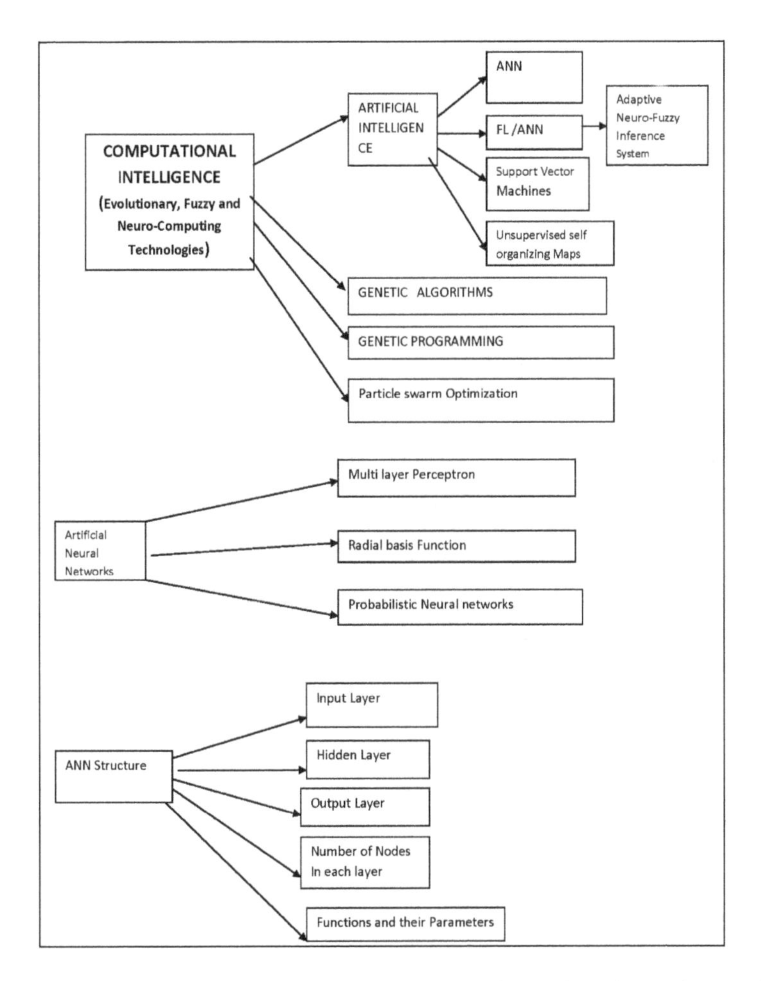

Genetic Programming (GP) is a branch of GA with a lot of similarities. The main difference of GP and GA is in the representation of the solution. In GA the output is in form of a string of numbers representing the solution. GP produces a computer program in the form of a tree-based structure [relating to the inputs or leaves, the mathematical functions (nodes) and the output (root node)].

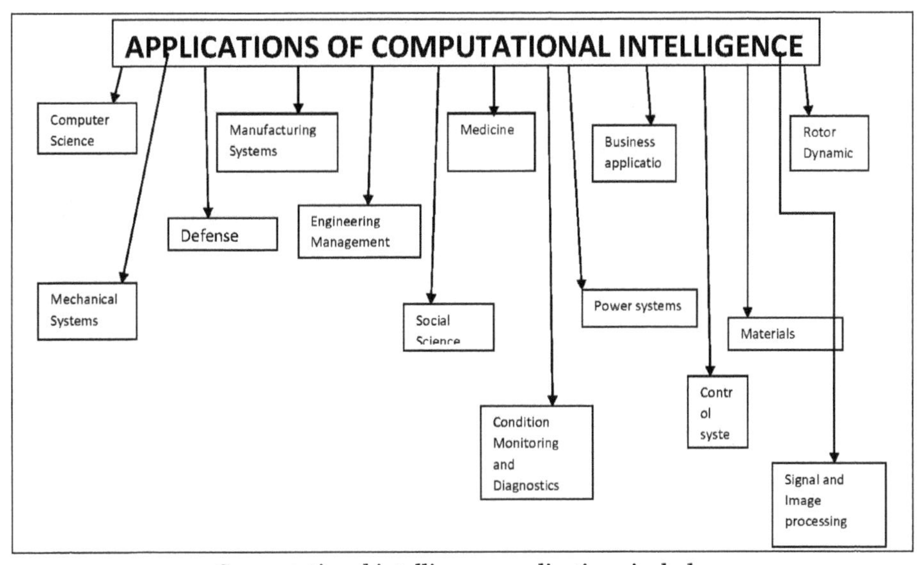

Computational intelligence applications include.

Applications

The main applications of C.I. include computer science , engineering, data analysis and bio-medicine. One must gain a good knowledge of the principles of C.I. like Fuzzy Logic, Neural Networks, Evolutionary computation, Learning Theory and Probabilistic methods to justify his process of research.

CI is responsible for solutions and decision making in several branches of science, engineering, business and management. There are many applications in Computer science, Mechanical systems, manufacturing systems, Engineering management, Medicines, social science and business. More specifically:

- Computer Science applications pertain to Pattern Recognition (PR), NLP, speaker verification, Data Mining, Knowledge Discovery / Machine Learning, Feature Extraction and Selection.
- Mechanical systems in which Condition monitoring and diagnostics, air pollution modeling, heating, ventilating, and air conditioning, Multi-objective optimization in design, Control System Design.
- Manufacturing Systems dealing with Development of data-driven models, Multiobjective optimization of machining parameters.
- Engineering management areas like Inventory management, Project selection, Facility layout design, Scheduling.
- Patient monitoring related to medicine, gene regulatory networks, molecular biology, kernels on protein structures, teaching & learning processes and also in business, economics and management.

Besides the above areas some other computer science applications of C.I. are in system modeling and simulations, network security, intrusion detection, robotics, modeling and optimization, multimedia processes, time series forecasting & power engineering.

References

- What-Is-a-Knowledge-Representation-2553185: researchgate.net, Retrieved 09, Aprril 2020
- Knowledge-representation-in-ai: javatpoint.com, Retrieved 16, Jan 2020
- Artificial-intelligence-agents-and-environments, artificial_intelligence: tutorialspoint.com, Retrieved 20, July 2020
- Agents-in-artificial-intelligence: codingninjas.com, Retrieved 17, Feb 2020
- Reasoning-in-artificial-intelligence: javatpoint.com, Retrieved 05, March 2020

2

Types of Artificial Intelligence

While all intelligent agents possessing artificial intelligence show a similarity in the way they mimic human intelligence to complete tasks, they can be differentiated into various categories based on their limits and capabilities. Artificial narrow intelligence, artificial general intelligence, artificial strong intelligence, reactive machines, united machines, self-aware machines, etc. are all different types of artificial intelligence which are covered in this chapter.

AI can be classified in any number of ways there are two types of main classification:

Type 1

- Weak AI or Narrow AI: It is focused on one narrow task, the phenomenon that machines which are not too intelligent to do their own work can be built in such a way that they seem smart. An example would be a poker game where a machine beats human where in which all rules and moves are fed into the machine. Here each and every possible scenario needs to be entered beforehand manually. Each and every weak AI will contribute to the building of strong AI.
- Strong AI: The machines that can actually think and perform tasks on its own just like a human being. There are no proper existing examples for this but some industry leaders are very keen on getting close to build a strong AI which has resulted in rapid progress.

Type 2 (Based on Functionalities)

- Reactive Machines: This is one of the basic forms of AI. It doesn't have past memory and cannot use past information to information for the future actions. Example: IBM chess program that beat Garry Kasparov in the 1990s.
- Limited Memory: AI systems can use past experiences to inform future decisions. Some of the decision-making functions in self-driving cars have been designed this way. Observations used to inform actions happening in the not so distant future, such as a car that has changed lanes. These observations are not stored permanently and also Apple's Chatbot Siri.
- Theory of Mind: This type of AI should be able to understand people's emotion, belief, thoughts, and expectations and be able to interact socially Even though a lot of improvements are there in this field this kind of AI is not complete yet.
- Self-awareness: An AI that has its own conscious, super intelligent, self-awareness and sentient (In simple words a complete human being). Of course, this kind of bot also doesn't exist and if achieved it will be one of the milestones in the field of AI.

There are many ways AI can be achieved some of them are as follows:

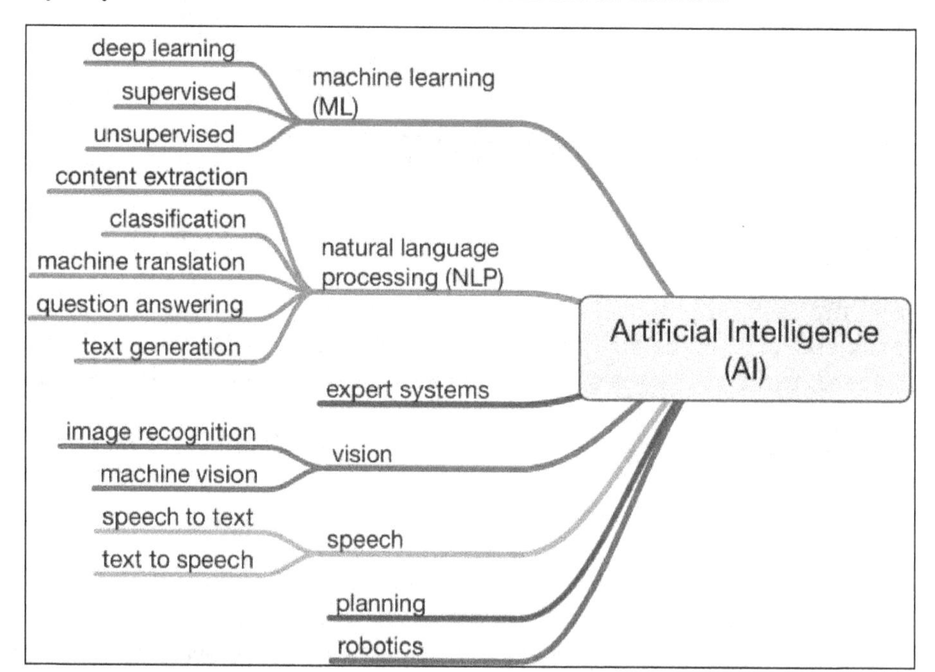

The most important among them are as follows:

- Machine Learning (ML): It is a method where the target (goal) is defined and the steps to reach that target are learned by the machine itself by training (gaining experience). For example to identify a simple object such as an apple or orange. The target is achieved not by explicitly specifying the details about it and coding it but it is just as we teach a child by showing multiple different pictures of it and therefore allowing the machine to define the steps to identify it like an apple or an orange.
- Natural Language Processing (NLP): Natural Language Processing is broadly defined as the automatic manipulation of natural language, like speech and text, by software. One of the well-known examples of this is email spam detection as we can see how it has improved in our mail system.
- Vision: It can be said as a field which enables the machines to see. Machine vision captures and analyses visual information using a camera, analog-to-digital conversion, and digital signal processing. It can be compared to human eyesight but it is not bound by the human limitation which can enable it to see through walls (now that would be interesting if we can have implants that can make us see through the wall). It is usually achieved through machine learning to get the best possible results so we could say that these two fields are interlinked.
- Robotics: It is a field of engineering focused on the design and manufacturing of robots. Robots are often used to perform tasks that are difficult for humans to perform or perform consistently. Examples include car assembly lines, in hospitals, office cleaner, serving foods, and preparing foods in hotels, patrolling farm areas and even as police officers. Recently machine learning has been used to achieve certain good results in building robots that interact socially.

- Autonomous Vehicles: This area of AI has gathered a lot of attention. The list of vehicles includes cars, buses, trucks, trains, ships, submarines, and autopilot flying drones etc.

Artificial Narrow Intelligence

Artificial Narrow Intelligence (ANI) also commonly known as weak AI or narrow AI. It is particularly that type of AI that we have been able to successfully realize and implement in the present date. It is a goal-oriented, narrow range ability holding perspective that executes specific focused tasks, without the ability to the self-expand mechanism (functionality). Machines that are focused on one narrow task operate under a narrow set of constraints and limitations, that's why they are commonly referred to as WEAK AI. Narrow AI doesn't replicate proper human intelligence; it basically simulates/mimics human behavior based on a narrow range of parameters.

Narrow AI has faced a lot of ups and downs in the past few decades incorporated by the progress made in machine learning and deep learning. Narrow AI is basically a combination of two words: AI meaning the technology to simulate human behavior in machines through a set of algorithms and the second word being Narrow, so it basically means implementing the concept of AI but with a narrow range of abilities.

Narrow AI's machine intelligence is basically achieved through the concept of Natural Language Processing (NLP). NLP concept is the common functionality in chatbots and similar AI domains in which the machines are basically programmed in a way to interact with humans using speech and text recognition mechanism.

Different Types of Narrow AI

Narrow AI has two possibilities, either it can be reactive or can have a limited amount of memory.

- Reactive AI: It is the basic version, having no memory or data storage capabilities. It emulates the human mind's behavior and responds to different interpretations without any prior experience.
- Limited Memory AI: It is more advanced, having great memory and data storage capabilities enabling machines to interpret precisely using statistical data. Most of the AI is the Limited Memory AI, enabling machines to use a large amount of data especially in the domains of Deep Learning to give results with utmost accuracy.

Examples of Narrow AI

- Virtual Assistants like Siri by Apple, Alexa by Amazon, Cortana by Microsoft, etc.
- Used in medications and prediction tools to diagnose cancer and other health-related issues with extreme accuracy through human behavior cognition, replication, and reasoning.
- IBM's Watson: It is capable of answering questions asked in natural language interpretations.

- Rankbrain: It is an algorithm used by Google to sort the search results.
- Self-Driven Cars.
- Facial/Image recognition and interpretation software.
- Social Media Marketing tools for keeping a check on violating contents and Email spam filters.
- Manufacturing and Drone-based robots.
- Tools for bringing out the best recommendations based on search results, purchases, history, etc. in the entertainment and marketing domains.

Limitations of Narrow AI

Weak AI has limitations because of its limited capabilities which add to the prospect of causing harm if a system fails. If we take into account an example of a driverless car that calculates the location of oncoming vehicles but somehow it miscalculates the location which causes a deadly collision or a system failure if it is used by some third party or destructive organizations, then it can lead to enormous destructions to the human mankind. Another drawback is to determine the faulty identity for a malfunction or a design flaw.

A further concern is regarding the huge loss of jobs caused by the automatic functionality and performance of an increasing number of tasks. Slowly the machines are taking over human manpower for intelligent automation through AI. So it must be thought-provoking that whether there will be an increase in the job opportunities or the machines will gradually take over the entire physical manpower with the emerging levels of AI.

Artificial General Intelligence

- General intelligence involves the ability to achieve a variety of goals, and carry out a variety of tasks, in a variety of different contexts and environments.
- A generally intelligent system should be able to handle problems and situations quite different from those anticipated by its creators.
- A generally intelligent system should be good at generalizing the knowledge it's gained, so as to transfer this knowledge from one problem or context to others.
- Arbitrarily general intelligence is not possible given realistic resource constraints.
- Real-world systems may display varying degrees of limited generality, but are inevitably going to be a lot more efficient at learning some sorts of things than others; and for any given real-world system, there will be some learning tasks on which it is unacceptably slow. So real-world general intelligences are inevitably somewhat biased toward certain sorts of goals and environments.
- Humans display a higher level of general intelligence than existing AI programs do, and apparently also a higher level than other animals.

- It seems quite unlikely that humans happen to manifest a maximal level of general intelligence, even relative to the goals and environment for which they have been evolutionarily adapted.

There is also a common intuition in the AGI community that various real-world general intelligences will tend to share certain common properties; though there is less agreement on what these properties are.

Within the scope of the core AGI hypothesis, a number of different approaches to defining and characterizing AGI are under current study, encompassing psychological, mathematical, pragmatic and cognitive architecture perspectives. Most contemporary approaches to designing AGI systems fall into four top-level categories: symbolic, emergentist, hybrid and Universalist.

Not all contemporary AGI approaches seek to create human-like general intelligence specifically. But it is argued here, that, for any approach which does, there is a certain set of key cognitive processes and interactions that it must come to grips with, including familiar constructs such as working and long-term memory, deliberative and reactive processing, perception, action and reinforcement learning, metacognition and so forth.

A robust theory of general intelligence, human-like or otherwise, remains elusive. Multiple approaches to defining general intelligence have been proposed, and in some cases these coincide with different approaches to designing AGI systems (so that various systems aim for general intelligence according to different definitions). The perspective presented here is that a mature theory of AGI would allow one to theoretically determine, based on a given environment and goal set and collection of resource constraints, the optimal AGI architecture for achieving the goals in the environments given the constraints. Lacking such a theory at present, researchers must conceive architectures via diverse theoretical paradigms and then evaluate them via practical metrics.

Finally, in order for a community to work together toward common goals, environments and metrics for evaluation of progress are necessary. Metrics for assessing the achievement of human level AGI are argued to be fairly straightforward, including e.g. the classic Turing test, and the test of operating a robot that can graduate from elementary school or university. On the other hand, metrics for assessing partial progress toward, human-level AGI are shown to be more controversial and problematic, with different metrics suiting different AGI approaches, and with the possibility of systems whose partial versions perform poorly on common sensical metrics, yet whose complete versions perform well. The problem of defining agreed-upon metrics for incremental progress remains largely open, and this constitutes a substantial challenge for the young field of AGI moving forward.

Characterizing AGI and General Intelligence

One interesting feature of the AGI community, allude to above, is that it does not currently agree on any single definition of the AGI concept – though there is broad agreement on the general intuitive nature of AGI and broad agreement that some form of the core AGI hypothesis is true. There is a mature theory of general intelligence in the psychology field and a literature in the AGI field on the formal mathematical definition of intelligence; however, none of the neither psychological nor mathematical conceptions of general intelligence are accepted as foundational in their details, by more than a small plurality of the AGI community. Rather, the formulation of a detailed and rigorous theory of "what AGI is" is a small but significant part of the AGI community's ongoing research. The bulk of the emerging AGI community's efforts are devoted to devising and implementing designs for AGI systems, and developing theories regarding the best way to do so; but the fleshing out of the concept of "AGI" is being accomplished alongside and in synergy with these other tasks.

The term "AI" also has many different meanings within the AI research community, with no clear agreement on the definition. George Lugar's popular AI textbook famously defined it as "that which AI practitioners do." The border between AI and advanced algorithmic is often considered unclear. A common joke is that, as soon as certain functionality has been effectively achieved by computers, it's no longer considered AI. The situation with the ambiguity of "AGI" is certainly no worse than that with the ambiguity of the term "AI" itself. In terms of basic semantics, the term "AGI" has been variously used to describe:

- A property of certain systems ("AGI" as the intersection of "artificial" (i.e. synthetic) and "Generally intelligent").
- A system that displays this property (an "AGI" meaning "an AGI system").
- The field of endeavour pursuing the creation of AGI systems, and the study of the nature of AGI.

AGI is related to many other terms and concepts. Joscha Bach has elegantly characterized it in terms of the quest to create "synthetic intelligence." One also finds communities of researchers working toward AGI-related goals under the labels "computational intelligence", "natural intelligence", "cognitive architecture", "biologically inspired cognitive architecture" (BICA), and many others. Each of these labels was introduced with a certain underlying purpose, and has a specific collection of concepts and approaches associated with it; each corresponds to a certain perspective or family of perspectives. The specific purpose underlying the concept and term "AGI" is to focus attention on the general scope and generalization capability of certain intelligent systems, such as humans, theoretical system like AIXI, and a subset of potential future synthetic intelligences. That is, roughly speaking, an AGI system is a synthetic intelligence that has a general scope and is good at generalization across various goals and contexts.

The ambiguity of the concept of "AGI" relates closely to the underlying ambiguity of the concepts of "intelligence" and "general intelligence." The AGI community has embraced, to varying extents, a variety of characterizations of general intelligence, finding each of them to contribute different insights to the AGI quest.

AGI Versus Human-Level Artificial Intelligence

One key distinction to be kept in mind as we review the various approaches to characterizing AGI, is the distinction between AGI and the related concept of "human-level AI" (which is usually used to mean, in effect: human-level, reasonably human-like AGI). AGI is a fairly abstract notion, which is not intrinsically tied to any particular characteristics of human beings. Some properties of human general intelligence may in fact be universal among all powerful AGIs, but given our current limited understanding of general intelligence, it's not yet terribly clears what these may be.

The concept of "human-level AGI", interpreted literally, is confusing and ill-defined. It's difficult to place the intelligences of all possible systems in a simple hierarchy, according to which the "intelligence level" of an arbitrary intelligence can be compared to the "intelligence level" of a human. Some researchers have proposed universal intelligence measures that could be used in this way; but currently the details and utility of such measures are both quite contentious. To keep things simpler, here we will interpret "human-level AI" as meaning "human-level and roughly human-like AGI," a restriction that makes the concept much easier to handle. For AGI systems that are supposed to operate in similar sorts of environments to humans, according to cognitive processes vaguely similar to those used by humans, the concept of "human level" is relatively easy to understand.

The concept of "AGI" appears more theoretically fundamental than "human-level AGI"; however, it's very breadth can also be problematic. "Human-level AGI" is more concrete and specific, which lets one take it in certain directions more easily than can be done with general AGI. In our discussions on evaluations and metrics below, for example, we will restrict attention to human-level AGI systems, because otherwise creating metrics to compare qualitatively different AGI systems becomes a much trickier problem.

The Pragmatic Approach to Characterizing General Intelligence

The pragmatic approach to conceptualizing general intelligence is typified by the AI Magazine article "Human Level Artificial Intelligence? Be Serious", written by Nils Nilsson, one of the early leaders of the AI field. Nilsson's view is that achieving real Human Level artificial intelligence would necessarily imply that most of the tasks "that humans perform for pay could be automated. Rather than work toward this goal of automation by building special-purpose systems, I argue for the development of general-purpose, educable systems that can learn and be taught to perform any of the thousands of jobs that humans can perform. Joining others who have made similar proposals, I advocate beginning with a system that has minimal, although extensive, built-in capabilities. These would have to include the ability to improve through learning along with many other abilities".

In this perspective, once an AI obsoletes humans in most of the practical things we do, it's got general Human Level intelligence. The implicit assumption here is that humans are the generally intelligent system we care about, so that the best practical way to characterize general intelligence is via comparison with human capabilities.

The classic Turing Test for machine intelligence – simulating human conversation well enough to fool human judges – is pragmatic in a similar sense to Nilsson. But the Turing test has a different focus, on emulating humans. Nilsson isn't interested in whether an AI system can fool people into thinking it's a human, but rather in whether an AI system can do the useful and important practical things that people can do.

Psychological Characterizations of General Intelligence

The psychological approach to characterizing general intelligence also focuses on human-like general intelligence; but rather than looking directly at practical capabilities, it tries to isolate deeper underlying capabilities that enable these practical capabilities. In practice it encompasses a broad variety of sub-approaches, rather than presenting a unified perspective.

Viewed historically, efforts to conceptualize, define, and measure intelligence in humans reflect a distinct trend from general to specific (it is interesting to note the similarity between historical trends in psychology and AI). Thus, early work in defining and measuring intelligence was heavily influenced by Spearman, who in 1904 proposed the psychological factor g (the "g factor", for general intelligence). Spearman argued that g was biologically determined, and represented the overall intellectual skill level of an individual. A related advance was made in 1905 by Binet and Simon, who developed a novel approach for measuring general intelligence in French schoolchildren. A unique feature of the Binet-Simon scale was that it provided comprehensive age norms, so that each child could be systematically compared with others across both age and intellectual skill level. In 1916, Terman introduced the notion of an intelligence quotient or IQ, which is computed by dividing the test-taker's mental age (i.e., their age-equivalent performance level) by their physical or chronological age.

In subsequent years, psychologists began to question the concept of intelligence as a single, undifferentiated capacity. There were two primary concerns. First, while performance within an individual across knowledge domains is somewhat correlated, it is not unusual for skill levels in one domain to be considerably higher or lower than in another (i.e., intra-individual variability). Second, two individuals with comparable overall performance levels might differ significantly across specific knowledge domains (i.e., inter-individual variability). These issues helped to motivate a number of alternative theories, definitions, and measurement approaches, which share the idea that intelligence is multifaceted and variable both within and across individuals. Of these approaches, a particularly well-known example is Gardner's theory of multiple intelligences, which proposes eight distinct forms or types of intelligence: linguistic, logical-mathematical, musical, bodily-kinaesthetic, spatial, interpersonal, intrapersonal, and naturalist. Gardner's theory suggests that each individual's intellectual skill is represented by an intelligence profile, that is, a unique mosaic or combination of skill levels across the eight forms of intelligence.

Competencies Characterizing Human-Level General Intelligence

Another approach to understanding general intelligence based on the psychology literature, is to look at the various competencies that cognitive scientists generally understand humans to display. The following list of competencies was assembled at the 2009 AGI Roadmap Workshop via a group of 12 experts, including AGI researchers and psychologists, based on a review of the AI and psychology literatures. The list is presented as a list of broad areas of capability, each one then subdivided into specific sub-areas:

- Perception:
  - Vision: Image and scene analysis and understanding.
  - Hearing: Identifying the sounds associated with common objects; understanding. which sounds come from which sources in a noisy environment.
  - Touch: Identifying common objects and carrying out common actions using touch alone.
  - Crossmodal: Integrating information from various senses.
  - Proprioception: Sensing and understanding what its body is doing.

- Actuation:
  - Physical skills: Manipulating familiar and unfamiliar objects.
  - Tool use, including the flexible use of ordinary objects as tools.
  - Navigation, including in complex and dynamic environments.
- Memory:
  - Implicit: Memory the content of which cannot be introspected.
  - Working: Short-term memory of the content of current/recent experience (awareness).
  - Episodic: Memory of a first-person experience (actual or imagined) attributed to a particular instance of the agent as the subject who had the experience.
  - Semantic: Memory regarding facts or beliefs.
  - Procedural: Memory of sequential/parallel combinations of (physical or mental) actions often habituated (implicit).
- Learning:
  - Imitation: Spontaneously adopt new behaviors that the agent sees others carrying out.
  - Reinforcement: Learn new behaviors from positive and/or negative reinforcement signals, delivered by teachers and/or the environment.
  - Interactive verbal instruction.
  - Learning from written media.
  - Learning via experimentation.
- Reasoning:
  - Deduction, from uncertain premises observed in the world.
  - Induction, from uncertain premises observed in the world.
  - Abduction, from uncertain premises observed in the world.
  - Causal reasoning, from uncertain premises observed in the world.
  - Physical reasoning, based on observed "fuzzy rules" of naive physics.
  - Associational reasoning, based on observed spatiotemporal associations.
- Planning:
  - Tactical.
  - Strategic.

    - Physical.
    - Social.
- Attention:
    - Visual Attention within the agent's observations of its environment.
    - Social Attention.
    - Behavioral Attention.
- Motivation:
    - Subgoal creation, based on the agent's preprogrammed goals and its reasoning and planning.
    - Affect-based motivation.
    - Control of emotions.
- Emotion:
    - Expressing Emotion.
    - Perceiving/Interpreting Emotion.
- Modeling Self and Other:
    - Self-Awareness.
    - Theory of Mind.
    - Self-Control.
    - Other-Awareness.
    - Empathy.
- Social Interaction:
    - Appropriate Social Behavior.
    - Communication about and oriented toward social relationships.
    - Inference about social relationships.
    - Group interactions (e.g. play) in loosely-organized activities.
- Communication:
    - Gestural communication to achieve goals and express emotions.
    - Verbal communication using natural language in its life-context.
    - Pictorial Communication regarding objects and scenes with.

- Language acquisition.
- Cross-modal communication.

- Quantitative:
    - Counting sets of objects in its environment.
    - Simple, grounded arithmetic with small numbers.
    - Comparison of observed entities regarding quantitative properties.
    - Measurement using simple, appropriate tools.
- Building/Creation:
    - Physical: Creative constructive play with objects.
    - Conceptual invention: Concept formation.
    - Verbal invention.
    - Social construction (e.g. assembling new social groups, modifying existing ones).

Different researchers have different views about which of the above competency areas is most critical, and as you peruse the list, you may feel that it over or under emphasizes certain aspects of intelligence. But it seems clear that any software system that could flexibly and robustly display competency in all of the above areas would be broadly considered a strong contender for possessing human-level general intelligence.

A Cognitive-Architecture Perspective on General Intelligence

Complementing the above perspectives, Laird et al have composed a list of "requirements for human-level intelligence" from the standpoint of designers of cognitive architectures. Their own work has mostly involved the SOAR cognitive architecture, which has been pursued from the AGI perspective, but also from the perspective of accurately simulating human cognition:

- R0: fixed structure for all tasks (i.e., explicit loading of knowledge files or software modification should not be done when the AGI system is presented with a new task).
- R1: Realize a symbol system (i.e., the system should be able to create symbolism and utilize symbolism internally, regardless of whether this symbolism is represented explicitly or implicitly within the system's knowledge representation).
- R2: Represent and effectively use modality-specific knowledge.
- R3: Represent and effectively use large bodies of diverse knowledge.
- R4: Represent and effectively use knowledge with different levels of generality.
- R5: Represent and effectively use diverse levels of knowledge.
- R6: Represent and effectively use beliefs independent of current perception.

- R7: Represent and effectively use rich, hierarchical control knowledge.
- R8: Represent and effectively use meta-cognitive knowledge.
- R9: Support a spectrum of bounded and unbounded deliberation (where "bounded" refers to computational space and time resource utilization).
- R10: Support diverse, comprehensive learning.
- R11: Support incremental, online learning.

There are no current AI systems that plainly fulfil all these requirements (although the precise definitions of these requirements may be open to a fairly broad spectrum of interpretations). It is worth remembering, in this context, Stan Franklin's careful articulation of the difference between software "agent" and a mere "program":

> "An autonomous agent is a system situated within and a part of an environment that senses that environment and acts on it, over time, in pursuit of its own agenda and so as to effect what it senses in the future".

Laird and Wray's requirements do not specify that the general intelligence must be an autonomous agent rather than a program. So, their requirements span both "agent AI" and "tool AI". However, if we piece together Franklin's definition with Laird and Wray's requirements, we get a reasonable stab at a characterization of a "generally intelligent agent", from the perspective of the cognitive architecture designer.

A Mathematical Approach to Characterizing General Intelligence

In contrast to approaches focused on human-like general intelligence, some researchers have sought to understand general intelligence in general. The underlying intuition here is that truly, absolutely general intelligence would only be achievable given infinite computational ability. For any computable system, there will be some contexts and goals for which it's not very intelligent However, some finite computational systems will be more generally intelligent than others, and it's possible to quantify this extent.

This approach is typified by the recent work of Legg and Hutter, who give a formal definition of general intelligence based on the Solomonoff-Levin prior. Put very roughly, they define intelligence as the average reward-achieving capability of a system, calculated by averaging over all possible reward-summable environments, where each environment is weighted in such a way that more compactly describable programs have larger weights.

According to this sort of measure, humans are nowhere near the maximally generally intelligent system. However, humans are more generally intelligent than, say, rocks or worms. While the original form of Legg and Hutter's definition of intelligence is impractical to compute, a more tractable approximation has recently been developed. Also, Achler has proposed an interesting, pragmatic AGI intelligence measurement approach explicitly inspired by these formal approaches, in the sense that it explicitly balances the effectiveness of a system at solving problems with the compactness of its solutions. This is similar to a common strategy in evolutionary program learning, where one uses a fitness function comprising an accuracy term and an "Occam's Razor" compactness term.

The Adaptationist Approach to Characterizing General Intelligence

Another perspective views general intelligence as closely tied to the environment in which it exists. Pei Wang has argued carefully for a conception of general intelligence as adaptation to the environment using insufficient resources. A system may be said to have greater general intelligence, if it can adapt effectively to a more general class of environments, within realistic resource constraints. The pragmatic general intelligence is defined relative to a given probability distribution over environments and goals, as the average goal-achieving capability of a system, calculated by weighted-averaging over all possible environments and goals, using the given distribution to determine the weights.

The generality of a system's intelligence is defined in a related way, as (roughly speaking) the entropy of the class of environments over which the system displays high pragmatic general intelligence. The efficient pragmatic general intelligence is defined relative to a given probability distribution over environments and goals, as the average effort-normalized goal-achieving capability of a system, calculated by weighted-averaging over all possible environments and goals, using the given distribution to determine the weights. The effort-normalized goal achieving capability of a system is defined by taking its goal-achieving capability (relative to a particular goal and environment), and dividing it by the computational effort the system must expend to achieve that capability.

Lurking in this vicinity are some genuine differences of perspective with the AGI community, regarding the proper way to conceive general intelligence. Some theorists argue that intelligence is purely a matter of capability, and that the intelligence of a system is purely a matter of its behaviors, and is independent of how much effort it expends in achieving its behaviors. On the other hand, some theorists (e.g. Wang) believe that the essence of general intelligence lies in the complex systems of compromises needed to achieve a reasonable degree of generality of adaptation using limited computational resources. In the latter, adaptationist view, the sorts of approaches to goal-achievement that are possible in the theoretical case of infinite or massive computational resources, have little to do with real-world general intelligence. But in the former view, real-world general intelligence can usefully be viewed as a modification of infinite-resources, infinitely-general intelligence to the case of finite resources.

The Embodiment Focused Approach to Characterizing General Intelligence

A close relative of the adaptationist approach, but with a very different focus that leads to some significant conceptual differences as well, is what we may call the embodiment approach to characterizing general intelligence. In brief this perspective holds that intelligence is something that physical bodies do in physical environments. It holds that intelligence is best understood via focusing on the modulation of the body-environment interaction that an embodied system carries out as it goes about in the world. Rodney Brooks is one of the better known advocates of this perspective.

Pfeifer and Bonard summarize the view of intelligence underlying this perspective adroitly as follows: " In spite of all the difficulties of coming up with a concise definition, and regardless of the enormous complexities involved in the concept of intelligence, it seems that whatever we intuitively view as intelligent is always vested with two particular characteristics: compliance and diversity. In short, intelligent agents always comply with the physical and social rules of their environment, and exploit those rules to produce diverse behavior. " For example, they note: "All animals, humans and robots have to comply with the fact that there is gravity and friction, and that locomotion requires energy. Adapting to these constraints and exploiting them in particular ways opens up the possibility of walking, running, drinking from a cup, putting dishes on a table, playing soccer, or riding a bicycle."

Pfeifer and Bonard go so far as to assert that intelligence, in the perspective they analyze it, doesn't apply to conventional AI software programs. "We ascribe intelligence only to real physical systems whose behavior can be observed as they interact with the environment. Software agents, and computer programs in general, are disembodied, and many of the conclusions drawn do not apply to them." Of course, this sort of view is quite contentious, and e.g. Pei Wang has argued against it in a paper titled "Does a Laptop Have a Body?" – the point being that any software program with any kind of user interface is interacting with the physical world via some kind of body, so the distinctions involved are not as sharp as embodiment-oriented researchers sometimes imply.

Philosophical points intersect here with issues regarding research focus. Conceptually, the embodiment perspective asks whether it even makes sense to talk about human-level or human-like AGI in a system that lacks a vaguely human-like body. Focus-wise, this perspective suggests that, if one is interested in AGI, it makes sense to put resources on achieving human-like intelligence the way evolution did, i.e. in the context of controlling a body with complex sensors and actuators in a complex physical world.

The overlap between the embodiment and adaptationist approaches is strong, because historically, human intelligence evolved specifically to adapt to the task of controlling a human body in certain sorts of complex environment, given limited energetic resources and subject to particular physical constraints. But, the two approaches are not identical, because the embodiment approach posits that adaptation to physical body-control tasks under physical constraints is a key whereas the adaptationist approach holds that the essential point is more broadly-conceived adaptation to environments subject to resource constraints.

Approaches to Artificial General Intelligence

As appropriate for an early-stage research field, there is a wide variety of different approaches to AGI in play. It compares a number of (sometimes quite loosely) biologically inspired cognitive architectures in terms of a feature checklist, and was created collaboratively with the creators of the architectures. Hugo de Garis. Duch's survey, divides existing approaches into three paradigms – symbolic, emergentist and hybrid. Whether this trichotomy has any fundamental significance is somewhat contentious, but it is convenient given the scope of approaches currently and historically pursued.

Symbolic AGI Approaches

A venerable tradition in AI focuses on the physical symbol system hypothesis, which states that minds exist mainly to manipulate symbols that represent aspects of the world or themselves. A physical symbol system has the ability to input, output, store and alter symbolic entities, and to execute appropriate actions in order to reach its goals. Generally, symbolic cognitive architectures focus on "working memory" that draws on long-term memory as needed, and utilize a centralized control over perception, cognition and action. Although in principle such architectures could be arbitrarily capable (since symbolic systems have universal representational and computational power, in theory), in practice symbolic architectures tend to be weak in learning, creativity, procedure learning, and episodic and associative memory. Decades of work in this tradition have not compellingly resolved these issues, which has led many researchers to explore other options.

Perhaps the most impressive successes of symbolic methods on learning problems have occurred in the areas of Genetic Programming (GP), Inductive Logic Programming, and probabilistic learning methods such as Markov Logic Networks (MLN). These techniques are interesting from a variety of theoretical and practical standpoints. For instance, it is notable that, GP and MLN have been usefully applied to high-level symbolic relationships, and also to quantitative data resulting directly from empirical observations, depending on how one configures them and how one prepares their inputs. Another important observation one may make about these methods is that, in each case, the ability to do data-driven learning using an underlying symbolic representation, comes along with a lack of transparency in how and why the learning algorithms come up with the symbolic constructs that they do. Nontrivially large GP program trees are generally quite opaque to the human reader, though in principle using a comprehensible symbolic formalism. The propositions making up a Markov Logic Network are easy to understand, but the reasons that MLN weight learning ranks one propositional rule higher than another over a given set of evidence, are obscure and not easily determinable from the results MLN produces. In some ways these algorithms blur the border between symbolic and sub symbolic, because they use underlying symbolic representation languages according to algorithms that produce large, often humanly inscrutable combinations of data elements in a manner conceptually similar to many sub symbolic learning algorithms.

Indeed, the complex, somewhat "emergentist" nature of "symbolic" algorithms like GP and MLN provides a worthwhile reminder that the "symbolic vs. sub symbolic" dichotomy, while heuristically valuable for describing the AI and AGI approaches existent at the current time, is not necessarily a clear, crisp, fundamentally grounded distinction. It is utilized here more for its sociological descriptive value, as for its core value as a scientific, mathematical or philosophical distinction. A few illustrative symbolic cognitive architectures are:

- ACT-R is fundamentally a symbolic system, but Duch classifies it as a hybrid system because it incorporates connectionist-style activation spreading in a significant role; and there is an experimental thoroughly connectionist implementation to complement the primary mainly-symbolic implementation. Its combination of SOAR-style "production rules" with large-scale connectionist dynamics allows it to simulate a variety of human psychological phenomena.
- Cyc is an AGI architecture based on predicate logic as a knowledge representation, and using logical reasoning techniques to answer questions and derive new knowledge from old. It has been connected to a natural language engine, and designs have been created for the connection of Cyc with Albus's 4D-RCS. Cyc's most unique aspect is the large database of common sense knowledge that Cycorp has accumulated (millions of pieces of knowledge, entered by specially trained humans in predicate logic format); part of the philosophy underlying Cyc is that once a sufficient quantity of knowledge is accumulated in the knowledge base, the problem of creating human-level general intelligence will become much less difficult due to the ability to leverage this knowledge.

- EPIC, a cognitive architecture aimed at capturing human perceptual, cognitive and motor activities through several interconnected processors working in parallel. The system is controlled by production rules for cognitive processor and a set of perceptual (visual, auditory, tactile) and motor processors operating on symbolically coded features rather than raw sensory data. It has been connected to SOAR for problem solving, planning and learning.
- ICARUS an integrated cognitive architecture for physical agents, with knowledge. Specified in the form of reactive skills, each denoting goal-relevant reactions to a class of problems. The architecture includes a number of modules: a perceptual system, a planning system, an execution system, and several memory systems.
- SNePS (Semantic Network Processing System) is a logic, frame and network-based knowledge representation, reasoning, and acting system that has undergone over three decades of development, and has been used for some interesting prototype experiments in language processing and virtual agent control.
- SOAR, a classic example of expert rule-based cognitive architecture. Designed to model general intelligence. It has recently been extended to handle sensorimotor functions and reinforcement learning.

A caricature of some common attitudes for and against the symbolic approach to AGI would be:

- For: Symbolic thought is what most strongly distinguishes humans from other animals; it's the crux of human general intelligence. Symbolic thought is precisely what lets us generalize most broadly. It's possible to realize the symbolic core of human general intelligence independently of the specific neural processes that realize this core in the brain, and independently of the sensory and motor systems that serve as (very sophisticated) input and output conduits for human symbol-processing.
- Against: While these symbolic AI architectures contain many valuable ideas and have yielded some interesting results, they seem to be incapable of giving rise to the emergent structures and dynamics required to yield humanlike general intelligence using feasible computational resources. Symbol manipulation emerged evolutionarily from simpler processes of perception and motivated action; and symbol manipulation in the human brain emerges from these same sorts of processes. Divorcing symbol manipulation from the underlying substrate of perception and motivated action doesn't make sense, and will never yield generally intelligent agents, at best only useful problem-solving tools.

Emergentist AGI Approaches

Another species of AGI design expects abstract symbolic processing – along with every other aspect of intelligence – to emerge from lower-level "sub symbolic" dynamics, which sometimes (but not always) are designed to simulate neural networks or other aspects of human brain function. Today's emergentist architectures are sometimes very strong at recognizing patterns in high-dimensional data, reinforcement learning and associative memory; but no one has yet compellingly shown how to achieve high-level functions such as abstract reasoning or complex language processing using a purely sub symbolic, emergentist approach. There are research results doing inference and language processing using sub symbolic architectures, some of which are reviewed in but these mainly involve relatively simplistic problem cases. The most broadly effective reasoning and language processing systems available are those utilizing various forms of symbolic representations, though often also involving forms of probabilistic, data-driven learning, as in examples like Markov Logic Networks and statistical language processing.

A few illustrative subsymbolic, emergentist cognitive architectures are:

- DeSTIN is hierarchical temporal pattern recognition architecture, with some similarities to HTM but featuring more complex learning mechanisms. It has been integrated into the CogPrime architecture to serve as a perceptual subsystem; but is primarily being developed to serve as the center of its own AGI design, assisted via action and reinforcement hierarchies.
- Hierarchical Temporal Memory (HTM) is hierarchical temporal pattern recognition architecture, presented as both an AI / AGI approach and a model of the cortex. So far it has been used exclusively for vision processing, but a conceptual framework has been outlined for extension to action and perception/action coordination.
- SAL based on the earlier and related IBCA (Integrated Biologically based Cognitive Architecture) is a large-scale emergent architecture that seeks to model distributed information processing in the brain, especially the posterior and frontal cortex and the hippocampus. So far the architectures in this lineage have been used to simulate various human psychological and psycholinguistic behaviors, but haven't been shown to give rise to higher-level behaviors like reasoning or subgoaling.
- NOMAD are based on Edelman's "Neural Darwinism" model of the brain, and feature large numbers of simulated neurons evolving by natural selection into configurations that carry out sensorimotor and categorization tasks. This work builds conceptually on prior work by Edelman and colleagues on the "Darwin" series of brain-inspired perception systems.
- Ben Kuipers and his colleagues have pursued an extremely innovative research program which combines qualitative reasoning and reinforcement learning to enable an intelligent agent to learn how to act, perceive and model the world. Kuipers' notion of "bootstrap learning" involves allowing the robot to learn almost everything about its world, including for instance the structure of 3D space and other things that humans and other animals obtain via their genetic endowments.
- Tsvi Achler has demonstrated neural networks whose weights adapt according to a different methodology than the usual, combining feedback and feed forward dynamics in a particular way, with the result that the weights in the network have a clear symbolic meaning. This provides a novel approach to bridging the symbolic-subsymbolic gap.

There has also been a great deal of work relevant to these sorts of architectures, done without explicit reference to cognitive architectures, under labels such as "deep learning" – e.g. Andrew Ng's well known work applying deep learning to practical vision processing problems, and the work of Tomasso Poggio and his team which achieves deep learning via simulations of visual cortex.

A caricature of some common attitudes for and against the emergentist approach to AGI would be:

- For: The brain consists of a large set of simple elements, complexly self-organizing into dynamical structures in response to the body's experience. So, the natural way to approach

AGI is to follow a similar approach: a large set of simple elements capable of appropriately adaptive self-organization. When a cognitive faculty is achieved via emergence from subsymbolic dynamics, then it automatically has some flexibility and adaptiveness to it (quite different from the "brittleness" seen in many symbolic AI systems). The human brain is actually very similar to the brains of other mammals, which are mostly involved in processing high-dimensional sensory data and coordinating complex actions; this sort of processing, which constitutes the foundation of general intelligence, is most naturally achieved via subsymbolic means.

- Against: The brain happens to achieve its general intelligence via self-organizing networks of neurons, but to focus on this underlying level is misdirected. What matters is the cognitive "software" of the mind, not the lower-level hardware or wetware that's used to realize it. The brain has a complex architecture that evolution has honed specifically to support advanced symbolic reasoning and other aspects of human general intelligence; what matters for creating human-level (or greater) intelligence is having the right information processing architecture, not the underlying mechanics via which the architecture is implemented.

Structures Underlying Human-Like General Intelligence

AGI is a very broad pursuit, not tied to the creation of systems emulating human-type general intelligence. However, if one temporarily restricts attention to AGI systems intended to vaguely emulate human functionality, then one can make significantly more intellectual progress in certain interesting directions. For example, by piecing together insights from the various architectures mentioned above, one can arrive at a rough idea regarding what are the main aspects that need to be addressed in creating a "human-level AGI" system.

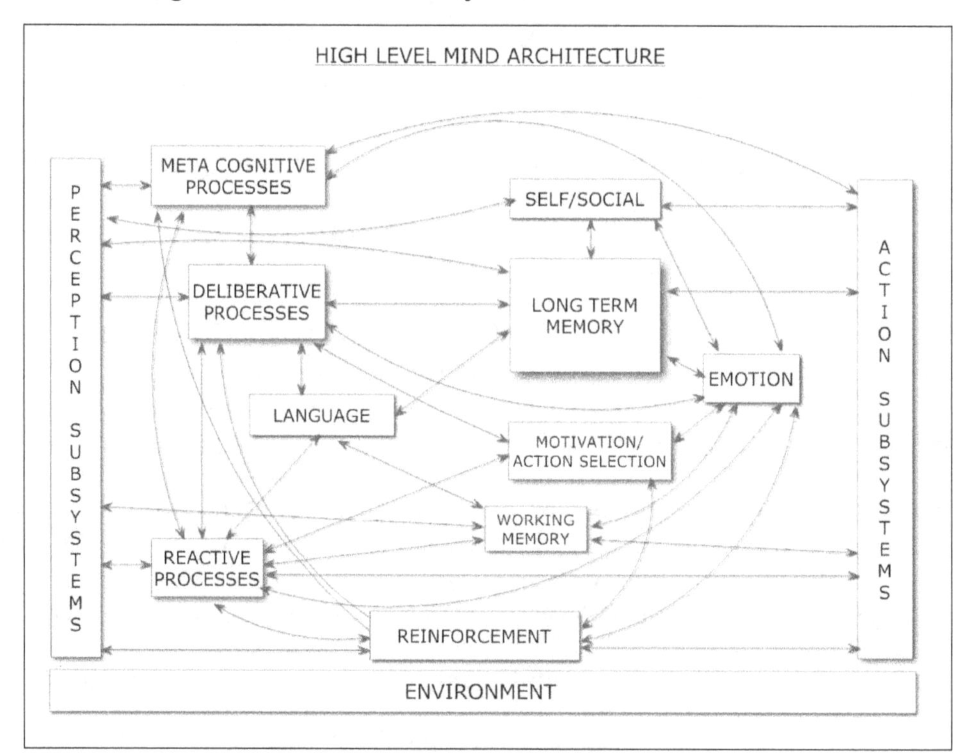

High-Level Structure of a Human-Like Mind.

We will present here my rough understanding of the key aspects of human-level AGI in a series of seven figures, each adapted from a figure used to describe (all or part of) one of the AGI approaches listed above. The collective of these seven figures we will call the "integrative diagram." When the term "architecture" is used in the context of these figures, it refers to an abstract cognitive architecture that may be realized in hardware, software, wetware or perhaps some other way. This "integrative diagram" is not intended as a grand theoretical conclusion, but rather as a didactic overview of the key elements involved in human-level general intelligence, expressed in a way that is not extremely closely tied to any one AGI architecture or theory, but represents a fair approximation of the AGI field's overall understanding (inasmuch as such a diverse field can be said to have a coherent "overall understanding").

First, figure above gives a high-level breakdown of a human-like mind into components, based on Aaron Sloman's high-level cognitive-architectural sketch. This diagram represents, roughly speaking, "modern common sense" about the architecture of a human-like mind. The separation between structures and processes, embodied in having separate boxes for Working Memory vs. Reactive Processes, and for Long Term Memory vs. Deliberative Processes, could be viewed as somewhat artificial, since in the human brain and most AGI architectures, memory and processing are closely integrated. However, the tradition in cognitive psychology is to separate out Working Memory and Long Term Memory from the cognitive processes acting thereupon, so we have adhered to that convention. The other changes from Sloman's diagram are the explicit inclusion of language, representing the hypothesis that language processing is handled in a somewhat special way in the human brain; and the inclusion of a reinforcement component parallel to the perception and action hierarchies, as inspired by intelligent control systems theory (e.g. Albus) and deep learning theory. Of course Sloman's high level diagram in its original form is intended as inclusive of language and reinforcement.

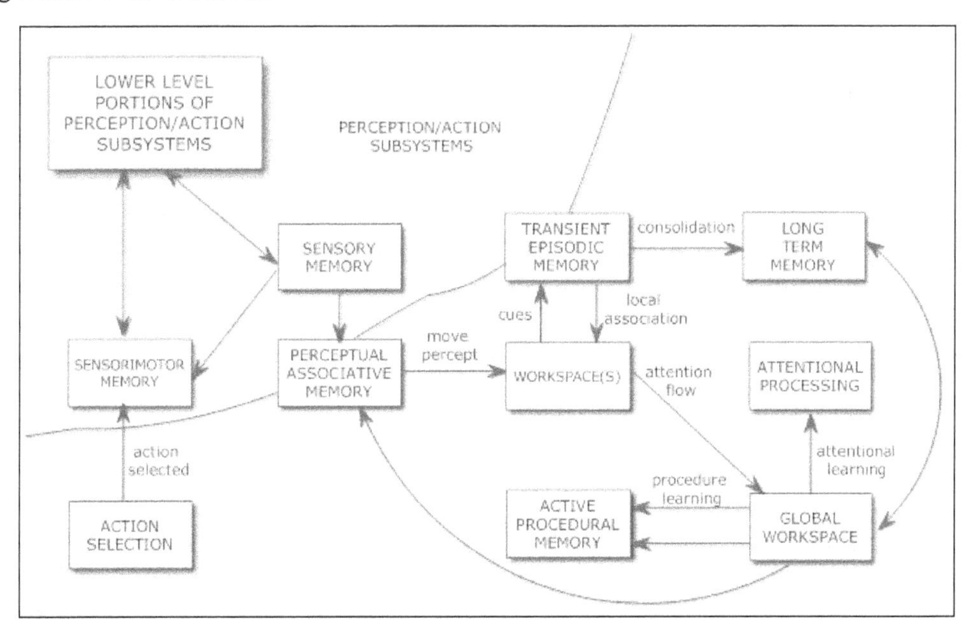

Architecture of Working Memory and Reactive Processing, closely modeled on the LIDA architecture.

Modeling working memory and reactive processing is essentially the LIDA diagram as given in prior papers by Stan Franklin, Bernard Baars and colleagues. The boxes in the upper left corner of the LIDA diagram pertain to sensory and motor processing, which LIDA does not handle in detail, and which are modeled more carefully by deep learning theory. The bottom left corner box refers to action selection, which in the integrative diagram is modeled in more detail by Psi. The top right corner box refers to Long-Term Memory, which the integrative diagram models in more detail as a synergetic multi-memory system.

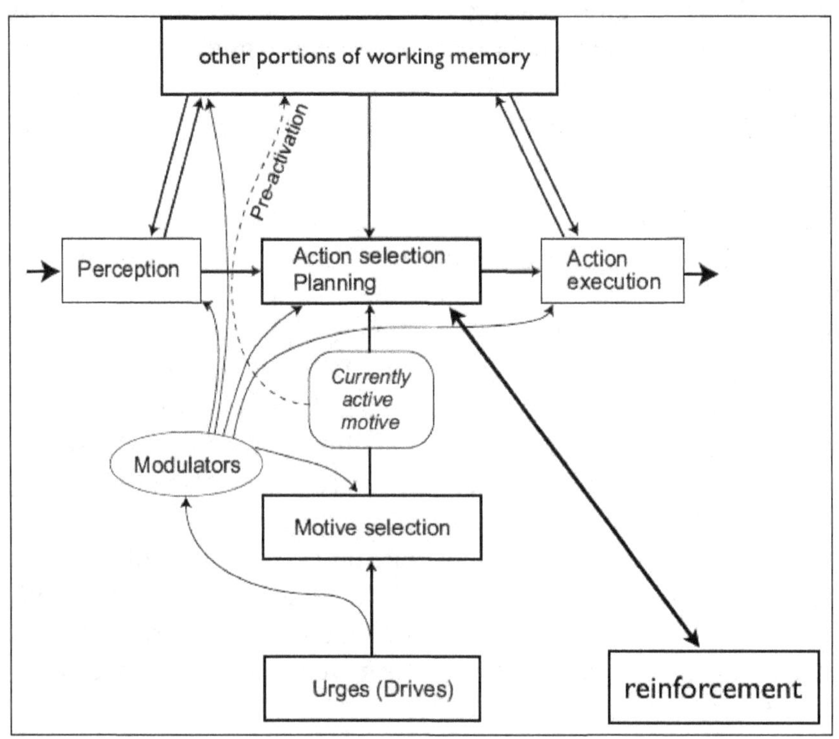

Architecture of Motivated Action.

Modeling motivation and action selection is a lightly modified version of the Psi diagram from Joscha Bach's book Principles of Synthetic Intelligence. The main difference from Psi is that in the integrative diagram the Psi motivated action framework is embedded in a larger, more complex cognitive model. Psi comes with its own theory of working and long-term memory, which is related to but different from the one given in the integrative diagram – it views the multiple memory types distinguished in the integrative diagram as emergent from a common memory substrate. Psi comes with its own theory of perception and action, which seems broadly consistent with the deep learning approach incorporated in the integrative diagram. Psi's handling of working memory lacks the detailed, explicit workflow of LIDA, though it seems broadly conceptually consistent with LIDA.

In Figure above the box labeled "Other parts of working memory" is labeled "Protocol and situation memory" in the original Psi diagram. The Perception, Action Execution and Action Selection boxes have fairly similar semantics to the similarly labeled boxes in the LIDA-like, so that these diagrams may be viewed as overlapping. The LIDA model doesn't explain action selection and planning in as much detail as Psi, so the Psi-like figure above could be viewed as an elaboration of the action-selection portion of the LIDA-like. In Psi, reinforcement is considered as part of the learning process involved in action selection and planning; in Figure an explicit "reinforcement box" has been added to the original Psi diagram, to emphasize this.

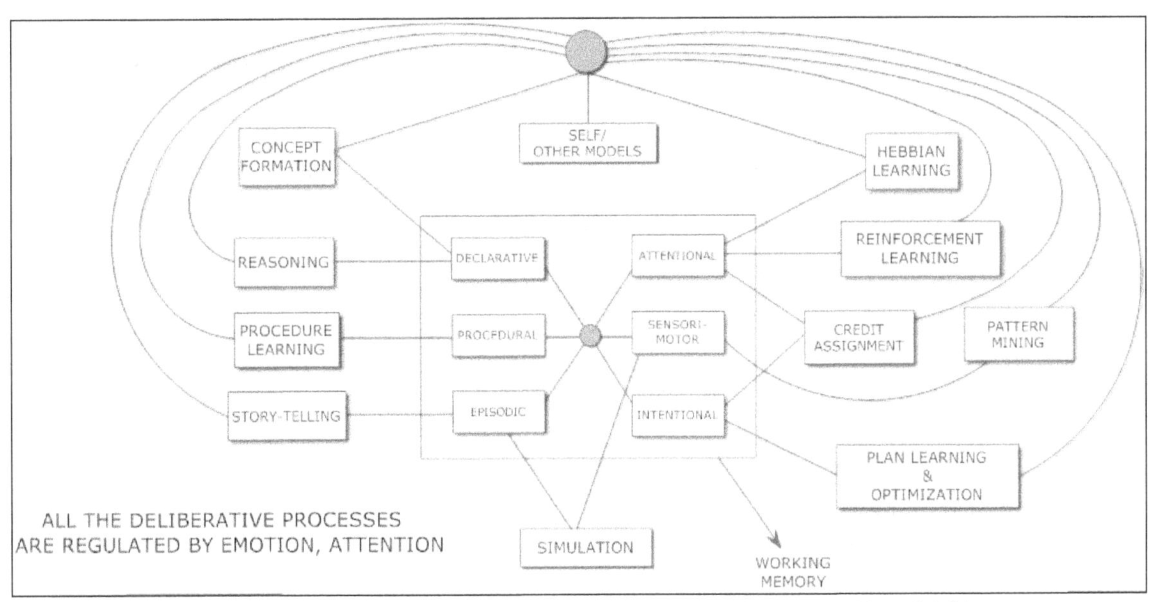

Architecture of Long-Term Memory and Deliberative and Metacognitive Thinking.

Figure above modeling long-term memory and deliberative processing, is derived from my own prior work studying the "cognitive synergy" between different cognitive processes associated with different types of memory, and seeking to embody this synergy into the OpenCog system. The division into types of memory is fairly standard in the cognitive science field. Declarative, procedural, episodic and sensorimotor memory are routinely distinguished; we like to distinguish attention memory and intentional (goal) memory as well, and view these as the interface between long-term memory and the mind's global control systems. One focus of our AGI design work has been on designing learning algorithms, corresponding to these various types of memory, that interact with each other in a synergetic way, helping each other to overcome their intrinsic combinatorial explosions. There is significant evidence that these various types of long-term memory are differently implemented in the brain, but the degree of structure and dynamical commonality underlying these different implementations remains unclear.

Each of these long-term memory types has its analogue in working memory as well. In some cognitive models, the working memory and long-term memory versions of a memory type and corresponding cognitive processes is basically the same thing. OpenCog is mostly like this – it implements working memory as a subset of long-term memory consisting of items with particularly high importance values. The distinctive nature of working memory is enforced via using slightly different dynamical equations to update the importance values of items with importance above a certain threshold. On the other hand, many cognitive models treat working and long term memory as more distinct than this, and there is evidence for significant functional and anatomical distinctness in the brain in some cases. So for the purpose of the integrative diagram, it seemed best to leave working and long-term memory subcomponents as parallel but distinguished.

Figure above may be interpreted to encompass both workaday deliberative thinking and metacognition ("thinking about thinking"), under the hypothesis that in human beings and human-like minds, metacognitive thinking is carried out using basically the same processes as plain ordinary deliberative thinking, perhaps with various tweaks optimizing them for thinking about thinking. If it turns out that humans have, say, a special kind of reasoning faculty exclusively for metacognition, then the diagram would need to be modified. Modeling of self and others is understood to occur via a combination of metacognition and deliberative thinking, as well as via implicit adaptation based on reactive processing.

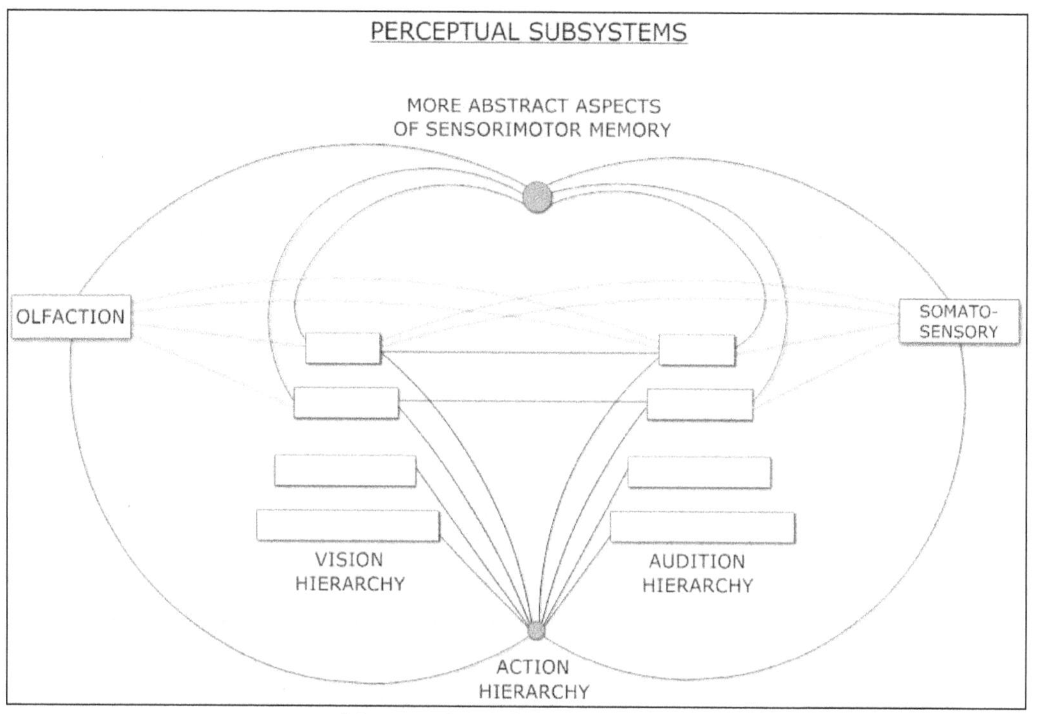

Architecture for Multimodal Perception.

Figure above models perception, according to the concept of deep learning. Vision and audition are modeled as deep learning hierarchies, with bottom-up and top-down dynamics. The lower layers in each hierarchy refer to more localized patterns recognized in, and abstracted from, sensory data. Output from these hierarchies to the rest of the mind is not just through the top layers, but via some sort of sampling from various layers, with a bias toward the top layers. The different hierarchies cross-connect, and are hence to an extent dynamically coupled together. It is also recognized that there are some sensory modalities that aren't strongly hierarchical, e.g. touch and smell (the latter being better modeled as something like an asymmetric Hopfield net, prone to frequent chaotic dynamics – these may also cross-connect with each other and with the more hierarchical perceptual sub networks. Of course the suggested architecture could include any number of sensory modalities; the diagram is restricted to four just for simplicity.

The self-organized patterns in the upper layers of perceptual hierarchies may become quite complex and may develop advanced cognitive capabilities like episodic memory, reasoning, language learning, etc. A pure deep learning approach to intelligence argues that all the aspects of intelligence emerge from this kind of dynamics (among perceptual, action and reinforcement hierarchies). My own view is that the heterogeneity of human brain architecture argues against this perspective, and that deep learning systems are probably better as models of perception and action than of general cognition. However, the integrative diagram is not committed to my perspective on this – a deep-learning theorist could accept the integrative diagram, but argue that all the other portions besides the perceptual, action and reinforcement hierarchies should be viewed as descriptions of phenomena that emerge in these hierarchies due to their interaction.

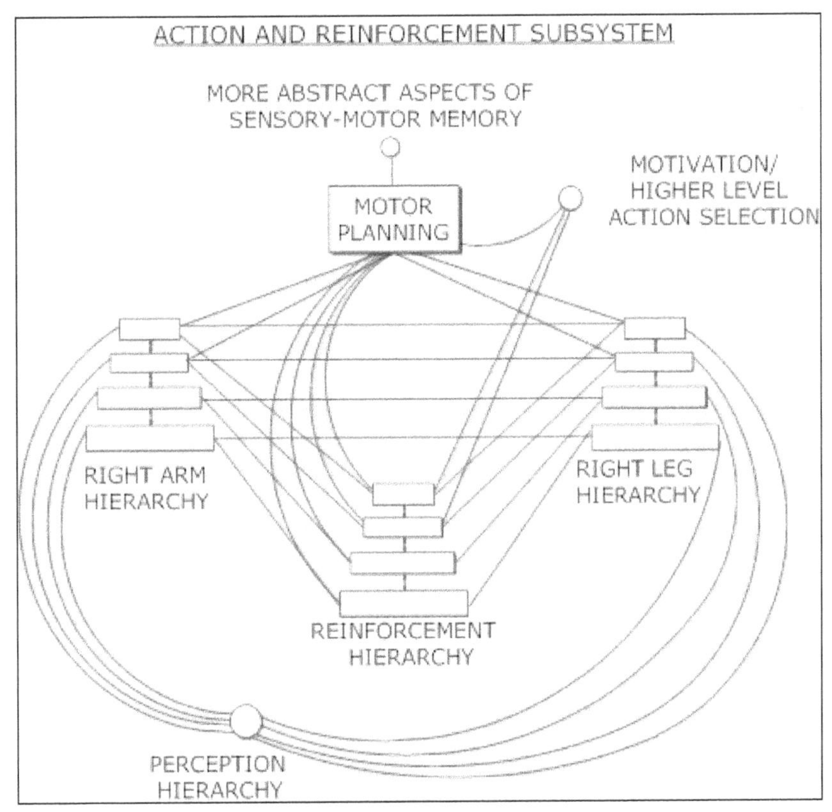

Architecture for Action and Reinforcement.

Figure above shows an action subsystem and a reinforcement subsystem, parallel to the perception subsystem. Two action hierarchies, one for an arm and one for a leg, are shown for concreteness, but of course the architecture is intended to be extended more broadly. In the hierarchy corresponding to an arm, for example, the lowest level would contain control patterns corresponding to individual joints, the next level up to groupings of joints (like fingers), the next level up to larger parts of the arm (hand, elbow). The different hierarchies corresponding to different body parts cross-link, enabling coordination among body parts; and they also connect at multiple levels to perception hierarchies, enabling sensorimotor coordination. Finally there is a module for motor planning, which links tightly with all the motor hierarchies, and also overlaps with the more cognitive, inferential planning activities of the mind, in a manner that is modeled different ways by different theorists. Albus has elaborated this kind of hierarchy quite elaborately. The reinforcement hierarchy in figure provides reinforcement to actions at various levels on the hierarchy, and includes dynamics for propagating information about reinforcement up and down the hierarchy.

Figure architecture for language processing deals with language, treating it as a special case of coupled perception and action. The traditional architecture of a computational language comprehension system is a pipeline, which is equivalent to a hierarchy with the lowest-level linguistic features (e.g. sounds, words) at the bottom, and the highest level features (semantic abstractions) at the top, and syntactic features in the middle. Feedback connections enable semantic and cognitive modulation of lower-level linguistic processing. Similarly, language generation is commonly modeled hierarchically, with the top levels being the ideas needing verbalization, and the bottom level corresponding to the actual sentence produced. In generation the primary flow is top-down, with bottom-up flow providing modulation of abstract concepts by linguistic surface forms.

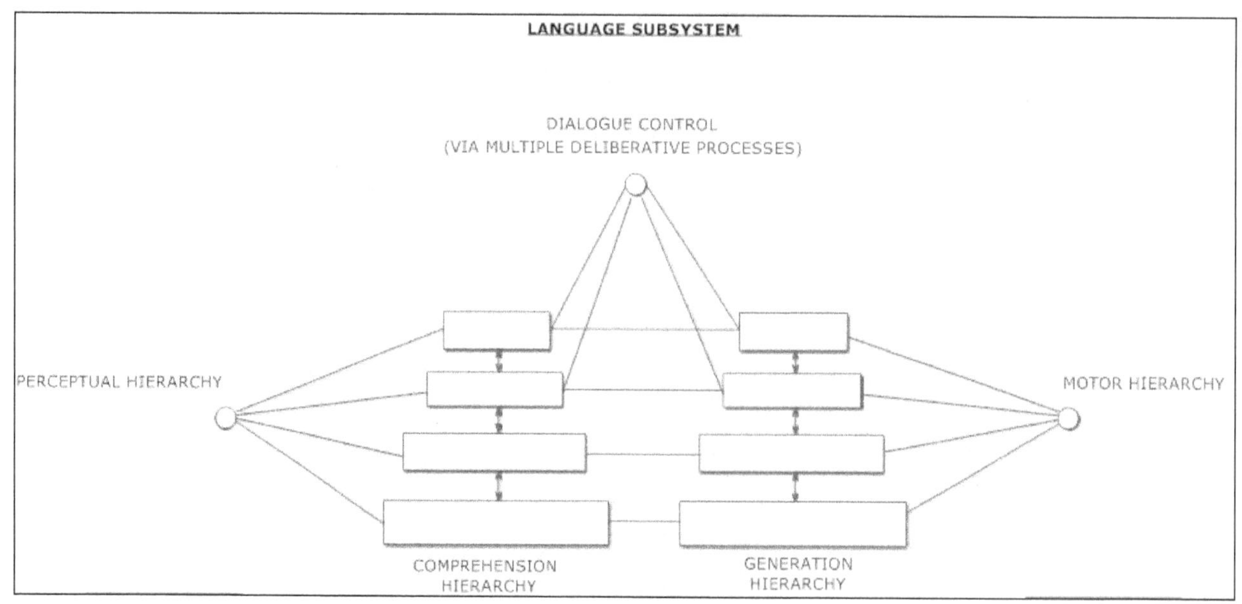

Architecture for Language Processing.

This completes the posited, rough integrative architecture diagram for human-like general intelligence, split among 7 different pictures, formed by judiciously merging together architecture diagrams produced via a number of cognitive theorists with different, overlapping foci and research paradigms. One may wonder: Is anything critical left out of the diagram? A quick perusal of the table of contents of cognitive psychology textbooks suggests that if anything major is left out, it's also unknown to current cognitive psychology. However, one could certainly make an argument for explicit inclusion of certain other aspects of intelligence, that in the integrative diagram are left as implicit emergent phenomena. For instance, creativity is obviously very important to intelligence, but, there is no "creativity" box in any of these diagrams – because in our view, and the view of the cognitive theorists whose work we've directly drawn on here, creativity is best viewed as a process emergent from other processes that are explicitly included in the diagrams.

A high-level "cognitive architecture diagram" like this is certainly not a design for an AGI. Rather, it is more like a pointer in the direction of a requirements specification. These are, to a rough approximation, the aspects that must be taken into account, by anyone who wants to create a human-level AGI; and this is how these aspects appear to interact in the human mind. Different AGI approaches may account for these aspects and their interactions in different ways – e.g. via explicitly encoding them, or creating a system from which they can emerge, etc.

Metrics and Environments for Human-Level AGI

Science hinges on measurement; so if AGI is a scientific pursuit, it must be possible to measure what it means to achieve it. Given the variety of approaches to AGI, it is hardly surprising that there are also multiple approaches to quantifying and measuring the achievement of AGI. However, things get a little simpler if one restricts attention to the sub problem of creating "human-level" AGI.

When one talk about AGI beyond the human level or AGI that is very qualitatively different from human intelligence, then the measurement issue becomes very abstract – one basically has to choose a mathematical measure of general intelligence, and adopt it as a measure of success. This is a meaningful approach, yet also worrisome, because it's difficult to tell, at this stage, what relation any of the existing mathematical measures of general intelligence is going to have to practical systems.

When one talks about human-level AGI, however, the measurement problem gets a lot more concrete: one can use tests designed to measure human performance, or tests designed relative to human behavior. The measurement issue then decomposes into two sub problems: quantifying achievement of the goal of human-level AGI, and measuring incremental progress toward that goal. The former sub problem turns out to be considerably more straightforward.

Metrics and Environments

The issue of metrics is closely tied up with the issue of "environments" for AGI systems. For AGI systems that are agents interacting with some environment, any method of measuring the general intelligence of these agents will involve the particulars of the AGI systems' environments. If an AGI is implemented to control video game characters, then its intelligence must be measured in the video game context. If an AGI is built with solely a textual user interface, then its intelligence must be measured purely via conversation, without measuring, for example, visual pattern recognition.

And the importance of environments for AGI goes beyond the value of metrics. Even if one doesn't care about quantitatively comparing two AGI systems, it may still be instructive to qualitatively observe the different ways they face similar situations in the same environment. Using multiple AGI systems in the same environment also increases the odds of code-sharing and concept sharing between different systems. It makes it easier to conceptually compare what different systems are doing and how they're working.

It is often useful to think in terms of "scenarios" for AGI systems, where a "scenario" means an environment plus a set of tasks defined in that environment, plus a set of metrics to measure performance on those tasks. At this stage, it is unrealistic to expect all AGI researchers to agree to conduct their research relative to the same scenario. The early-stage manifestations of different AGI approaches tend to fit naturally with different sorts of environments and tasks. However, to whatever extent it is sensible for multiple AGI projects to share common environments or scenarios, this sort of cooperation should be avidly pursued.

Quantifying the Milestone of Human-Level AGI

A variety of metrics, relative to various different environments, may be used to measure achievement of the goal of "human-level AGI." Examples include:

- The classic Turing Test conceived as (roughly) "fooling a panel of college-educated human judges, during a one hour long interrogation, that one is a human being".
- The Virtual World Turing Test occurring in an online virtual world, where the AGI and the human controls are controlling avatars (this is inclusive of the standard Turing Test if one assumes the avatars can use language).
- Shane Legg's AIQ measure Legg and Veness, which is a computationally practical approximation to the algorithmic information theory based formalization of general intelligence. Work by Hernandez-Orallo and Dowe pursues a similar concept with different technical details.

- Text compression: The idea being that any algorithm capable of understanding text should be transformable into an algorithm for compressing text based on the patterns it recognizes therein. This is the basis of the Hutter Prize a cash prize funded by Marcus Hutter which rewards data compression improvements on a specific 100 MB English text file.
- The Online University Student Test, where an AGI has to obtain a college degree at an online university, carrying out the same communications with the professors and the other students as a human student would (including choosing its curriculum, etc).
- The Robot University Student Test, where an AGI has to obtain a college degree at a physical university, carrying out the same communications with the professors and the other students as a human student would, and also moving about the campus and handling relevant physical objects in a sufficient manner to complete the coursework.
- The Artificial Scientist Test, where an AGI that can do high-quality, original scientific research, including choosing the research problem, reading the relevant literature, writing and publishing the paper, etc. (this may be refined to a Nobel Prize Test, where the AGI has do original scientific research that wins a Nobel Prize).

Each of these approaches has its pluses and minuses. None of them can sensibly be considered necessary conditions for human-level intelligence, but any of them may plausibly be considered sufficient conditions. The latter three have the disadvantage that they may not be achievable by every human – so they may set the bar a little too high. The former two have the disadvantage of requiring AGI systems to imitate humans, rather than just honestly being themselves; and it may be that accurately imitating humans when one does not have a human body or experience requires significantly greater than human level intelligence. Regardless of the practical shortcomings of the above measures, though, we believe they are basically adequate as precipitations of "what it means to achieve human-level general intelligence."

Metrics Assessing Generality of Machine Learning Capability

Complementing the above tests that are heavily inspired by human everyday life, there is also some more computer science oriented evaluation paradigms aimed at assessing AI systems going beyond specific tasks. For instance, there is a literature on multitask learning, where the goal for an AI is to learn one task quicker given another task solved previously. There is a literature on shaping, where the idea is to build up the capability of an AI by training it on progressively more difficult versions of the same tasks. Also, Achler has proposed criteria measuring the "flexibility of recognition" and posited this as a key measure of progress toward AGI.

While we applaud the work done in these areas, we also note it is an open question whether exploring these sorts of processes using mathematical abstractions, or in the domain of various machine-learning or robotics test problems, is capable of adequately addressing the problem of AGI. The potential problem with this kind of approach is that generalization among tasks, or from simpler to more difficult versions of the same task, is a process whose nature may depend strongly on the overall nature of the set of tasks and task-versions involved. Real-world humanly-relevant tasks have a subtlety of interconnectedness and developmental course that is not captured in current mathematical learning frameworks or standard AI test problems.

To put it a little differently, it is possible that all of the following hold:

- The universe of real-world human tasks may possess a host of "special statistical properties that have implications regarding what sorts of AI programs will be most suitable.
- Exploring and formalizing and generalizing these statistical properties are an important research area.
- An easier and more reliable approach to AGI testing is to create a testing environment that embodies these properties implicitly, via constituting an emulation of the most cognitively meaningful aspects of the real-world human learning environment.

Another way to think about these issues is to contrast the above-mentioned "AGI Roadmap Workshop" ideas with the "General Game Player (GGP) AI competition, in which AIs seek to learn to play games based on formal descriptions of the rules. Clearly doing GGP well requires powerful AGI; and doing GGP even mediocrely probably requires robust multitask learning and shaping. But it is unclear whether GGP constitutes a good approach to testing early-stage AI programs aimed at roughly humanlike intelligence. This is because, unlike the tasks involved in, say, making coffee in an arbitrary house, or succeeding in preschool or university, the tasks involved in doing simple instances of GGP seem to have little relationship to humanlike intelligence or real-world human tasks.

So, an important open question is whether the class of statistical biases present in the set of real-world human environments tasks, has some sort of generalizable relevance to AGI beyond the scope of human-like general intelligence, or is informative only about the particularities of human-like intelligence. Currently we seem to lack any solid, broadly accepted theoretical framework for resolving this sort of question.

Why is Measuring Incremental Progress Toward AGI so Hard?

A question raised by these various observations is whether there is some fundamental reason why it's hard to make an objective, theory-independent measure of intermediate progress toward advanced AGI, which respects the environment and task biased nature of human intelligence as well as the mathematical generality of the AGI concept. Is it just that we haven't been smart enough to figure out the right test – or is there some conceptual reason why the very notion of such a test is problematic?

Why might a solid, objective empirical test for intermediate progress toward humanly meaningful AGI be such a difficult project? One possible reason could be the phenomenon of "cognitive synergy" briefly noted above. In this hypothesis, for instance, it might be that there are 10 critical components required for a human-level AGI system. Having all 10 of them in place results in human-level AGI, but having only 8 of them in place results in having a dramatically impaired system – and maybe having only 6 or 7 of them in place results in a system that can hardly do anything at all.

Of course, the reality is not as strict as the simplified example in the above paragraph suggests. No AGI theorist has really posited a list of 10 crisply-defined subsystems and claimed them necessary and sufficient for AGI. We suspect there are many different routes to AGI, involving integration of different sorts of subsystems. However, if the cognitive synergy hypothesis is correct, then human-level AGI behaves roughly like the simplistic example in the prior paragraph suggests. Perhaps instead of using the 10 components, you could achieve human-level AGI with 7 components, but having only 5 of these 7 would yield drastically impaired functionality – etc. To mathematically formalize the cognitive synergy hypothesis becomes complex, but here we're only aiming for a qualitative argument. So for illustrative purposes, we'll stick with the "10 components" example, just for communicative simplicity.

Next, let's additionally suppose that for any given task, there are ways to achieve this task using a system that is much simpler than any subset of size 6 drawn from the set of 10 components needed for human-level AGI, but works much better for the task than this subset of 6 components (assuming the latter are used as a set of only 6 components, without the other 4 components).

This additional supposition is a good bit stronger than mere cognitive synergy. Tricky cognitive synergy would be the case if, for example, the following possibilities were true:

- Creating components to serve as parts of a synergetic AGI is harder than creating components intended to serve as parts of simpler AI systems without synergetic dynamics.
- Components capable of serving as parts of a synergetic AGI are necessarily more complicated than components intended to serve as parts of simpler AI systems.

These certainly seem reasonable possibilities, since to serve as a component of a synergetic AGI system; a component must have the internal flexibility to usefully handle interactions with a lot of other components as well as to solve the problems that come its way. If tricky cognitive synergy holds up as a property of human-level general intelligence, the difficulty of formulating tests for intermediate progress toward human-level AGI follows as a consequence. Because, according to the tricky cognitive synergy hypothesis, any test is going to be more easily solved by some simpler narrow AI process than by a partially complete human-level AGI system.

At the current stage in the development of AGI, we don't really know how big a role "tricky cognitive synergy" plays in the general intelligence. Quite possibly, 5 or 10 years from now someone will have developed wonderfully precise and practical metrics for the evaluation of incremental progress toward human-level AGI. However, it's worth carefully considering the possibility that fundamental obstacles, tied to the nature of general intelligence, stand in the way of this possibility.

What would a General Theory of General Intelligence Look Like?

While most approaches to creating AGI are theoretically motivated in one way or another, nobody would claim there currently exists a thorough and systematic theory of AGI in the same sense that there exist theories of say, sorting algorithms, respiration, genetics, or near-equilibrium thermodynamics. Current AGI theory is a patchwork of overlapping concepts, frameworks and hypotheses, often synergetic and sometimes mutually contradictory. Current AGI system designs are usually inspired by theories, but do not have all their particulars derived from theories.

The creation of an adequate theoretical foundation for AGI is far beyond the scope of this review paper; however, it does seem worthwhile to briefly comment on what we may hope to get out of such a theory once it has been developed. Or in other words: What might a general theory of general intelligence look like? Some of the things AGI researchers would like to do with a general theory of general intelligence are:

- Given a description of a set of goals and environments (and perhaps a probability distribution over these), and a set of computational resource restrictions, determine what is the system architecture that will display the maximum general intelligence relative to these goals and environments, subject to the given restrictions.

- Given a description of system architecture, figure out what are the goals and environments, with respect to which it will reach a relatively high level of general intelligence.
- Given intelligent system architecture, determine what sort of subjective experience the system will likely report having, in various contexts.
- Given a set of subjective experiences and associated environments, determine what sort of intelligent system will likely have those experiences in those environments.
- Find a practical way to synthesize a general-intelligence test appropriate for a given class of reasonably similar intelligent systems.
- Identify the implicit representations of abstract concepts, arising within emergentist, hybrid, program learning based or other non-wholly-symbolic intelligent systems.
- Given a certain intelligent system in a certain environment, predict the likely course of development of that system as it learns experiences and grows.
- Given a set of behavioral constraints (for instance, ethical constraints), estimate the odds that a given system will obey the constraints given certain assumptions about its environment. Determine architectures that, consistent with given computational resource constraints, provide an optimal balance between general intelligence for specified goals and environments, and adherence to given behavioral constraints.
- What are the key structures and dynamics required for an AGI system to achieve human-level, human-like general intelligence within feasible computational resources?
- Predict the consequences of releasing an AGI into the world, depending on its level of intelligence and some specificities of its design.
- Determine methods of assessing the ethical character of an AGI system, both in its current form and in future incarnations likely to develop from its current form.

Anyone familiar with the current state of AGI research will find it hard to suppress a smile at this ambitious list of objectives. At the moment we would seem very far from having a theoretical understanding capable of thoroughly addressing any of these points, in a practically useful way. It is unclear to how far the limits of mathematics and computing will allow us to progress toward theoretical goals such as these. However: the further we can get in this direction, the better off the AGI field will be.

At the moment, AGI system design is as much artistic as scientific, relying heavily on the designer's scientific intuition. AGI implementation and testing are interwoven with (more or less) inspired tinkering, according to which systems are progressively improved internally as their behaviors are observed in various situations. This sort of approach is not unworkable, and many great inventions have been created via similar processes. It's unclear how necessary or useful a more advanced AGI theory will be for the creation of practical AGI systems. But it seems likely that, the further we can get toward a theory providing tools to address questions like those listed above, the more systematic and scientific the AGI design process will become, and the more capable the resulting systems.

It's possible that a thorough, rigorous theory of AGI will emerge from the mind of some genius AGI researcher, in one fell swoop – or from the mind of one of the early AGI successes itself! However, it appears more probable that the emergence of such a theory will be a gradual process, in which theoretical and experimental developments progress hand in hand.

Strong Artificial Intelligence

Strong Artificial Intelligence (AI) is a theoretical form of machine intelligence that is equal to human intelligence. Key characteristics of Strong AI include the ability to reason, solve puzzles, make judgments, plan, learn, and communicate. It should also have consciousness, objective thoughts, self-awareness, sentience, and sapience. Strong AI is also called True Intelligence or Artificial General Intelligence (AGI).

Strong AI does not currently exist. Some experts predict it may be developed by 2030 or 2045. Others more conservatively predict that it may be developed within the next century, or that the development of Strong AI may not be possible at all.

Some theorists argue that a machine with Strong AI should be able to go through the same development process as a human, starting with a childlike mind and developing an adult mind through learning. It should be able to interact with the world and learn from it, acquiring its own common sense and language. Another argument is that we will not know when we have developed strong AI (if it can indeed be developed) because there is no consensus on what constitutes intelligence.

While Weak AI merely simulates human cognition, Strong AI would actually have human cognition. With Strong AI, a single system could theoretically handle all the same problems that a single human could. While Weak AI can replace many low- and medium-skilled workers, Strong AI might be necessary to replace certain categories of highly skilled workers.

Risks and Rewards of Strong AI

The possibility of Strong AI comes with major potential benefits and serious concerns. Some people fear that if Strong AI becomes a reality, AI may become more intelligent than humans, a phenomenon known as the singularity. The idea is that Strong AI will be so intelligent that it can alter itself and pursue its own goals without human intervention, possibly in ways that are harmful to humans. Could Strong AI be developed with constraints to prevent such outcomes? Could Strong AI be programmed with desirable moral values, and could humanity agree on what those desirable values would be? Further research into these issues could help prevent the possibility of robots that turn against us, or determine if they could even ever exist.

Another major concern is that AI will increasingly take jobs away from people, resulting in high unemployment – even for knowledge-intensive white-collar work, especially if Strong AI becomes a reality. However, just as the Industrial Revolution dramatically changed the types of jobs workers performed, an AI Revolution could result not in massive unemployment, but in a massive employment shift. Strong AI could have a significant positive impact on society by increasing productivity and wealth. Humans could perform jobs that we cannot even imagine today and will not have a need for until we see all that AI can do for us. Another possibility is that the government will have to step in a provide a safety net for those displaced by AI.

Observe: Sentient Surveillance Systems

To observe is more than just to see. It is the active surveillance of the situation, which is the combination of focusing attention at key areas and making connections between disparate sources. In the big data era, the exponential growth in sensory data available has outpaced humans' ability to manually process it. Today, AI systems are deployed to aid human operations by automating the manual processes in a single system. Tomorrow, the mass proliferation of sensors will mean that the AI will be needed to orchestrate the data collection effort on top of processing in multiple systems and domains.

At present, AIs successes in a specific task prediction performance usually involve deep neural networks that depend on having large amounts of annotated training datasets and high-quality data. However, in certain contexts, it can be difficult, if not impossible, to obtain large training data. Hence, the AIs of tomorrow will have to overcome this hurdle by employing the techniques of transfer learning, or domain adaptation and "few-shot" learning. For example, in the prediction of age from images of faces, Rothe et al. starts from a neural network trained on general images adapts it to the task of face and age estimation using data automatically obtained from the Internet (0.5 million age-annotated face images in IMDB); and tunes the model for the particular dataset of 2.5 thousand images. The extreme case is training AIs with no data, in what is called zero-shot learning. In such a case, the adaptation is done via constraining the algorithms and extracting features of the algorithm to be used in the new task. This requires mimicking human ingenuity in understanding the relation between different tasks and exploiting the latent features induced by the learning algorithm.

Orient: Emotionally Intelligent Cyborgs

To orient to a new situation, is to analyze past experiences and synthesize them with the current observations. The real operating environment is not a clinical environment. It is further complicated by human actors, who have different dynamic behaviors. To have the correct orientation in a complex situation requires tacit understanding of human emotions.

The AI needs to be emotionally aware to be an effective team player alongside its human counterparts. It needs to comprehend human idiosyncrasies and biases in complex situations, and exploit human weaknesses when necessary. The aim is not to build a machine that can cry or express its emotions to make it look more human-like, but rather to detect and recognize a particular state of emotion the human user is in and use the additional information to adjust its actions. In addition, human emotions can lower the quality of his decision-making ability, and at the critical juncture, the AI system can step up to complement or augment the decisions made. Emotional intelligence in AI systems can also have other usages like detecting the emotional states of social groups or even to encourage pro-social behavior in a population by the use of large-scale emotional AI.

Decide: Imaginative Machines

Decide is the generation of the courses of actions or hypotheses after orientating to the situation. Hypotheses generation is not a regurgitation of experiences, for the environment is dynamic and reactive. In the military context, the thinking enemy is part of the equation. Inspired decision-making requires imagination, one of the hallmarks of human intelligence. With the ability to imagine, humans can mentally transcend space and time, and dream of something novel. Current advancements in data analytics address the "what is" and some of the "what" that are embedded in the data. With imagination, it can bring out the why. In addition, an imaginative AI is able to create new problems to solve, which could be viewed as a form of exploration with no explicit objective functions, and could eventually lead to better methods and solutions.

One area of active research is learning affordance — the ability to perceive an object as in not only its current state, but also what can be done with it. This gives the machine the flexibility it needs to "think out of the data" and manipulate objects or its environment beyond statically defined tasks. While this idea of an imagination machine is not a novel idea, these ideas have been explored in an area known as computational creativity. This creativity has been expressed in areas such as music, novels, paintings, and engineering. We hope future AI could "imagine" and produce strategies and operating concepts, aid in the design of advanced materials and equipment, and aid in cryptanalysis by thinking out of the data.

Act: Robots/Actuator

Act is to carry out the decided course of action. For the modern military, "act" includes the use of unmanned systems and robotics. Today, robotic systems that operate autonomously are typically pre-programmed to perform well-defined actions. Future robotic systems have to operate autonomously under varying mission outcomes that deviate from pre-programmed tasks. Mission planning that is dynamically modifiable is a requirement for the autonomous system to cope with changing mission outcomes. Additionally, dynamic re-tasking of sensors and payloads may be needed to support aided target recognition, identification and tracking. Precise navigation and timing is another key enabler for autonomous systems operation that allows understanding of the operational area, sensor cueing and collision avoidance. Cognitive techniques and algorithms are needed to integrate sensing, perceiving, analyzing, communicating, planning, decision-making, and executing, in order to fully realize the operational benefits of robotic systems.

In the near future, robotic systems have to work autonomously and collaboratively in executing missions. For example, applications such as surveillance and reconnaissance, search and rescue, mapping unknown environments and payload transportation can be performed by having a collaborative system consisting of Unmanned Surface Vehicles (USV) and Unmanned Aerial Vehicles (UAV). By having a USV—UAV collaborative system which leverages on their complementary properties, it provides humans at the higher command center with richer information to achieve the mission of a patrol system.

Closing the Loop: Self-referential and Self-reflecting AI System

After every action by the AI system, the environment would react. The AI system would then observe those phenomena and the decision cycle repeats. This closes the OODA loop. However, without a means of self-inspection, such an AI system would be susceptible to being trapped in a closed loop. A common quote that perfectly sums this up is insanity is doing the same thing over and expecting a different result. Fortunately, humans have the capacity to exercise introspection, to learn and improve their internal states and purpose. The introspective ability is a defining feature of future Strong AIs.

Introspection can be defined as self-referencing and self-reflecting. Building Strong AI with self-referential ability will allow its function to refer to itself, like recursion in programming, but the ultimate aim is to give it its own ability to modify its function by rewriting its own source code. An AI system with self-referential ability should be able to represent its own state in its own native memory representation. States within the AI system could represent error rates, utility values over time, metadata pertaining to the environment, and an embedding of the system's Finite state machine.

Man—Machine Collaboration

To achieve Strong AI would require a partnership between Man and Machine. For example, to imbue AIs with emotional intelligence would require factoring of humans idiosyncrasies and biases. This can be achieved with interactive reinforcement learning where the human acts as a critic of the AI training process. However, this interactive process, while necessary, may introduce human tendencies problems such as:

- Humans tend to reward good actions that have diminishing returns over time but consistently punish bad actions.
- Reward hacking (gaming the system).
- Contradictory constraints (yes means no).

Additionally, humans are subjective, and behavioral differences between different people might taint the human-in-the-loop learning process. When building AI with emotional intelligence, the training phase with human-in-the-loop should be designed around human trainers rather than the human trainers simply being a small component in the training process.

For an effective partnership between Man and Machine, the evolving AI agent needs to be trusted by the human. Such trust is more readily established if the agent can explain the manner in which it arrives at its decision or recommendation. While the previous generation of tools based on their human engineered set of rules can generate plausible explanations, the increasing use of deep learning methods due to their superior performance is making this harder to accomplish. With explanations, one may envision tighter man—machine interaction to achieve better results. For example, Malasky has designed a resource allocation and planning strategy where humans are involved in selecting options and variables proposed by an algorithm in an iterative manner. For the task of inferring the relation between two entities in a natural language text, Sameer has proposed that humans study the chain of reasoning given by the algorithm and correcting only the part of the reasoning that is wrong. Enabling humans to examine the explanations and correct the algorithms is one manner to overcome the challenge of low-data regime. These are examples of Man-Machine collaborative reasoning, which is part of an emerging field known as collaborative and coactive AI systems. The idea is to bring out the best of both worlds by considering the advantages and disadvantages of both human and machine processes when designing AI systems.

Reliable and Safe AI Systems

As AI sees wide adoption, there will be an increased competition in AI systems, not only between industries and countries, but from malicious actors as well. Adversarial AI is an emerging field that uses AI techniques for the attack and defense of AI models. Examples of attacks can range from evading spam filter, to tricking the AI into seeing something that is not, like misclassifying a turtle as a rifle. Such adversarial attacks could be employed by terrorists to avoid automated detection when publishing online materials or by adversaries to sabotage the perception system of autonomous vehicles during times of conflict. On the other hand, there are advances in adversarial defenses, too. This form of defense includes pre-processing-based methods to remove the adversarial signal, adversarial training to make the AI more robust, and the use of conceptual reasoning to form a secondary check. Future AI systems will likely be complex and incomprehensible to most humans. Thus, other AI systems would be needed to secure the operational AI systems using adversarial defense techniques and be qualified as safe from adversarial attacks.

Can Strong AI Achieve Consciousness?

Building AI systems as an aid to humans and more towards a man—machine collaboration such as augmented intelligence, leads to the amplification of human intelligence. It is more human centric than the AI system centric design. The AI system centric design concept has the ultimate quest of building a Strong AI or AGI where the AI has super intelligence, autonomy and human-like consciousness. Can humans build such an AI system that has consciousness?

- What is consciousness and why are we conscious? Thus far, nobody has any idea exactly what is consciousness in humans. Thus, that brings us back to the basic problem, i.e. we do not have the know-how to design the AI system with the same consciousness as humans, since we do not know it ourselves. However, assuming in the future, humans are able to use material means to design Strong AI-like human intelligence, can the Strong AI intelligence achieve consciousness? That leads to the fundamental question of whether pure material means of intelligence give rise to consciousness; or is consciousness more than just material? This is related to the Mind–Brain (or Mind–Body) problem. Lewis said, “Consciousness is either inexplicable illusion, or else revelation”.

- On the Mind–Brain Problem: The Mind–Brain problem breaks down into two possibilities, i.e. the materialism view and the non-materialism view. Hence, we are faced with the question of how our minds have self-awareness and self-dialogue capabilities, a mind that asks questions such as, “What, Who and Why am I?” All matter originates and exists only by virtue of a force. We must assume behind this force the existence of a conscious and intelligent mind.” Hence, there exists something beyond materialism.

- Intelligence and Consciousness: In our biological brain, the intelligence and consciousness that have “conscience” is connected. In today’s AI system, the designs of intelligence and “conscience” are separated; and we do not yet know how to design it as a tightly connected structure. As intelligence and consciousness are linked and not separated, our purpose and value of doing intelligence work are governed by our conscience. Would AI systems be able to have this capability?

- Legal and Moral Law: One of our greatest fears of building Strong AI is the total autonomy of the AI system. Hence, we have debates on legality and morality for autonomous systems such as self-driving cars if an accident were to occur on the road. Can we mirror the human system by building morality rules into the AI system? Picard said, "The greater the freedom of a machine, the more it will need moral standards." Can AI systems reach full autonomy and have freedom to make its own decisions?
- Full AI System Autonomy: Boddington's account reflects the human situation, "For if we see the Genesis account of the Fall of man as foreshadowing our fears about robots, then Genesis gets the problem exactly right, for exactly the right reasons – it's a worry about autonomy itself: what might robots do if we can't control them fully? Will they adhere to the same value system as us? Will they decide to disobey us? What will our relationship with our creations be? We can thank the Hebrew account of Genesis for pre-warning us thousands and thousands of years ago." Boddington brought up an interesting point on human freedom and turning his back to his creator. However, this will not happen in the AI system because of the gaps mention and at best, governing rules will be built into the AI system in its decision process.

Symbolic Artificial Intelligence

Symbolic AI involves the explicit embedding of human knowledge and behavior rules into computer programs. The practice showed a lot of promise in the early decades of AI research. But in recent years, as neural networks, also known as connectionist AI, gained traction, symbolic AI has fallen by the wayside.

The Role of Symbols in Artificial Intelligence

Symbols are things we use to represent other things. Symbols play a vital role in the human thought and reasoning process. We use symbols all the time to define things (cat, car, airplane, etc.) and people (teacher, police, and salesperson). Symbols can represent abstract concepts (bank transaction) or things that don't physically exist (web page, blog post, etc). They can also describe actions (running) or states (inactive). Symbols can be organized into hierarchies (a car is made of doors, windows, tires, seats, etc). They can also be used to describe other symbols (a cat with fluffy ears, a red carpet, etc).

Being able to communicate in symbols is one of the main things that make us intelligent. Therefore, symbols have also played a crucial role in the creation of artificial intelligence. The early pioneers of AI believed that "every aspect of learning or any other feature of intelligence can in principle be so precisely described that a machine can be made to simulate it." Therefore, symbolic AI took center stage and became the focus of research projects. Scientists developed tools to define and manipulate symbols.

Many of the concepts and tools you find in computer science are the results of these efforts. Symbolic AI programs are based on creating explicit structures and behavior rules. An example of symbolic AI tools is object-oriented programming. OOP languages allow you to define classes, specify their properties, and organize them in hierarchies. You can create instances of these classes (called objects) and manipulate their properties. Class instances can also perform actions, also known as functions, methods, or procedures. Each method executes a series of rule-based instructions that might read and change the properties of the current and other objects. Using OOP, you can create extensive and complex symbolic AI programs that perform various tasks.

The Benefits and Limits of Symbolic AI

Symbolic artificial intelligence showed early progress at the dawn of AI and computing. You can easily visualize the logic of rule-based programs, communicate them, and troubleshoot them. Symbolic artificial intelligence is very convenient for settings where the rules are very clear cut, and you can easily obtain input and transform it into symbols. In fact, rule-based systems still account for most computer programs today, including those used to create deep learning applications.

But symbolic AI starts to break when you must deal with the messiness of the world. For instance, consider computer vision, the science of enabling computers to make sense of the content of images and video. Say you have a picture of your cat and want to create a program that can detect images that contain your cat. You create a rule-based program that takes new images as inputs, compares the pixels to the original cat image, and responds by saying whether your cat is in those images.

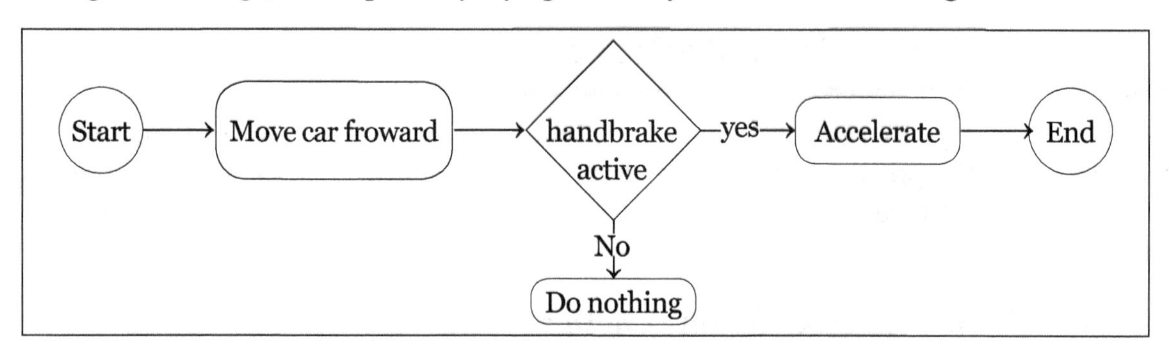

Flowcharts can depict the logic of symbolic AI programs very clearly.

This will only work as you provide an exact copy of the original image to your program. A slightly different picture of your cat will yield a negative answer. For instance, if you take a picture of your cat from a somewhat different angle, the program will fail.

One solution is to take pictures of your cat from different angles and create new rules for your application to compare each input against all those images. Even if you take a million pictures of your cat, you still won't account for every possible case. A change in the lighting conditions or the background of the image will change the pixel value and cause the program to fail. You'll need millions of other pictures and rules for those. And what if you wanted to create a program that could detect any cat? How many rules would you need to create for that?

The cat example might sound silly, but these are the kinds of problems that symbolic AI programs have always struggled with. You can't define rules for the messy data that exists in the real world. For instance, how can you define the rules for a self-driving car to detect all the different pedestrians it might face? Also, some tasks can't be translated to direct rules, including speech recognition and natural language processing.

There have been several efforts to create complicated symbolic AI systems that encompass the multitudes of rules of certain domains. Called expert systems, these symbolic AI models use hardcoded knowledge and rules to tackle complicated tasks such as medical diagnosis. But they require a huge amount of effort by domain experts and software engineers and only work in very narrow use cases. As soon as you generalize the problem, there will be an explosion of new rules to add (remember the cat detection problem?), which will require more human labor. As some AI scientists point out, symbolic AI systems don't scale.

Neural Networks vs. Symbolic AI

Neural networks are almost as old as symbolic AI, but they were largely dismissed because they were inefficient and required compute resources that weren't available at the time. In the past decade, thanks to the large availability of data and processing power, deep learning has gained popularity and has pushed past symbolic AI systems.

The advantage of neural networks is that they can deal with messy and unstructured data. Take the cat detector example. Instead of manually laboring through the rules of detecting cat pixels, you can train a deep learning algorithm on many pictures of cats. The neural network then develops a statistical model for cat images. When you provide it with a new image, it will return the probability that it contains a cat.

Deep learning and neural networks excel at exactly the tasks that symbolic AI struggles with. They have created a revolution in computer vision applications such as facial recognition and cancer detection. Deep learning has also driven advances in language-related tasks.

Deep neural networks are also very suitable for reinforcement learning, AI models that develop their behavior through numerous trial and errors. This is the kind of AI that masters complicated games such as Go, StarCraft, and Dota.

But the benefits of deep learning and neural networks are not without tradeoffs. Deep learning has several deep challenges and disadvantages in comparison to symbolic AI. Notably, deep learning algorithms are opaque, and figuring out how they work perplexes even their creators. And it's very hard to communicate and troubleshoot their inner-workings.

Neural networks are also very data-hungry. And unlike symbolic AI, neural networks have no notion of symbols and hierarchical representation of knowledge. This limitation makes it very hard to apply neural networks to tasks that require logic and reasoning, such as science and high-school math.

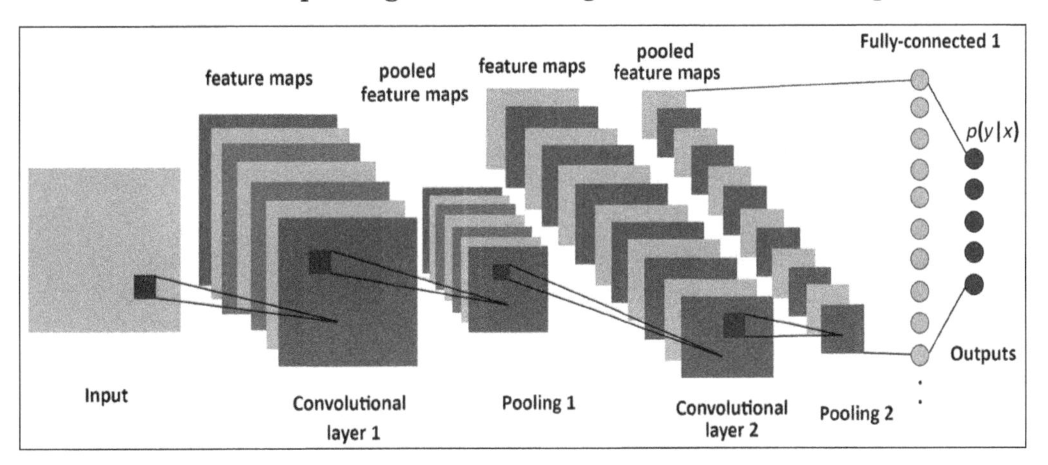

The Current State of Symbolic AI

Some believe that symbolic AI is dead. But this assumption couldn't be farther from the truth. In fact, rule-based AI systems are still very important in today's applications. Many leading scientists believe that symbolic reasoning will continue to remain a very important component of artificial intelligence.

There are now several efforts to combine neural networks and symbolic AI. One such project is the Neuro-Symbolic Concept Learner (NSCL), a hybrid AI system developed by the MIT-IBM Watson AI Lab. NSCL uses both rule-based programs and neural networks to solve visual question-answering problems. As opposed to pure neural network–based models, the hybrid AI can learn new tasks with less data and is explainable. And unlike symbolic-only models, NSCL doesn't struggle to analyze the content of images.

3

Significant Aspects of Machine Learning

Machine Learning can be defined as an application of artificial intelligence that provides machine systems the ability to automatically learn and improve from experience. According to this concept a computer program can learn and adapt to new data without human intervention given the right set of algorithms. This chapter has been carefully written to provide an easy understanding of machine learning and its related concepts.

Machine learning is an application of artificial intelligence (AI) that provides systems the ability to automatically learn and improve from experience without being explicitly programmed. Machine learning focuses on the development of computer programs that can access data and use it learn for themselves.

The process of learning begins with observations or data, such as examples, direct experience, or instruction, in order to look for patterns in data and make better decisions in the future based on the examples that we provide. The primary aim is to allow the computers learn automatically without human intervention or assistance and adjust actions accordingly.

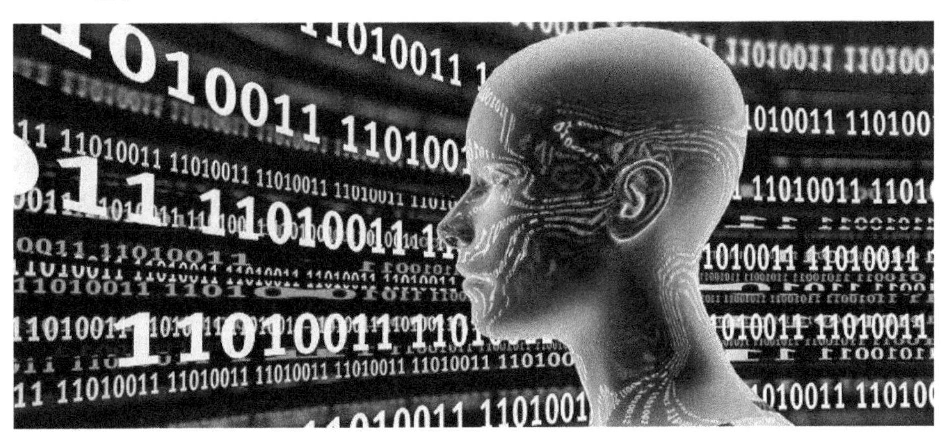

Machine learning enables analysis of massive quantities of data. While it generally delivers faster, more accurate results in order to identify profitable opportunities or dangerous risks, it may also require additional time and resources to train it properly. Combining machine learning with AI and cognitive technologies can make it even more effective in processing large volumes of information.

Tom M. Mitchell provided a widely quoted, more formal definition of the algorithms studied in the machine learning field: "A computer program is said to learn from experience E with respect to some class of tasks T and performance measure P if its performance at tasks in *T*, as measured by *P*, improves with experience *E*." This definition of the tasks in which machine learning is concerned offers a fundamentally operational definition rather than defining the field in cognitive terms. This follows Alan Turing's proposal in his paper "Computing Machinery and Intelligence", in which the question "Can machines think?" is replaced with the question "Can machines do what we (as thinking entities) can do?". In Turing's proposal the various characteristics that could be possessed by a *thinking machine* and the various implications in constructing one are exposed.

Machine Learning Tasks

Machine learning tasks are typically classified into two broad categories, depending on whether there is a learning "signal" or "feedback" available to a learning system:

- Supervised learning: The computer is presented with example inputs and their desired outputs, given by a "teacher", and the goal is to learn a general rule that maps inputs to outputs. As special cases, the input signal can be only partially available, or restricted to special feedback:
    - Semi-supervised learning: the computer is given only an incomplete training signal: a training set with some (often many) of the target outputs missing.
    - Active learning: the computer can only obtain training labels for a limited set of instances (based on a budget), and also has to optimize its choice of objects to acquire labels for. When used interactively, these can be presented to the user for labeling.
    - Reinforcement learning: training data (in form of rewards and punishments) is given only as feedback to the program's actions in a dynamic environment, such as driving a vehicle or playing a game against an opponent.
- Unsupervised learning: No labels are given to the learning algorithm, leaving it on its own to find structure in its input. Unsupervised learning can be a goal in itself (discovering hidden patterns in data) or a means towards an end (feature learning).

Machine Learning Applications

Another categorization of machine learning tasks arises when one considers the desired *output* of a machine-learned system:

- In classification, inputs are divided into two or more classes, and the learner must produce a model that assigns unseen inputs to one or more (multi-label classification) of these classes. This is typically tackled in a supervised manner. Spam filtering is an example of classification, where the inputs are email (or other) messages and the classes are "spam" and "not spam".

- In regression, also a supervised problem, the outputs are continuous rather than discrete.
- In clustering, a set of inputs is to be divided into groups. Unlike in classification, the groups are not known beforehand, making this typically an unsupervised task.
- Density estimation finds the distribution of inputs in some space.
- Dimensionality reduction simplifies inputs by mapping them into a lower-dimensional space. Topic modeling is a related problem, where a program is given a list of human language documents and is tasked with finding out which documents cover similar topics.

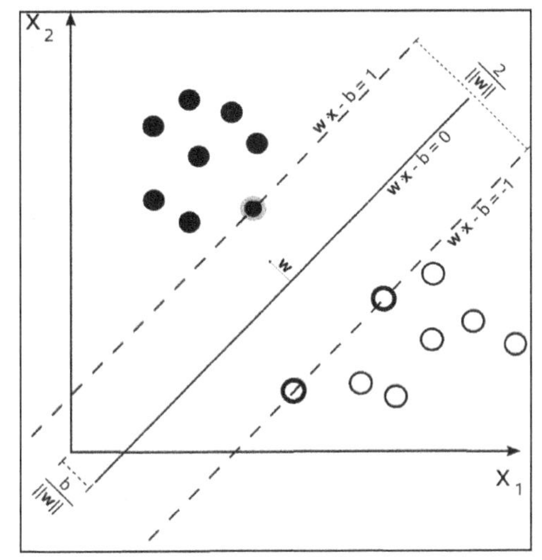

A support vector machine is a classifier that divides its input space into two regions, separated by a linear boundary. Here, it has learned to distinguish black and white circles.

Among other categories of machine learning problems, learning to learn learns its own inductive bias based on previous experience. Developmental learning, elaborated for robot learning, generates its own sequences (also called curriculum) of learning situations to cumulatively acquire repertoires of novel skills through autonomous self-exploration and social interaction with human teachers and using guidance mechanisms such as active learning, maturation, motor synergies, and imitation.

Machine Learning Algorithms

Decision Tree Learning

Decision tree learning uses a decision tree as a predictive model, which maps observations about an item to conclusions about the item's target value.

Association Rule Learning

Association rule learning is a method for discovering interesting relations between variables in large databases.

Artificial Neural Networks

An artificial neural network (ANN) learning algorithm, usually called "neural network" (NN), is a learning algorithm that is vaguely inspired by biological neural networks. Computations are structured in terms of an interconnected group of artificial neurons, processing information using a connectionist approach to computation. Modern neural networks are non-linear statistical data modeling tools. They are usually used to model complex relationships between inputs and outputs, to find patterns in data, or to capture the statistical structure in an unknown joint probability distribution between observed variables.

Deep Learning

Falling hardware prices and the development of GPUs for personal use in the last few years have contributed to the development of the concept of deep learning which consists of multiple hidden layers in an artificial neural network. This approach tries to model the way the human brain processes light and sound into vision and hearing. Some successful applications of deep learning are computer vision and speech recognition.

Inductive Logic Programming

Inductive logic programming (ILP) is an approach to rule learning using logic programming as a uniform representation for input examples, background knowledge, and hypotheses. Given an encoding of the known background knowledge and a set of examples represented as a logical database of facts, an ILP system will derive a hypothesized logic program that entails all positive and no negative examples. Inductive programming is a related field that considers any kind of programming languages for representing hypotheses (and not only logic programming), such as functional programs.

Support Vector Machines

Support vector machines (SVMs) are a set of related supervised learning methods used for classification and regression. Given a set of training examples, each marked as belonging to one of two categories, an SVM training algorithm builds a model that predicts whether a new example falls into one category or the other.

Clustering

Cluster analysis is the assignment of a set of observations into subsets (called *clusters*) so that observations within the same cluster are similar according to some predesignated criterion or criteria, while observations drawn from different clusters are dissimilar. Different clustering techniques make different assumptions on the structure of the data, often defined by some *similarity metric* and evaluated for example by *internal compactness* (similarity between members of the same cluster) and *separation* between different clusters. Other methods are based on *estimated density* and *graph connectivity*. Clustering is a method of unsupervised learning, and a common technique for statistical data analysis.

Bayesian Networks

A Bayesian network, belief network or directed acyclic graphical model is a probabilistic graphical model that represents a set of random variables and their conditional independencies via a directed acyclic graph (DAG). For example, a Bayesian network could represent the probabilistic relationships between diseases and symptoms. Given symptoms, the network can be used to compute the probabilities of the presence of various diseases. Efficient algorithms exist that perform inference and learning.

Reinforcement Learning

Reinforcement learning is concerned with how an *agent* ought to take *actions* in an *environment* so as to maximize some notion of long-term *reward*. Reinforcement learning algorithms attempt to find a *policy* that maps *states* of the world to the actions the agent ought to take in those states. Reinforcement learning differs from the supervised learning problem in that correct input/output pairs are never presented, nor sub-optimal actions explicitly corrected.

Representation Learning

Several learning algorithms, mostly unsupervised learning algorithms, aim at discovering better representations of the inputs provided during training. Classical examples include principal components analysis and cluster analysis. Representation learning algorithms often attempt to preserve the information in their input but transform it in a way that makes it useful, often as a pre-processing step before performing classification or predictions, allowing reconstruction of the inputs coming from the unknown data generating distribution, while not being necessarily faithful for configurations that are implausible under that distribution.

Manifold learning algorithms attempt to do so under the constraint that the learned representation is low-dimensional. Sparse codingalgorithms attempt to do so under the constraint that the learned representation is sparse (has many zeros). Multilinear subspace learningalgorithms aim to learn low-dimensional representations directly from tensor representations for multidimensional data, without reshaping them into (high-dimensional) vectors. Deep learning algorithms discover multiple levels of representation, or a hierarchy of features, with higher-level, more abstract features defined in terms of (or generating) lower-level features. It has been argued that an intelligent machine is one that learns a representation that disentangles the underlying factors of variation that explain the observed data.

Similarity and Metric Learning

In this problem, the learning machine is given pairs of examples that are considered similar and pairs of less similar objects. It then needs to learn a similarity function (or a distance metric function) that can predict if new objects are similar. It is sometimes used in Recommendation systems.

Sparse Dictionary Learning

In this method, a datum is represented as a linear combination of basis functions, and the coefficients are assumed to be sparse. Let x be a d-dimensional datum, D be a d by n matrix, where each column of D represents a basis function. r is the coefficient to represent x using D. Mathematically, sparse dictionary learning means solving where r is sparse. Generally speaking, n is assumed to be larger than d to allow the freedom for a sparse representation.

Learning a dictionary along with sparse representations is strongly NP-hard and also difficult to solve approximately. A popular heuristic method for sparse dictionary learning is K-SVD.

Sparse dictionary learning has been applied in several contexts. In classification, the problem is to determine which classes a previously unseen datum belongs to. Suppose a dictionary for each class has already been built. Then a new datum is associated with the class such that it's best sparsely represented by the corresponding dictionary. Sparse dictionary learning has also been applied in image de-noising. The key idea is that a clean image patch can be sparsely represented by an image dictionary, but the noise cannot.

Genetic Algorithms

A genetic algorithm (GA) is a search heuristic that mimics the process of natural selection, and uses methods such as mutation and crossover to generate new genotype in the hope of finding good solutions to a given problem. In machine learning, genetic algorithms found some uses in the 1980s and 1990s. Conversely, machine learning techniques have been used to improve the performance of genetic and evolutionary algorithms.

Rule-based Machine Learning

Rule-based machine learning is a general term for any machine learning method that identifies, learns, or evolves "rules" to store, manipulate or apply, knowledge. The defining characteristic of a rule-based machine learner is the identification and utilization of a set of relational rules that collectively represent the knowledge captured by the system. This is in contrast to other machine learners that commonly identify a singular model that can be universally applied to any instance in order to make a prediction. Rule-based machine learning approaches include learning classifier systems, association rule learning, and artificial immune systems.

Learning Classifier Systems

Learning classifier systems (LCS) are a family of rule-based machine learning algorithms that combine a discovery component (e.g. typically a genetic algorithm) with a learning component (performing either supervised learning, reinforcement learning, or unsupervised learning). They seek to identify a set of context-dependent rules that collectively store and apply knowledge in a piecewise manner in order to make predictions.

Feature Selection Approach

Feature selection is the process of selecting an optimal subset of relevant features for use in model construction. It is assumed the data contains some features that are either redundant or irrelevant, and can thus be removed to reduce calculation cost without incurring much loss of information. Common optimality criteria include accuracy, similarity and information measures.

Applications

Applications for machine learning include:

- Agriculture.
- Automated theorem proving.
- Adaptive websites.
- Affective computing.
- Bioinformatics.
- Brain–machine interfaces.
- Cheminformatics.
- Classifying DNA sequences.
- Computational anatomy.
- Computer Networks.
- Telecommunication.
- Computer vision, including object recognition.
- Detecting credit-card fraud.
- General game playing.
- Information retrieval.

- Internet fraud detection.
- Linguistics.
- Marketing.
- Machine learning control.
- Machine perception.
- Medical diagnosis.
- Economics.
- Insurance.
- Natural language processing.
- Natural language understanding.
- Optimization and metaheuristic.
- Online advertising.
- Recommender systems.
- Robot locomotion.
- Search engines.
- Sentiment analysis (or opinion mining).
- Multimodal sentiment analysis.
- Sequence mining.
- Software engineering.
- Speech and handwriting recognition.
- Space mapping.
- Financial market analysis.
- Structural health monitoring.
- Syntactic pattern recognition.
- Time series forecasting.
- User behavior analytics.
- Translation.

In 2006, the online movie company Netflix held the first "Netflix Prize" competition to find a program to better predict user preferences and improve the accuracy on its existing Cinematch movie recommendation algorithm by at least 10%. A joint team made up of researchers from AT&T Labs-Research in collaboration with the teams Big Chaos and Pragmatic Theory built an ensemble model to win the Grand Prize in 2009 for $1 million. Shortly after the prize was awarded, Netflix realized that viewers' ratings were not the best indicators of their viewing patterns ("everything is a recommendation") and they changed their recommendation engine accordingly.

In 2010 The Wall Street Journal wrote about the firm Rebellion Research and their use of Machine Learning to predict the financial crisis.

In 2012, co-founder of Sun Microsystems Vinod Khosla predicted that 80% of medical doctors jobs would be lost in the next two decades to automated machine learning medical diagnostic software.

In 2014, it has been reported that a machine learning algorithm has been applied in Art History to study fine art paintings, and that it may have revealed previously unrecognized influences between artists.

Model Assessments

Although machine learning has been very transformative in some fields, effective machine learning is difficult because finding patterns is hard and often not enough training data are available; as a result, machine-learning programs often fail to deliver.

Classification machine learning models can be validated by accuracy estimation techniques like the Holdout method, which splits the data into a training and test sets (conventionally 2/3 training set and 1/3 test set designation) and evaluates the performance of the training model on the test set. In comparison, the k-fold-cross-validation method randomly splits the data into k subsets where the k - 1 instances of the data subsets are used to train the model while the kth subset instance is used to test the predictive ability of the training model. In addition to the holdout and cross-validation methods, bootstrap, which samples n instances with replacement from the dataset, can be used to assess model accuracy.

In addition to overall accuracy, investigators frequently report sensitivity and specificity meaning True Positive Rate (TPR) and True Negative Rate (TNR) respectively. Similarly, investigators sometimes report the False Positive Rate (FPR) as well as the False Negative Rate (FNR). However, these rates are ratios that fail to reveal their numerators and denominators. The Total Operating Characteristic(TOC) is an effective method to express a model's diagnostic ability. TOC shows the numerators and denominators of the previously mentioned rates, thus TOC provides more information than the commonly used Receiver Operating Characteristic (ROC) and ROC's associated Area Under the Curve (AUC).

Examples of Machine Learning

Machine learning is being used in a wide range of applications today. One of the most well-known examples is Facebook's News Feed. The News Feed uses machine learning to personalize each member's feed. If a member frequently stops scrolling to read or like a particular friend's posts, the News Feed will start to show more of that friend's activity earlier in the feed. Behind the scenes, the software is simply using statistical analysis and predictive analytics to identify patterns in the user's data and use those patterns to populate the News Feed. Should the member no longer stop to read, like or comment on the friend's posts, that new data will be included in the data set and the News Feed will adjust accordingly.

Machine learning is also entering an array of enterprise applications. Customer relationship management (CRM) systems use learning models to analyze email and prompt sales team members to respond to the most important messages first. More advanced systems can even recommend potentially effective responses. Business intelligence (BI) and analytics vendors use machine learning in their software to help users automatically identify potentially important data points. Human resource (HR) systems use learning models to identify characteristics of effective employees and rely on this knowledge to find the best applicants for open positions.

Machine learning also plays an important role in self-driving cars. Deep learning neural networks are used to identify objects and determine optimal actions for safely steering a vehicle down the road.

Virtual assistant technology is also powered through machine learning. Smart assistants combine several deep learning models to interpret natural speech, bring in relevant context -- like a user's personal schedule or previously defined preferences -- and take an action, like booking a flight or pulling up driving directions.

Automated Machine Learning

AutoML is not automated data science. While there is undoubtedly overlap, machine learning is but one of many tools in the data science toolkit, and its use does not actually factor in to all data science tasks. For example, if prediction will be part of a given data science task, machine learning will be a useful component; however, machine learning may not play in to a descriptive analytics task at all.

Even for predictive tasks, data science encompasses much more than the actual predictive modeling. Data scientist Sandro Saitta, when discussing the potential confusion between AutoML and automated data science, had this to say:

> "The misconception comes from the confusion between the whole Data Science process and the sub-tasks of data preparation (feature extraction, etc.) and modeling (algorithm selection, hyper-parameters tuning, etc.) which I call Machine Learning."

Further, data scientist and leading automated machine learning proponent Randy Olson states that effective machine learning design requires us to:

1. Always tune the hyperparameters for our models.
2. Always try out many different models.
3. Always explore numerous feature representations for our data.

Taking all of the above into account, if we consider AutoML to be the tasks of algorithm selection, hyperparameter tuning, iterative modeling, and model assessment, we can start to define what AutoML actually is. There will not be total agreement on this definition (for comparison, ask 10 people to define "data science," and then compare the 11 answers you get), but it arguably starts us off on the right foot.

Automated machine learning represents a fundamental shift in the way organizations of all sizes approach machine learning and data science. Applying traditional machine learning methods to real-world business problems is time-consuming, resource-intensive, and challenging. It requires experts in the several disciplines, including data scientists – some of the most sought-after professionals in the job market right now.

Automated machine learning changes that, making it easier to build and use machine learning models in the real world by running systematic processes on raw data and selecting models that pull the most relevant information from the data – what is often referred to as "the signal in the noise." Automated machine learning incorporates machine learning best practices from top-ranked data scientists to make data science more accessible across the organization.

Here is the standard machine learning process at a high level:

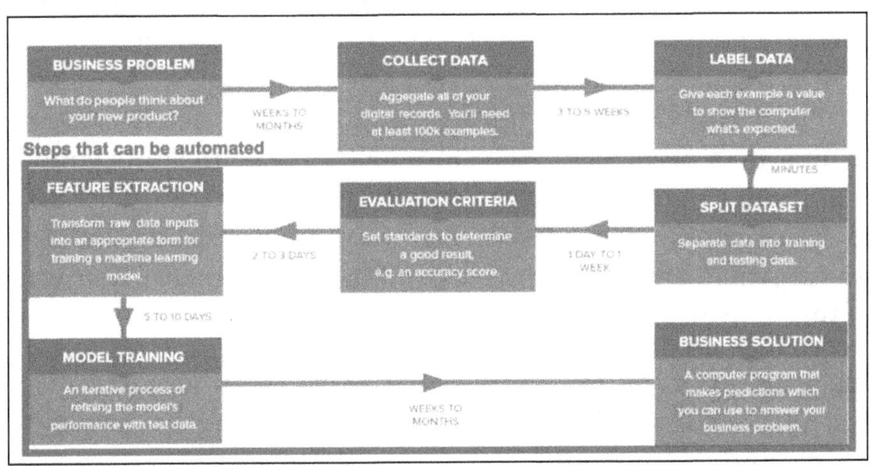

When developing a model with the traditional process, as you can see from figure above, the only automatic task is model training. Automated machine learning software automatically executes all the steps outlined in red – manual, tedious modeling tasks that used to require skilled data scientists. The traditional process often takes weeks or months, but with automated machine learning, it takes days at most for business professionals and data scientists to develop and compare dozens of models, find insights and predictions, and solve more business problems much faster.

shows the automated machine learning process after uploading a dataset and choose the target variable for the business problem:

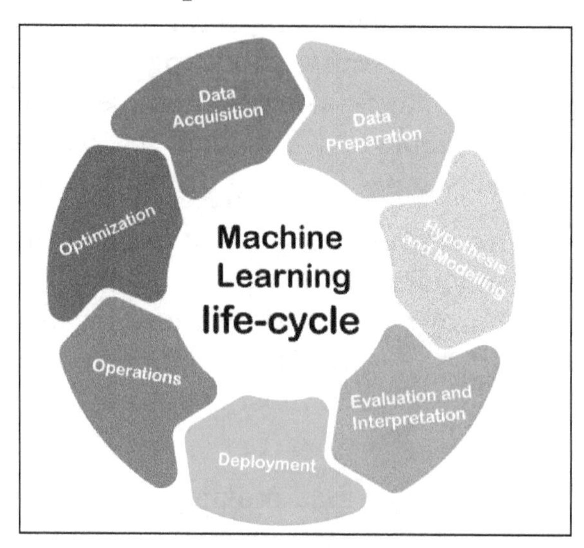

Automating these steps allows for greater agility in problem-solving and the democratization of data science to include those without extensive programming knowledge.

Importance of Machine Learning

Manually constructing a machine learning model is a multistep process that requires domain knowledge, mathematical expertise, and computer science skills – which is a lot to ask of one company, let alone one data scientist (provided you can hire and retain one). Not only that, there are countless opportunities for human error and bias, which gets in the way of model accuracy and devalues the insights you might get from the model. Automated machine learning enables organizations to use the baked-in knowledge of data scientists without having to develop the capabilities themselves, simultaneously improving return on investment in data science initiatives and reducing the amount of time it takes to capture value.

Automated machine learning makes it possible for businesses in every industry – healthcare, fintech, banking, the public sector, marketing, and more – to leverage machine learning and AI technology that was previously limited to organizations with vast resources at their disposal. By automating most of the manual modeling tasks that used to be necessary in order to develop and deploy machine learning models, automated machine learning enables business users to implement machine learning solutions with ease and frees up data scientists to focus on more complex problems.

Targets of Automation

Automated machine learning can target various stages of the machine learning process:

- Automated data preparation and ingestion (from raw data and miscellaneous formats):
    - Automated column type detection; e.g., boolean, discrete numerical, continuous numerical, or text.
    - Automated column intent detection; e.g., target/label, stratification field, numerical feature, categorical text feature, or free text feature.
    - Automated task detection; e.g., binary classification, regression, clustering, or ranking.
- Automated feature engineering:
    - Feature selection.
    - Feature extraction.
    - Meta learning and transfer learning.
    - Detection and handling of skewed data and/or missing values.
- Automated model selection.
- Hyperparameter optimization of the learning algorithm and featurization.
- Automated pipeline selection under time, memory, and complexity constraints.
- Automated selection of evaluation metics / validation procedures.
- Automated problem checking:
    - Leakage detection.
    - Misconfiguration detection.
- Automated analysis of results obtained.
- User interfaces and visualizations for automated machine learning.

Examples

Software tackling various stages of AutoML:

Hyperparameter optimization and model selection

- H2O AutoML provides automated data preparation, hyperparameter tuning via random search, and stacked ensembles in a distributed machine learning platform.

- Mlr is a R package that contains several hyperparameter optimization techniques for machine learning problems.

Full Pipeline Optimization

- Auto-WEKA is a Bayesian hyperparameter optimization layer on top of WEKA.
- Auto-sklearn is a Bayesian hyperparameter optimization layer on top of scikit-learn.
- TPOT is a Python library that automatically creates and optimizes full machine learning pipelines using genetic programming.

Deep Neural Network Architecture Search

- Devol is a Python package that performs Deep Neural Network architecture search using genetic programming.
- Google AutoML for deep learning model architecture selection.

Automated Machine Learning will lessen the scientists' and programmers' dependency on intuition by trying out an algorithm, scoring, testing and refining other models. In fact, it will automate the machine learning process of the data science workflow in the organisation.

Randy Olson, Senior Data Scientist at University of Pennsylvania Institute for Biomedical Informatics, and lead developer of TPOT has gone on record to say:

"In the near future, I see automated machine learning (AutoML) taking over the machine learning model-building process: once a data set is in a (relatively) clean format, the AutoML system will be able to design and optimise a machine learning pipeline faster than 99% of the humans out there. Perhaps AutoML systems will be able to expand out to cover a larger portion of the data cleaning process, but many tasks — such as being able to pose a problem as a machine learning problem in the first place — will remain solely a human endeavour in the near future."

Feature

In machine learning, feature vectors are used to represent numeric or symbolic characteristics, called features, of an object in a mathematical, easily analyzable way. They are important for many different areas of machine learning and pattern processing. Machine learning algorithms typically require a numerical representation of objects in order for the algorithms to do processing and statistical analysis. Feature vectors are the equivalent of vectors of explanatory variables that are used in statistical procedures such as linear regression.

An example of a feature vector you might be familiar with is RGB (red-green-blue) color descriptions. A color can be described by how much red, blue, and green there is in it. A feature vector for this would be color = [R, G, B].

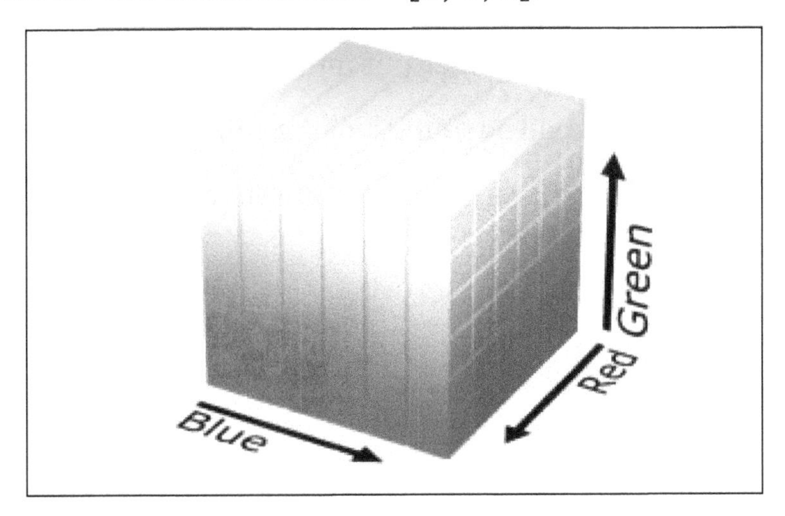

A vector is a series of numbers, like a matrix with one column but multiple rows, that can often be represented spatially. A feature is a numerical or symbolic property of an aspect of an object. A feature vector is a vector containing multiple elements about an object. Putting feature vectors for objects together can make up a feature space.

The features may represent, as a whole, one mere pixel or an entire image. The granularity depends on what someone is trying to learn or represent about the object. You could describe a 3-dimensional shape with a feature vector indicating its height, width, depth, etc.

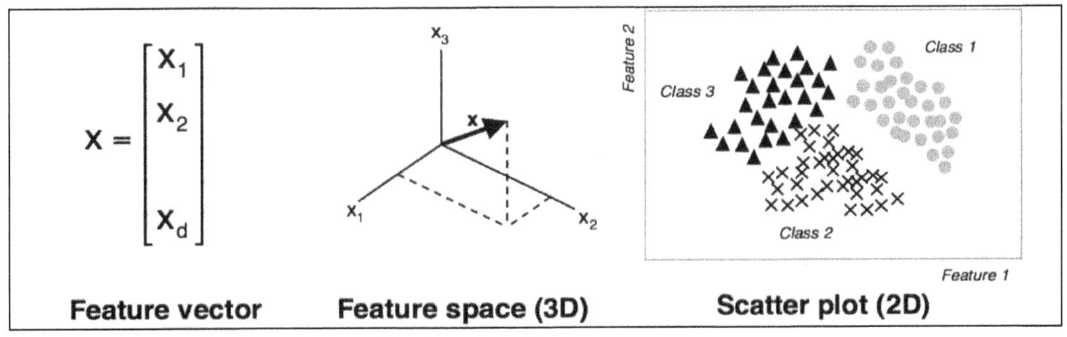

The basics of feature vectors.

Uses of Feature Vectors

Feature vectors are used widely in machine learning because of the effectiveness and practicality of representing objects in a numerical way to help with many kinds of analyses. They are good for analysis because there are many techniques for comparing feature vectors. One simple way to compare the feature vectors of two objects is to take the Euclidean distance.

In image processing, features can be gradient magnitude, color, grayscale intensity, edges, areas, and more. Feature vectors are particularly popular for analyses in image processing because of the convenient way attributes about an image, like the examples listed, can be compared numerically once put into feature vectors.

In speech recognition, features can be sound lengths, noise level, noise ratios, and more.

In spam-fighting initiatives, features are abundant. They can be IP location, text structure, frequency of certain words, or certain email headers.

Feature vectors are used in classification problems, artificial neural networks, and k-nearest neighbors algorithms in machine learning.

Examples

In character recognition, features may include histograms counting the number of black pixels along horizontal and vertical directions, number of internal holes, stroke detection and many others.

In speech recognition, features for recognizing phonemes can include noise ratios, length of sounds, relative power, filter matches and many others.

In spam detection algorithms, features may include the presence or absence of certain email headers, the email structure, the language, the frequency of specific terms, the grammatical correctness of the text.

In computer vision, there are a large number of possible features, such as edges and objects.

Extensions

In pattern recognition and machine learning, a feature vector is an n-dimensional vector of numerical features that represent some object. Many algorithms in machine learning require a numerical representation of objects, since such representations facilitate processing and statistical analysis. When representing images, the feature values might correspond to the pixels of an image, while when representing texts the features might be the frequencies of occurrence of textual terms. Feature vectors are equivalent to the vectors of explanatory variables used in statistical procedures such as linear regression. Feature vectors are often combined with weights using a dot product in order to construct a linear predictor function that is used to determine a score for making a prediction.

The vector space associated with these vectors is often called the feature space. In order to reduce the dimensionality of the feature space, a number of dimensionality reduction techniques can be employed.

Higher-level features can be obtained from already available features and added to the feature vector; for example, for the study of diseases the feature 'Age' is useful and is defined as *Age = 'Year of death' minus 'Year of birth'*. This process is referred to as feature construction. Feature construction is the application of a set of constructive operators to a set of existing features resulting in construction of new features. Examples of such constructive operators include checking for the equality conditions {=, ≠}, the arithmetic operators {+,−,×, /}, the array operators {max(S), min(S), average(S)} as well as other more sophisticated operators, for example count(S,C) that counts the number of features in the feature vector S satisfying some condition C or, for example, distances to other recognition classes generalized by some accepting device. Feature construction has long been considered a powerful tool for increasing both accuracy and understanding of structure, particularly in high-dimensional problems. Applications include studies of disease and emotion recognition from speech.

Selection and Extraction

The initial set of raw features can be redundant and too large to be managed. Therefore, a preliminary step in many applications of machine learning and pattern recognition consists of selecting a subset of features, or constructing a new and reduced set of features to facilitate learning, and to improve generalization and interpretability.

Extracting or selecting features is a combination of art and science; developing systems to do so is known as feature engineering. It requires the experimentation of multiple possibilities and the combination of automated techniques with the intuition and knowledge of the domain expert. Automating this process is feature learning, where a machine not only uses features for learning, but learns the features itself.

Importance of Feature Selection

Machine learning works on a simple rule – if you put garbage in, you will only get garbage to come out.

This becomes even more important when the number of features are very large. You need not use every feature at your disposal for creating an algorithm. You can assist your algorithm by feeding in only those features that are really important.

Not only in the competitions but this can be very useful in industrial applications as well. You not only reduce the training time and the evaluation time, you also have less things to worry about.

Top reasons to use feature selection are:

- It enables the machine learning algorithm to train faster.
- It reduces the complexity of a model and makes it easier to interpret.
- It improves the accuracy of a model if the right subset is chosen.
- It reduces overfitting.

Filter Methods

Filter methods are generally used as a preprocessing step. The selection of features is independent of any machine learning algorithms. Instead, features are selected on the basis of their scores in various statistical tests for their correlation with the outcome variable. The correlation is a subjective term here. For basic guidance, you can refer to the following table for defining correlation co-efficients.

Feature\Response	Continuous	Categorical
Continuous	Pearson's Correlation	LDA
Categorical	Anova	Chi-Square

- Pearson's Correlation: It is used as a measure for quantifying linear dependence between two continuous variables X and Y. Its value varies from -1 to +1. Pearson's correlation is given as:

$$\rho_{X,Y} = \frac{\text{cov}(X,Y)}{\sigma_X \sigma_Y}$$

- LDA: Linear discriminant analysis is used to find a linear combination of features that characterizes or separates two or more classes (or levels) of a categorical variable.

- ANOVA: ANOVA stands for Analysis of variance. It is similar to LDA except for the fact that it is operated using one or more categorical independent features and one continuous dependent feature. It provides a statistical test of whether the means of several groups are equal or not.

- Chi-Square: It is a is a statistical test applied to the groups of categorical features to evaluate the likelihood of correlation or association between them using their frequency distribution.

One thing that should be kept in mind is that filter methods do not remove multicollinearity. So, you must deal with multicollinearity of features as well before training models for your data.

Wrapper Methods

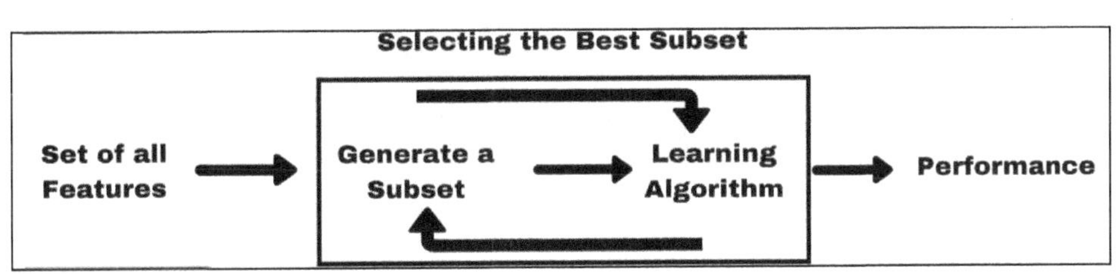

In wrapper methods, we try to use a subset of features and train a model using them. Based on the inferences that we draw from the previous model, we decide to add or remove features from your subset. The problem is essentially reduced to a search problem. These methods are usually computationally very expensive.

Some common examples of wrapper methods are forward feature selection, backward feature elimination, recursive feature elimination, etc.

- Forward Selection: Forward selection is an iterative method in which we start with having no feature in the model. In each iteration, we keep adding the feature which best improves our model till an addition of a new variable does not improve the performance of the model.
- Backward Elimination: In backward elimination, we start with all the features and removes the least significant feature at each iteration which improves the performance of the model. We repeat this until no improvement is observed on removal of features.
- Recursive Feature elimination: It is a greedy optimization algorithm which aims to find the best performing feature subset. It repeatedly creates models and keeps aside the best or the worst performing feature at each iteration. It constructs the next model with the left features until all the features are exhausted. It then ranks the features based on the order of their elimination.

One of the best ways for implementing feature selection with wrapper methods is to use Boruta package that finds the importance of a feature by creating shadow features.

It works in the following steps:

- Firstly, it adds randomness to the given data set by creating shuffled copies of all features (which are called shadow features).
- Then, it trains a random forest classifier on the extended data set and applies a feature importance measure (the default is Mean Decrease Accuracy) to evaluate the importance of each feature where higher means more important.

- At every iteration, it checks whether a real feature has a higher importance than the best of its shadow features (i.e. whether the feature has a higher Z-score than the maximum Z-score of its shadow features) and constantly removes features which are deemed highly unimportant.
- Finally, the algorithm stops either when all features get confirmed or rejected or it reaches a specified limit of random forest runs.

For more information on the implementation of Boruta package, you can refer to this article:

Embedded Methods

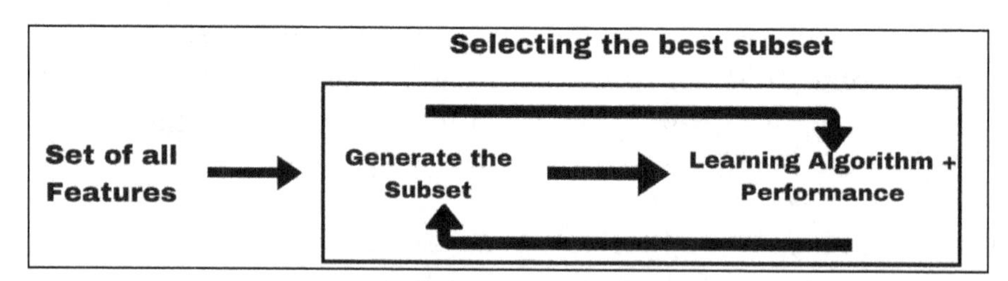

Embedded methods combine the qualities' of filter and wrapper methods. It's implemented by algorithms that have their own built-in feature selection methods.

Some of the most popular examples of these methods are LASSO and RIDGE regression which have inbuilt penalization functions to reduce overfitting.

- Lasso regression performs L1 regularization which adds penalty equivalent to absolute value of the magnitude of coefficients.
- Ridge regression performs L2 regularization which adds penalty equivalent to square of the magnitude of coefficients.

Other examples of embedded methods are Regularized trees, Memetic algorithm, Random multinomial logit.

Difference between Filter and Wrapper methods

The main differences between the filter and wrapper methods for feature selection are:

- Filter methods measure the relevance of features by their correlation with dependent variable while wrapper methods measure the usefulness of a subset of feature by actually training a model on it.
- Filter methods are much faster compared to wrapper methods as they do not involve training the models. On the other hand, wrapper methods are computationally very expensive as well.

- Filter methods use statistical methods for evaluation of a subset of features while wrapper methods use cross validation.
- Filter methods might fail to find the best subset of features in many occasions but wrapper methods can always provide the best subset of features.
- Using the subset of features from the wrapper methods make the model more prone to overfitting as compared to using subset of features from the filter methods.

Hyperparameter

Model optimization is one of the toughest challenges in the implementation of machine learning solutions. Entire branches of machine learning and deep learning theory have been dedicated to the optimization of models. Typically, we think about model optimization as a process of regularly modifying the code of the model in order to minimize the testing error. However, the are of machine learning optimization often entails fine tuning elements that live outside the model but that can heavily influence its behavior. Machine learning often refers to those hidden elements as hyperparameters as they are one of the most critical components of any machine learning application.

Hyperparameters are settings that can be tuned to control the behavior of a machine learning algorithm. Conceptually, hyperparameters can be considered orthogonal to the learning model itself in the sense that, although they live outside the model, there is a direct relationship between them.

The criteria of what defines a hyperparameter is incredibly abstract and flexible. Sure, there are well established hyperparameters such as the number of hidden units or the learning rate of a model but there are also an arbitrarily number of settings that can play the role of hyperparameters for specific models. In general, hyperparameters are very specific to the type of machine learning mode you are trying to optimize. Sometimes, a setting is modeled as a hyperparameter because is not appropriate to learn it from the training set. A classic example are settings that control the capacity of a model(the spectrum of functions that the model can represent). If a machine learning algorithm learns those settings directly from the training set, then it is likely to try to maximize them which will cause the model to overfit(poor generalization).

If hyperparameters are not learned from the training set, then how does a model learn them? Remember that classic role in machine learning models to split the input dataset in an 80/20 percent ratio between the training set and the validation set respectively? Well, part of the role of that 20% validation set is to guide the selection of hyperparameters. Technically, the validation set is used to "train" the hyperparameters prior to optimization.

Types

Most hyperparameters are one of two types (Fred et. al):

- Numerical (H_{num}): can be a real number or an integer value; these are usually bounded by a reasonable minimum value and maximum value.
- Categorical (H_{cat}): one value is chosen from a set of possible values.

Considerations

The time required to train and test a model can depend upon the choice of its hyperparameters. A hyperparameter is usually of continuous or integer type, leading to mixed-type optimization problems. The existence of some hyperparameters is conditional upon the value of others, e.g. the size of each hidden layer in a neural network can be conditional upon the number of layers.

Tunability

Most performance variation can be attributed to just a few hyperparameters. The tunability of an algorithm, hyperparameter, or interacting hyperparameters is a measure of how much performance can be gained by tuning it. For an LSTM, while the learning rate followed by the network size are its most crucial hyperparameters, whereas batching and momentum have no significant effect on its performance.

Although some research has advocated the use of mini-batch sizes in the thousands, other work has found the best performance with mini-batch sizes between 2 and 32.

Robustness

An inherent stochasticity in learning directly implies that the empirical hyperparameter performance is not necessarily its true performance. Methods that are not robust to simple changes in hyperparameters, random seeds, or even different implementations of the same algorithm cannot be integrated into mission critical control systems without significant simplification and robustification.

Reinforcement learning algorithms, in particular, require measuring their performance over a large number of random seeds, and also measuring their sensitivity to choices of hyperparameters. Their evaluation with a small number of random seeds does not capture performance adequately due to high variance. Some reinforcement learning methods, e.g. DDPG (Deep Deterministic Policy Gradient), are more sensitive to hyperparameter choices than others.

Optimization

Hyperparameter optimization finds a tuple of hyperparameters that yields an optimal model which minimizes a predefined loss function on given test data. The objective function takes a tuple of hyperparameters and returns the associated loss.

Reproducibility

Apart from tuning hyperparameters, machine learning involves storing and organizing the parameters and results, and making sure they are reproducible. In the absence of a robust infrastructure for this purpose, research code often evolves quickly and compromises essential aspects like bookkeeping and reproducibility. Online collaboration platforms for machine learning go further by allowing scientists to automatically share, organize and discuss experiments, data, and algorithms.

A number of relevant services and open source software exist:

Services

Name	Interfaces
Comet ml	Pylthon
OpenML	REST, Python, Java, R

Software

Name	Interfaces	Store
OpenMl Docker	REST, Python, Java, R	MySQL
sacred	Python	file, MongoDB, TinyDB, SQL

Examples

The number and diversity of hyperparameters in machine learning algorithms is very specific to each model. However, there some classic hyperparameters that we should always keep our eyes on and that should help you think about this aspect of machine learning solutions:

- Learning Rate: The mother of all hyperparameters, the learning rate quantifies the learning progress of a model in a way that can be used to optimize its capacity.
- Number of Hidden Units: A classic hyperparameter in deep learning algorithms, the number of hidden units is key to regulate the representational capacity of a model.
- Convolution Kernel Width: In convolutional Neural Networks(CNNs), the Kernel Width influences the number of parameters in a model which, in turns, influences its capacity.

Ensemble Averaging

In general, ensembling is a technique of combining two or more algorithms of similar or dissimilar types called base learners. This is done to make a more robust system which incorporates the predictions from all the base learners. It can be understood as conference room meeting between multiple traders to make a decision on whether the price of a stock will go up or not.

Since all of them have a different understanding of the stock market and thus a different mapping function from the problem statement to the desired outcome. Therefore, they are supposed to make varied predictions on the stock price based on their own understandings of the market.

Now we can take all of these predictions into account while making the final decision. This will make our final decision more robust, accurate and less likely to be biased. The final decision would have been opposite if one of these traders would have made this decision alone.

You can consider another example of a candidate going through multiple rounds of job interviews. The final decision of candidate's ability is generally taken based on the feedback of all the interviewers. Although a single interviewer might not be able to test the candidate for each required skill and trait. But the combined feedback of multiple interviewers usually helps in better assessment of the candidate.

Ensemble averaging is one of the simplest types of committee machines. Along with boosting, it is one of the two major types of static committee machines. In contrast to standard network design in which many networks are generated but only one is kept, ensemble averaging keeps the less satisfactory networks around, but with less weight. The theory of ensemble averaging relies on two properties of artificial neural networks:

1. In any network, the bias can be reduced at the cost of increased variance.
2. In a group of networks, the variance can be reduced at no cost to bias.

Ensemble averaging creates a group of networks, each with low bias and high variance, then combines them to a new network with (hopefully) low bias and low variance. It is thus a resolution of the bias-variance dilemma. The idea of combining experts has been traced back to Pierre-Simon Laplace.

Method

Create a set of experts with low bias and high variance, and then average them. Generally, what this means is to create a set of experts with varying parameters; frequently, these are the initial synaptic weights, although other factors (such as the learning rate, momentum etc.) may be varied as well. Some authors recommend against varying weight decay and early stopping. The steps are therefore:

1. Generate *N* experts, each with their own initial values. (Initial values are usually chosen randomly from a distribution.)

2. Train each expert separately.

3. Combine the experts and average their values.

Alternatively, domain knowledge may be used to generate several *classes* of experts. An expert from each class is trained, and then combined.

A more complex version of ensemble average views the final result not as a mere average of all the experts, but rather as a weighted sum. If each expert is y_i, then the overall result $\tilde{y}$ can be defined as:

$$\tilde{y}(\mathrm{X};\alpha)=\sum_{j=1}^{p}\alpha_j y_j(\mathrm{X})$$

where α is a set of weights. The optimization problem of finding alpha is readily solved through neural networks, hence a "meta-network" where each "neuron" is in fact an entire neural network can be trained, and the synaptic weights of the final network is the weight applied to each expert. This is known as a *linear combination of experts.*

It can be seen that most forms of neural networks are some subset of a linear combination: the standard neural net (where only one expert is used) is simply a linear combination with all $\alpha_j = 0$ and one $\alpha_k = 1$. A raw average is where all α_j are equal to some constant value, namely one over the total number of experts.

A more recent ensemble averaging method is negative correlation learning, proposed by Y. Liu and X. Yao. Now this method has been widely used in evolutionary computing.

Benefits

- The resulting committee is almost always less complex than a single network which would achieve the same level of performance.

- The resulting committee can be trained more easily on smaller input sets.

- The resulting committee often has improved performance over any single network.

- The risk of overfitting is lessened, as there are fewer parameters (weights) which need to be set.

Types of Ensembling

Some of the basic concepts which you should be aware of before we go into further detail are:

- Averaging: It's defined as taking the average of predictions from models in case of regression problem or while predicting probabilities for the classification problem.

Model1	Model2	Model3	AveragePrediction
45	40	65	50

- Majority vote: It's defined as taking the prediction with maximum vote / recommendation from multiple models predictions while predicting the outcomes of a classification problem.

Model1	Model2	Model3	VotingPrediction
1	0	1	1

- Weighted average: In this, different weights are applied to predictions from multiple models then taking the average which means giving high or low importance to specific model output.

	Model1	Model2	Model3	WeightAveragePrediction
Weight	0.4	0.3	0.3	
Prediction	45	40	60	48

Practically speaking, there can be a countless number of ways in which you can ensemble different models. But these are some techniques that are mostly used:

1. Bagging: Bagging is also referred to as bootstrap aggregation. To understand bagging, we first need to understand bootstrapping. Bootstrapping is a sampling technique in which we choose 'n' observations or rows out of the original dataset of 'n' rows as well. But the key is that each row is selected with replacement from the original dataset so that each row is equally likely to be selected in each iteration. Let's say we have 3 rows numbered 1, 2 and 3.

Data		Bootstraped Sample
Row 1		
Row 2		
Row 3		

For bootstrapped sample, we choose one out of these three randomly. Say we chose Row

Data	Bootstraped Sample
Row 1	Row 2
Row 2	
Row 3	

You see that even though Row 2 is chosen from the data to the bootstrap sample, it's still present in the data. Now, each of the three:

Data	Bootstraped Sample
Row 1	Row 2
Row 2	Row 1
Row 3	

Rows have the same probability of being selected again. Let's say we choose Row 1 this time.

Again, each row in the data has the same probability to be chosen for Bootstrapped sample. Let's say we randomly choose Row 1 again.

Data	Bootstraped Sample
Row 1	Row 2
Row 2	Row 1
Row 3	Row 1

Thus, we can have multiple bootstrapped samples from the same data. Once we have these multiple bootstrapped samples, we can grow trees for each of these bootstrapped samples and use the majority vote or averaging concepts to get the final prediction. This is how bagging works.

One important thing to note here is that it's done mainly to reduce the variance. Now, random forest actually uses this concept but it goes a step ahead to further reduce the variance by randomly choosing a subset of features as well for each bootstrapped sample to make the splits while training.

2. Boosting: Boosting is a sequential technique in which, the first algorithm is trained on the entire dataset and the subsequent algorithms are built by fitting the residuals of the first algorithm, thus giving higher weight to those observations that were poorly predicted by the previous model.

It relies on creating a series of weak learners each of which might not be good for the entire dataset but is good for some part of the dataset. Thus, each model actually boosts the performance of the ensemble.

It's really important to note that boosting is focused on reducing the bias. This makes the boosting algorithms prone to overfitting. Thus, parameter tuning becomes a crucial part of boosting algorithms to make them avoid overfitting.

Some examples of boosting are XGBoost, GBM, ADABOOST, etc.

3. Stacking: In stacking multiple layers of machine learning models are placed one over another where each of the models passes their predictions to the model in the layer above it and the top layer model takes decisions based on the outputs of the models in layers below it.

Let's understand it with an example:

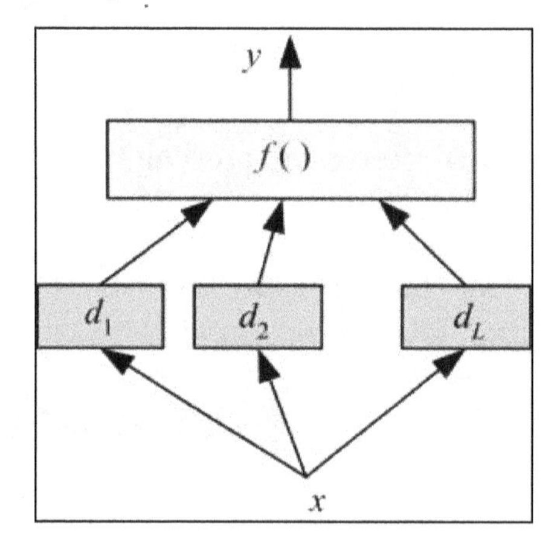

Here, we have two layers of machine learning models:

- Bottom layer models (d_1, d_2, d_3) which receive the original input features(x) from the dataset.
- Top layer model, f() which takes the output of the bottom layer models (d_1, d_2, d_3) as its input and predicts the final output.
- One key thing to note here is that out of fold predictions are used while predicting for the training data.

Here, we have used only two layers but it can be any number of layers and any number of models in each layer. Two of the key principles for selecting the models:

- The individual models fulfill particular accuracy criteria.
- The model predictions of various individual models are not highly correlated with the predictions of other models.

One thing that you might have realized is that we have used the top layer model which takes as input the predictions of the bottom layer models. This top layer model can also be replaced by many other simpler formulas like:

- Averaging.
- Majority vote.
- Weighted average.

Advantages and Disadvantages of ensembling

Advantages:

- Ensembling is a proven method for improving the accuracy of the model and works in most of the cases.
- It is the key ingredient for winning almost all of the machine learning hackathons.
- Ensembling makes the model more robust and stable thus ensuring decent performance on the test cases in most scenarios.
- You can use ensembling to capture linear and simple as well non-linear complex relationships in the data. This can be done by using two different models and forming an ensemble of two.

Disadvantages:

- Ensembling reduces the model interpretability and makes it very difficult to draw any crucial business insights at the end.
- It is time-consuming and thus might not be the best idea for real-time applications.
- The selection of models for creating an ensemble is an art which is really hard to master.

Supervised Learning

Supervised learning, in the context of artificial intelligence (AI) and machine learning, is a type of system in which both input and desired output data are provided. Input and output data are labelled for classification to provide a learning basis for future data processing.

Supervised learning is where you have input variables (x) and an output variable (Y) and you use an algorithm to learn the mapping function from the input to the output.

$$Y = f(X)$$

The goal is to approximate the mapping function so well that when you have new input data (x) that you can predict the output variables (Y) for that data.

It is called supervised learning because the process of an algorithm learning from the training dataset can be thought of as a teacher supervising the learning process. We know the correct answers, the algorithm iteratively makes predictions on the training data and is corrected by the teacher. Learning stops when the algorithm achieves an acceptable level of performance.

Steps

In order to solve a given problem of supervised learning, one has to perform the following steps:

1. Determine the type of training examples. Before doing anything else, the user should decide what kind of data is to be used as a training set. In case of handwriting analysis, for example, this might be a single handwritten character, an entire handwritten word, or an entire line of handwriting.
2. Gather a training set. The training set needs to be representative of the real-world use of the function. Thus, a set of input objects is gathered and corresponding outputs are also gathered, either from human experts or from measurements.
3. Determine the input feature representation of the learned function. The accuracy of the learned function depends strongly on how the input object is represented. Typically, the input object is transformed into a feature vector, which contains a number of features that are descriptive of the object. The number of features should not be too large, because of the curse of dimensionality; but should contain enough information to accurately predict the output.
4. Determine the structure of the learned function and corresponding learning algorithm. For example, the engineer may choose to use support vector machines or decision trees.
5. Complete the design. Run the learning algorithm on the gathered training set. Some supervised learning algorithms require the user to determine certain control parameters. These parameters may be adjusted by optimizing performance on a subset (called a *validation* set) of the training set, or via cross-validation.
6. Evaluate the accuracy of the learned function. After parameter adjustment and learning, the performance of the resulting function should be measured on a test set that is separate from the training set.

Algorithm Choice

A wide range of supervised learning algorithms are available, each with its strengths and weaknesses. There is no single learning algorithm that works best on all supervised learning problems.

There are four major issues to consider in supervised learning:

Bias-variance Tradeoff

A first issue is the tradeoff between *bias* and *variance*. Imagine that we have available several different, but equally good, training data sets. A learning algorithm is biased for a particular input x if, when trained on each of these data sets, it is systematically incorrect when predicting the correct output for x. A learning algorithm has high variance for a particular input x if it predicts different output values when trained on different training sets. The prediction error of a learned classifier is related to the sum of the bias and the variance of the learning algorithm. Generally, there is a tradeoff between bias and variance. A learning algorithm with low bias must be "flexible" so that it can fit the data well. But if the learning algorithm is too flexible, it will fit each training data set differently, and hence have high variance. A key aspect of many supervised learning methods is that they are able to adjust this tradeoff between bias and variance (either automatically or by providing a bias/variance parameter that the user can adjust).

Function Complexity and Amount of Training Data

The second issue is the amount of training data available relative to the complexity of the "true" function (classifier or regression function). If the true function is simple, then an "inflexible" learning algorithm with high bias and low variance will be able to learn it from a small amount of data. But if the true function is highly complex (e.g., because it involves complex interactions among many different input features and behaves differently in different parts of the input space), then the function will only be learnable from a very large amount of training data and using a "flexible" learning algorithm with low bias and high variance.

Dimensionality of the Input Space

A third issue is the dimensionality of the input space. If the input feature vectors have very high dimension, the learning problem can be difficult even if the true function only depends on a small number of those features. This is because the many "extra" dimensions can confuse the learning algorithm and cause it to have high variance. Hence, high input dimensionality typically requires tuning the classifier to have low variance and high bias. In practice, if the engineer can manually remove irrelevant features from the input data, this is likely to improve the accuracy of the learned function. In addition, there are many algorithms for feature selection that seek to identify the relevant features and discard the irrelevant ones. This is an instance of the more general strategy of dimensionality reduction, which seeks to map the input data into a lower-dimensional space prior to running the supervised learning algorithm.

Noise in the Output Values

A fourth issue is the degree of noise in the desired output values (the supervisory target variables). If the desired output values are often incorrect (because of human error or sensor errors), then the learning algorithm should not attempt to find a function that exactly matches the training examples. Attempting to fit the data too carefully leads to overfitting. You can overfit even when there are no measurement errors (stochastic noise) if the function you are trying to learn is too complex for your learning model. In such a situation, the part of the target function that cannot be modeled "corrupts" your training data - this phenomenon has been called deterministic noise. When either type of noise is present, it is better to go with a higher bias, lower variance estimator.

In practice, there are several approaches to alleviate noise in the output values such as early stopping to prevent overfitting as well as detecting and removing the noisy training examples prior to training the supervised learning algorithm. There are several algorithms that identify noisy training examples and removing the suspected noisy training examples prior to training has decreased generalization error with statistical significance.

Other Factors to Consider

Other factors to consider when choosing and applying a learning algorithm include the following:

- Heterogeneity of the data. If the feature vectors include features of many different kinds (discrete, discrete ordered, counts, continuous values), some algorithms are easier to apply than others. Many algorithms, including Support Vector Machines, linear regression, logistic regression, neural networks, and nearest neighbor methods, require that the input features be numerical and scaled to similar ranges (e.g., to the [-1,1] interval). Methods that employ a distance function, such as nearest neighbor methods and support vector machines with Gaussian kernels, are particularly sensitive to this. An advantage of decision trees is that they easily handle heterogeneous data.
- Redundancy in the data. If the input features contain redundant information (e.g., highly correlated features), some learning algorithms (e.g., linear regression, logistic regression, and distance based methods) will perform poorly because of numerical instabilities. These problems can often be solved by imposing some form of regularization.
- Presence of interactions and non-linearities. If each of the features makes an independent contribution to the output, then algorithms based on linear functions

(e.g., linear regression, logistic regression, Support Vector Machines, naive Bayes) and distance functions (e.g., nearest neighbor methods, support vector machines with Gaussian kernels) generally perform well. However, if there are complex interactions among features, then algorithms such as decision trees and neural networks work better, because they are specifically designed to discover these interactions. Linear methods can also be applied, but the engineer must manually specify the interactions when using them.

When considering a new application, the engineer can compare multiple learning algorithms and experimentally determine which one works best on the problem at hand. Tuning the performance of a learning algorithm can be very time-consuming. Given fixed resources, it is often better to spend more time collecting additional training data and more informative features than it is to spend extra time tuning the learning algorithms.

Algorithms

The most widely used learning algorithms are:

- Support Vector Machines.
- linear regression.
- logistic regression.
- naive Bayes.
- linear discriminant analysis.
- decision trees.
- k-nearest neighbor algorithm.
- Neural Networks (Multilayer perceptron).

Working of Supervised Learning Algorithms

Given a set of N training examples of the form $\{(x_1, y_1), \ldots, (x_N, y_N)\}$ such that x_i is the feature vector of the i-th example and y_i is its label (i.e., class), a learning algorithm seeks a function $g: X \to Y$, where X is the input space and Y is the output space. The function g is an element of some space of possible functions G, usually called the *hypothesis space*. It is sometimes convenient to represent g using a scoring function $f: X \times Y \to \mathbb{R}$ such that g is defined as returning the y value that gives the highest score: $g(x) = \arg\max_y f(x, y)$. Let F denote the space of scoring functions.

Although G and F can be any space of functions, many learning algorithms are probabilistic models where g takes the form of a conditional probability model $g(x) = P(y \mid x)$, or f takes the form of a joint probability model $f(x, y) = P(x, y)$. For example, naive

Bayes and linear discriminant analysis are joint probability models, whereas logistic regression is a conditional probability model.

There are two basic approaches to choosing f or g: empirical risk minimization and structural risk minimization. Empirical risk minimization seeks the function that best fits the training data. Structural risk minimization includes a *penalty function* that controls the bias/variance tradeoff.

In both cases, it is assumed that the training set consists of a sample of independent and identically distributed pairs, (x_i, y_i). In order to measure how well a function fits the training data, a loss function $L: Y \times Y \rightarrow \mathbb{R}^{\geq 0}$ is defined. For training example (x_i, y_i), the loss of predicting the value $\hat{y}$ is $L(y_i, \hat{y})$.

The *risk* $R(g)$ of function g is defined as the expected loss of g. This can be estimated from the training data as

$$R_{emp}(g) = \frac{1}{N}\sum_i L(y_i, g(x_i)).$$

Empirical Risk Minimization

In empirical risk minimization, the supervised learning algorithm seeks the function g that minimizes $R(g)$. Hence, a supervised learning algorithm can be constructed by applying an optimization algorithm to find g.

When g is a conditional probability distribution $P(y \mid x)$ and the loss function is the negative log likelihood: $L(y, \hat{y}) = -\log P(y \mid x)$, then empirical risk minimization is equivalent to maximum likelihood estimation.

When G contains many candidate functions or the training set is not sufficiently large, empirical risk minimization leads to high variance and poor generalization. The learning algorithm is able to memorize the training examples without generalizing well. This is called overfitting.

Structural Risk Minimization

Structural risk minimization seeks to prevent overfitting by incorporating a regularization penalty into the optimization. The regularization penalty can be viewed as implementing a form of Occam's razor that prefers simpler functions over more complex ones.

A wide variety of penalties have been employed that correspond to different definitions of complexity. For example, consider the case where the function g is a linear function of the form,

$$g(x) = \sum_{j=1}^{d} \beta_j x_j .$$

A popular regularization penalty is $\sum_j \beta_j^2$, which is the squared Euclidean norm of the weights, also known as the L_2 norm. Other norms include the L_1 norm, $\sum_j |\beta_j|$, and the L_0 norm, which is the number of non-zero β_j s. The penalty will be denoted by $C(g)$.

The supervised learning optimization problem is to find the function g that minimizes

$$J(g) = R_{emp}(g) + \lambda C(g).$$

The parameter λ controls the bias-variance tradeoff. When $\lambda = 0$, this gives empirical risk minimization with low bias and high variance. When λ is large, the learning algorithm will have high bias and low variance. The value of λ can be chosen empirically via cross validation.

The complexity penalty has a Bayesian interpretation as the negative log prior probability of g, $-\log P(g)$, in which case $J(g)$ is the posterior probabability of g.

Generative Training

The training methods described above are *discriminative training* methods, because they seek to find a function g that discriminates well between the different output values. For the special case where $f(x, y) = P(x, y)$ is a joint probability distribution and the loss function is the negative log likelihood $-\sum \log P(x_i, y_i)$, a risk minimization algorithm is said to perform *generative training*, because f can be regarded as a generative model that explains how the data were generated. Generative training algorithms are often simpler and more computationally efficient than discriminative training algorithms. In some cases, the solution can be computed in closed form as in naive Bayes and linear discriminant analysis.

Generalizations

There are several ways in which the standard supervised learning problem can be generalized:

- Semi-supervised learning: In this setting, the desired output values are provided only for a subset of the training data. The remaining data is unlabeled.
- Active learning: Instead of assuming that all of the training examples are given at the start, active learning algorithms interactively collect new examples, typically by making queries to a human user. Often, the queries are based on unlabeled data, which is a scenario that combines semi-supervised learning with active learning.
- Structured prediction: When the desired output value is a complex object, such as a parse tree or a labeled graph, then standard methods must be extended.

- Learning to rank: When the input is a set of objects and the desired output is a ranking of those objects, then again the standard methods must be extended.

Approaches and Algorithms

- Analytical learning.
- Artificial neural network.
- Backpropagation.
- Boosting (meta-algorithm).
- Bayesian statistics.
- Case-based reasoning.
- Decision tree learning.
- Inductive logic programming.
- Gaussian process regression.
- Genetic Programming.
- Group method of data handling.
- Kernel estimators.
- Learning Automata.
- Learning Classifier Systems.
- Minimum message length (decision trees, decision graphs, etc.).
- Multilinear subspace learning.
- Naive bayes classifier.
- Maximum entropy classifier.
- Conditional random field.
- Nearest Neighbor Algorithm.
- Probably approximately correct learning (PAC) learning.
- Ripple down rules, a knowledge acquisition methodology.
- Symbolic machine learning algorithms.
- Subsymbolic machine learning algorithms.
- Support vector machines.
- Minimum Complexity Machines (MCM).
- Random Forests.

- Ensembles of Classifiers.
- Ordinal classification.
- Data Pre-processing.
- Handling imbalanced datasets.
- Statistical relational learning.
- Proaftn, a multicriteria classification algorithm.

Applications

- Bioinformatics.
- Cheminformatics:
    - Quantitative structure–activity relationship.
- Database marketing.
- Handwriting recognition.
- Information retrieval:
    - Learning to rank.
- Information extraction.
- Object recognition in computer vision.
- Optical character recognition.
- Spam detection.
- Pattern recognition.
- Speech recognition.
- Supervised learning is a special case of Downward causation in biological systems.

Semi-supervised Learning

Semi-supervised learning(SSL) is one of the artificial intelligence(AI) methods that have become popular in the last few months. Companies such as Google have been advancing the tools and frameworks relevant for building semi-supervised learning applications. Google Expander is a great example of a tool that reflects the advancements in semi-supervised learning applications.

Conceptually, semi-supervised learning can be positioned halfway between unsupervised and supervised learning models. A semi-supervised learning problem starts with a series of labeled data points as well as some data point for which labels are not known.

The goal of a semi-supervised model is to classify some of the unlabeled data using the labeled information set.

Some AI practitioners see semi-supervised learning as a form of supervised learning with additional information. At the end, the goal of semi-supervised learning models is to sesame as supervised ones: to predict a target value for a specific input data set. Alternatively, other segments of the AI community see semi-supervised learning as a form of unsupervised learning with constraints.

Assumptions used

In order to make any use of unlabeled data, we must assume some structure to the underlying distribution of data. Semi-supervised learning algorithms make use of at least one of the following assumptions.

Continuity Assumption

Points which are close to each other are more likely to share a label. This is also generally assumed in supervised learning and yields a preference for geometrically simple decision boundaries. In the case of semi-supervised learning, the smoothness assumption additionally yields a preference for decision boundaries in low-density regions, so that there are fewer points close to each other but in different classes.

Cluster Assumption

The data tend to form discrete clusters, and points in the same cluster are more likely to share a label (although data sharing a label may be spread across multiple clusters). This is a special case of the smoothness assumption and gives rise to feature learning with clustering algorithms.

Manifold Assumption

The data lie approximately on a manifold of much lower dimension than the input space. In this case we can attempt to learn the manifold using both the labeled and unlabeled data to avoid the curse of dimensionality. Then learning can proceed using distances and densities defined on the manifold.

The manifold assumption is practical when high-dimensional data are being generated by some process that may be hard to model directly, but which only has a few degrees of freedom. For instance, human voice is controlled by a few vocal folds, and images of various facial expressions are controlled by a few muscles. We would like in these cases to use distances and smoothness in the natural space of the generating problem, rather than in the space of all possible acoustic waves or images respectively.

Methods

Generative Models

Generative approaches to statistical learning first seek to estimate $p(x \mid y)$, the distribution of data points belonging to each class. The probability $p(y \mid x)p(y \mid x)$ that a given point has label y is then proportional $p(x \mid y)p(y)$ to by Bayes' rule. Semi-supervised learning with generative models can be viewed either as an extension of supervised learning (classification plus information about $p(x)$) or as an extension of unsupervised learning (clustering plus some labels).

Generative models assume that the distributions take some particular form $p(x \mid y, \theta)$ parameterized by the vector θ. If these assumptions are incorrect, the unlabeled data may actually decrease the accuracy of the solution relative to what would have been obtained from labeled data alone. However, if the assumptions are correct, then the unlabeled data necessarily improves performance.

The unlabeled data are distributed according to a mixture of individual-class distributions. In order to learn the mixture distribution from the unlabeled data, it must be identifiable, that is, different parameters must yield different summed distributions. Gaussian mixture distributions are identifiable and commonly used for generative models.

The parameterized joint distribution can be written as $p(x, y \mid \theta) = p(y \mid \theta)p(x \mid y, \theta)p(x, y \mid \theta)$ by using the Chain rule. Each parameter vector θ is associated with a decision function $f_\theta(x) = \operatorname{argmax} \, p(y \mid x, \theta)$. The parameter is then chosen based on fit to both the labeled and unlabeled data, weighted by λ:

$$\underset{\Theta}{\operatorname{argmax}}\left(\log p(\{x_i, y_i\}_{i=l}^{l} \mid \theta) + \lambda \log p(\{x_i\}_{i=l+1}^{l+u} \mid \theta)\right)$$

Low-density Separation

Another major class of methods attempts to place boundaries in regions where there are few data points (labeled or unlabeled). One of the most commonly used algorithms is the transductive support vector machine, or TSVM (which, despite its name, may be used for inductive learning as well). Whereas support vector machines for supervised learning seek a decision boundary with maximal margin over the labeled data, the goal of TSVM is a labeling of the unlabeled data such that the decision boundary has maximal margin over all of the data. In addition to the standard hinge loss $(1 - yf(x))_+$ for labeled data, a loss function $(1 - |f(x)|)_+$ is introduced over the unlabeled data by letting $y = \operatorname{sign} f(x)$. TSVM then selects $f^*(x) = h^*(x) + b$ from a reproducing kernel Hilbert space $\mathcal{H}$ by minimizing the regularized empirical risk:

$$f^* = \underset{f}{\operatorname{argmin}}\left(\sum_{i=1}^{l}(1 - y_i f(x_i))_+ + \lambda_1 \|h\|_{\mathcal{H}}^2 + \lambda_2 \sum_{i=l+1}^{l+u}(1 - |f(x_i)|)_+\right)$$

An exact solution is intractable due to the non-convex term $(1-|f(x)|)_+$, so research has focused on finding useful approximations.

Other approaches that implement low-density separation include Gaussian process models, information regularization, and entropy minimization (of which TSVM is a special case).

Graph-based Methods

Graph-based methods for semi-supervised learning use a graph representation of the data, with a node for each labeled and unlabeled example. The graph may be constructed using domain knowledge or similarity of examples; two common methods are to connect each data point to its k nearest neighbors or to examples within some distance ϵ. The weight W_{ij} of an edge between x_i and x_j is then set to.

$$e^{\frac{-\|x_i - x_j\|^2}{\epsilon}}.$$

Within the framework of manifold regularization, the graph serves as a proxy for the manifold. A term is added to the standard Tikhonov regularization problem to enforce smoothness of the solution relative to the manifold (in the intrinsic space of the problem) as well as relative to the ambient input space. The minimization problem becomes,

$$\underset{f \in \mathcal{H}}{\operatorname{argmin}} \left(\frac{1}{l} \sum_{i=1}^{l} V(f(x_i), y_i) + \lambda_A \| f \|_{\mathcal{H}}^2 + \lambda_I \int_{\mathcal{M}} \| \nabla_{\mathcal{M}} f(x) \|^2 dp(x) \right)$$

where $\mathcal{H}$ is a reproducing kernel Hilbert space and $\mathcal{M}$ is the manifold on which the data lie. The regularization parameters λ_A and λ_I control smoothness in the ambient and intrinsic spaces respectively. The graph is used to approximate the intrinsic regularization term. Defining the graph Laplacian $L = D - W$ where $D_{ii} = \sum_{j=1}^{l+u} W_{ij}$ and f the vector $[f(x_1) \dots f(x_{l+u})]$ we have:

$$\mathrm{f}^T L \mathrm{f} = \sum_{i,j=1}^{l+u} W_{ij}(f_i - f_j)^2 \approx \int_{\mathcal{M}} \| \nabla_{\mathcal{M}} f(x) \|^2 dp(x)$$

The Laplacian can also be used to extend the supervised learning algorithms: regularized least squares and support vector machines (SVM) to semi-supervised versions Laplacian regularized least squares and Laplacian SVM.

Heuristic Approaches

Some methods for semi-supervised learning are not intrinsically geared to learning from both unlabeled and labeled data, but instead make use of unlabeled data within a supervised learning framework. For instance, the labeled and unlabeled examples may inform a choice of representation, distance metric, or kernel for the data in an unsupervised first step. Then supervised learning proceeds from only the labeled examples.

Self-training is a wrapper method for semi-supervised learning. First a supervised learning algorithm is trained based on the labeled data only. This classifier is then applied to the unlabeled data to generate more labeled examples as input for the supervised learning algorithm. Generally only the labels the classifier is most confident of are added at each step.

Co-training is an extension of self-training in which multiple classifiers are trained on different (ideally disjoint) sets of features and generate labeled examples for one another.

In Human Cognition

Human responses to formal semi-supervised learning problems have yielded varying conclusions about the degree of influence of the unlabeled data. More natural learning problems may also be viewed as instances of semi-supervised learning. Much of human concept learning involves a small amount of direct instruction (e.g. parental labeling of objects during childhood) combined with large amounts of unlabeled experience (e.g. observation of objects without naming or counting them, or at least without feedback).

Human infants are sensitive to the structure of unlabeled natural categories such as images of dogs and cats or male and female faces. More recent work has shown that infants and children take into account not only the unlabeled examples available, but the sampling process from which labeled examples arise.

Semi-Supervised Learning in the Real World

Semi-supervised learning models are becoming widely applicable in scenarios across a large variety of industries. Let's explore a few of the most well-known examples:

- Speech Analysis: Speech analysis is a classic example of the value of semi-supervised learning models. Labeling audio files typically is a very intensive tasks that requires a lot of human resources. Applying SSL techniques can really help to improve traditional speech analytic models.
- Protein Sequence Classification: Inferring the function of proteins typically requires active human intervention.
- Web Content Classification: Organizing the knowledge available iun billions of web pages will advance different segments of AI. Unfortunately, that task typically requires human intervention to classify the content.

There are plenty of other scenarios for SSL models. However, not all AI scenarios can directly be tackled using SSL. There are a few essential characteristics that should be present on a problem to be effectively solvable using SSL.

- Sizable Unlabeled Dataset: In SSL scenarios, the seize of the unlabeled dataset should be substantially bigger than the labeled data. Otherwise, the problem can be simply addressed using supervised algorithms.

- Input-Output Proximity Symmetry: SSL operates by inferring classification for unlabeled data based on proximity with labeled data points. Inverting that reasoning, SSL scenarios entail that if two data points are part of the same cluster (determined by a K-means algo or similar) their outputs are likely to be in close proximity as well. Complementarily, if two data points are separated by a low density area, their output should not be close.
- Relatively Simple Labeling & Low-Dimension Nature of the Problem: In SSL scenarios, it is important that the inference of the labeled data doesn't become a problem more complicated than the original problem. This is known in AI circles as the "Vapnik Principle" which essentially states that in order to solve a problem we should not pick an intermediate problem of a higher order of complexity. Also, problems that use datasets with many dimensions or attributes are likely to become really challenging for SSL algorithms as the labeling task will become very complex.

Active Learning

The main hypothesis in active learning is that if a learning algorithm can choose the data it wants to learn from, it can perform better than traditional methods with substantially less data for training.

But what are these traditional methods exactly?

These are tasks which involve gathering a large amount of data randomly sampled from the underlying distribution and using this large dataset to train a model that can perform some sort of prediction. You will call this typical method *passive learning*.

One of the more time-consuming tasks in passive learning is collecting labelled data. In many settings, there can be limiting factors that hamper gathering large amounts of labelled data.

Let's take the example of studying pancreatic cancer. You might want to predict whether a patient will get pancreatic cancer, however, you might only have the opportunity to give a small number of patients further examinations to collect features, etc. In this case, rather than selecting patients at random, we can select patients based on certain criteria. An example criteria might be if the patient drinks alcohol and is over 40 years. This criteria does not have to be static but can change depending on results from previous patients. For example, if you realised that your model is good at predicting pancreatic cancer for those over 50 years, but struggle to make accurate prediction for those between 40-50 years, this might be your new criteria.

The process of selecting these patients (or more generally instances) based upon the data we have collected so far is called *active learning*.

Let *T* be the total set of all data under consideration. For example, in a protein engineering problem, *T* would include all proteins that are known to have a certain interesting activity and all additional proteins that one might want to test for that activity.

During each iteration, *i*, *T* is broken up into three subsets:

- $T_{K,i}$: Data points where the label is known.
- $T_{U,i}$: Data points where the label is unknown.
- $T_{C,i}$: A subset of $T_{U,i}$ that is chosen to be labeled.

Most of the current research in active learning involves the best method to choose the data points for $T_{C,i}$.

Query Strategies

Algorithms for determining which data points should be labeled can be organized into a number of different categories:

- Uncertainty sampling: label those points for which the current model is least certain as to what the correct output should be.
- Query by committee: a variety of models are trained on the current labeled data, and vote on the output for unlabeled data; label those points for which the "committee" disagrees the most.
- Expected model change: label those points that would most change the current model.
- Expected error reduction: label those points that would most reduce the model's generalization error.
- Variance reduction: label those points that would minimize output variance, which is one of the components of error.
- Balance exploration and exploitation: the choice of examples to label is seen as a dilemma between the exploration and the exploitation over the data space representation. This strategy manages this compromise by modelling the active learning problem as a contextual bandit problem. For example, Bouneffouf et al. propose a sequential algorithm named Active Thompson Sampling (ATS), which, in each round, assigns a sampling distribution on the pool, samples one point from this distribution, and queries the oracle for this sample point label.
- Exponentiated Gradient Exploration for Active Learning: In this paper, the author proposes a sequential algorithm named exponentiated gradient (EG)-active that can improve any active learning algorithm by an optimal random exploration.
- Querying from diverse subspaces or partitions: When the underlying model is a forest of trees, the leaf nodes might represent (overlapping) partitions of

the original feature space. This offers the possibility of selecting instances from non-overlapping or minimally overlapping partitions for labeling.

A wide variety of algorithms have been studied that fall into these categories.

Minimum Marginal Hyperplane

Some active learning algorithms are built upon Support vector machines (SVMs) and exploit the structure of the SVM to determine which data points to label. Such methods usually calculate the margin, W, of each unlabeled datum in $T_{U,i}$ and treat W as an n-dimensional distance from that datum to the separating hyperplane.

Minimum Marginal Hyperplane methods assume that the data with the smallest W are those that the SVM is most uncertain about and therefore should be placed in $T_{C,i}$ to be labeled. Other similar methods, such as Maximum Marginal Hyperplane, choose data with the largest W. Tradeoff methods choose a mix of the smallest and largest Ws.

Applications and Modern Research into Active Learning

One of the most popular areas in active learning is natural language processing (NLP). This is because many applications in NLP require lots of labelled data (for example, Part-of-Speech Tagging, Named Entity Recognition) and there is a very high cost to labelling this data.

In fact, there are only a handful datasets in NLP that are freely available and fully tagged for these applications. Hence, using active learning can significantly reduce the amount of labelled data that is needed and the experts required to accurately label them. This same reasoning can be applied to many speech recognition tasks and even tasks such as information retrieval.

Active learning is still being heavily researched. Many people have begun research into using different deep learning algorithms like CNNs and LSTMS as the learner and how to improve their efficiency when using active learning frameworks. There is also research being done on implementing Generative Adversarial Networks (GANs) into the active learning framework. With the increasing interest into deep reinforcement learning, researchers are trying to reframe active learning as a reinforcement learning problem. Also, there are papers which try to learn active learning strategies via a meta-learning setting.

Reinforcement Learning

Reinforcement learning, in the context of artificial intelligence, is a type of dynamic programming that trains algorithms using a system of reward and punishment.

A reinforcement learning algorithm, or agent, learns by interacting with its environment. The agent receives rewards by performing correctly and penalties for performing incorrectly. The agent learns without intervention from a human by maximizing its reward and minimizing its penalty.

Reinforcement learning is an approach to machine learning that is inspired by behaviorist psychology. It is similar to how a child learns to perform a new task. Reinforcement learning contrasts with other machine learning approaches in that the algorithm is not explicitly told how to perform a task, but works through the problem on its own.

As an agent, which could be a self-driving car or a program playing chess, interacts with its environment, receives a reward state depending on how it performs, such as driving to destination safely or winning a game. Conversely, the agent receives a penalty for performing incorrectly, such as going off the road or being checkmated.

The agent over time makes decisions to maximize its reward and minimize its penalty using dynamic programming. The advantage of this approach to artificial intelligence is that it allows an AI program to learn without a programmer spelling out how an agent should perform the task.

In machine learning, the environment is typically formulated as a Markov Decision Process (MDP), as many reinforcement learning algorithms for this context utilize dynamic programming techniques. The main difference between the classical dynamic programming methods and reinforcement learning algorithms is that the latter do not assume knowledge of an exact mathematical model of the MDP and they target large MDPs where exact methods become infeasible.

Reinforcement learning differs from standard supervised learning in that correct input/output pairs need not be presented, and sub-optimal actions need not be explicitly corrected. Instead the focus is on performance, which involves finding a balance between exploration (of uncharted territory) and exploitation (of current knowledge). The exploration vs. exploitation trade-off has been most thoroughly studied through the multi-armed bandit problem and in finite MDPs.

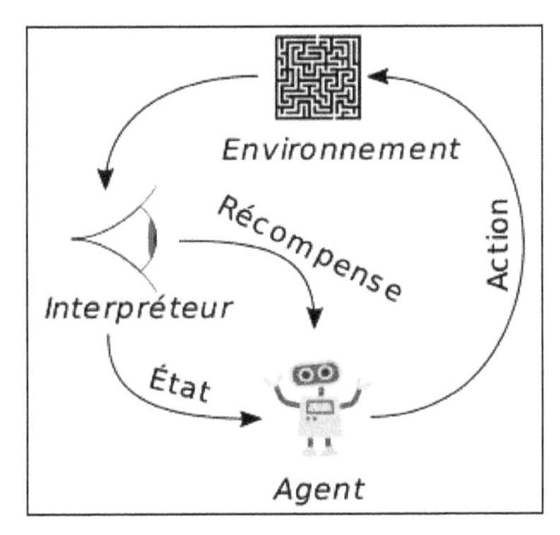

The typical framing of a Reinforcement Learning (RL) scenario: an agent takes actions in an environment, which is interpreted into a reward and a representation of the state, which are fed back into the agent.

Basic reinforcement is modeled as a Markov decision process:

- A set of environment and agent states, *S*.
- A set of actions, *A*, of the agent.
- $P_a(s,s') = Pr(s_{t+1} = s' \mid s_t = s, a_t = a)$ is the probability of transition from state s to state s' under action a.
- $R_a(s,s')$ is the immediate reward after transition from s to s' with action a.
- Rules that describe what the agent observes.

Rules are often stochastic. The observation typically involves the scalar, immediate reward associated with the last transition. In many works, the agent is assumed to observe the current environmental state (*full observability*). If not, the agent has *partial observability*. Sometimes the set of actions available to the agent is restricted (a zero balance cannot be reduced).

A reinforcement learning agent interacts with its environment in discrete time steps. At each time *t*, the agent receives an observation o_t which typically includes the reward r_t. It then chooses an action a_t from the set of available actions, which is subsequently sent to the environment. The environment moves to a new state s_{t+1} and the reward r_{t+1} associated with the *transition* (s_t, a_t, s_{t+1}) is determined. The goal of a reinforcement learning agent is to collect as much reward as possible. The agent can (possibly randomly) choose any action as a function of the history.

When the agent's performance is compared to that of an agent that acts optimally, the difference in performance gives rise to the notion of *regret*. In order to act near optimally, the agent must reason about the long term consequences of its actions (i.e., maximize future income), although the immediate reward associated with this might be negative.

Thus, reinforcement learning is particularly well-suited to problems that include a long-term versus short-term reward trade-off. It has been applied successfully to various problems, including robot control, elevator scheduling, telecommunications, backgammon, checkers and go (AlphaGo).

Two elements make reinforcement learning powerful: the use of samples to optimize performance and the use of function approximation to deal with large environments. Thanks to these two key components, reinforcement learning can be used in large environments in the following situations:

- A model of the environment is known, but an analytic solution is not available.

- Only a simulation model of the environment is given (the subject of simulation-based optimization).
- The only way to collect information about the environment is to interact with it.

The first two of these problems could be considered planning problems (since some form of model is available), while the last one could be considered to be a genuine learning problem. However, reinforcement learning converts both planning problems to machine learning problems.

Exploration

Reinforcement learning requires clever exploration mechanisms. Randomly selecting actions, without reference to an estimated probability distribution, shows poor performance. The case of (small) finite Markov decision processes is relatively well understood. However, due to the lack of algorithms that provably scale well with the number of states (or scale to problems with infinite state spaces), simple exploration methods are the most practical.

One such method is $\epsilon-$greedy, when the agent chooses the action that it believes has the best long-term effect with probability $1-\epsilon$, and it chooses an action uniformly at random, otherwise. Here, $0<\epsilon<1$ is a tuning parameter, which is sometimes changed, either according to a fixed schedule (making the agent explore progressively less), or adaptively based on heuristics.

Algorithms for Control Learning

Even if the issue of exploration is disregarded and even if the state was observable (assumed hereafter), the problem remains to use past experience to find out which actions are good.

Criterion of Optimality

Policy

The agent's action selection is modeled as a map called *policy*:

$$\pi : S \times A \rightarrow [0,1]$$

$$\pi(a \mid s) = P(a_t = a \mid s_t = s)$$

The policy map gives the probability of taking action a when in state s. There are also non-probabilistic policies.

State-value Function

Value function $V_\pi(s)$ is defined as the *expected return* starting with state s, i.e. $s_0 = s$, and successively following policy π. Hence, roughly speaking, the value function estimates "how good" it is to be in a given state.

$$V_\pi(s) = E[R] = E[\sum_{t=0}^{\infty} \gamma^t r_t \mid s_0 = s],$$

where the random variable R denotes the return, and is defined as the sum of future discounted rewards:

$$R = \sum_{t=0}^{\infty} \gamma^t r_t,$$

where r_t is the reward at step t, $\gamma \in [0,1]$ is the discount-rate.

The algorithm must find a policy with maximum expected return. From the theory of MDPs it is known that, without loss of generality, the search can be restricted to the set of so-called *stationary* policies. A policy is *stationary* if the action-distribution returned by it depends only on the last state visited (from the observation agent's history). The search can be further restricted to *deterministic* stationary policies. A *deterministic stationary* policy deterministically selects actions based on the current state. Since any such policy can be identified with a mapping from the set of states to the set of actions, these policies can be identified with such mappings with no loss of generality.

Brute Force

The brute force approach entails two steps:

- For each possible policy, sample returns while following it.
- Choose the policy with the largest expected return.

One problem with this is that the number of policies can be large, or even infinite. Another is that variance of the returns may be large, which requires many samples to accurately estimate the return of each policy.

These problems can be ameliorated if we assume some structure and allow samples generated from one policy to influence the estimates made for others. The two main approaches for achieving this are value function estimation and direct policy search.

Value Function

Value function approaches attempt to find a policy that maximizes the return by maintaining a set of estimates of expected returns for some policy (usually either the "current" [on-policy] or the optimal [off-policy] one).

These methods rely on the theory of MDPs, where optimality is defined in a sense that is stronger than the above one: A policy is called optimal if it achieves the best expected return from *any* initial state (i.e., initial distributions play no role in this definition). Again, an optimal policy can always be found amongst stationary policies.

To define optimality in a formal manner, define the value of a policy π by:

$$V^{\pi}(s) = E[R \mid s, \pi],$$

where R stands for the random return associated with following π from the initial state. Defining s as the maximum possible value of $V^{*}(s)$, where π is allowed to change,

$$V^{*}(s) = \max_{\pi} V^{\pi}(s).$$

A policy that achieves these optimal values in each state is called *optimal.* Clearly, a policy that is optimal in this strong sense is also optimal in the sense that it maximizes the expected return ρ^{π}, since $\rho^{\pi} = E[V^{\pi}(S)]$, where S is a state randomly sampled from the distribution μ.

Although state-values suffice to define optimality, it is useful to define action-values. Given a state s, an action a and a policy π, the action-value of the pair (s,a) under π is defined by,

$$Q^{\pi}(s,a) = E[R \mid s, a, \pi],$$

where R now stands for the random return associated with first taking action a in state s and following π, thereafter.

The theory of MDPs states that if π^{*} is an optimal policy, we act optimally (take the optimal action) by choosing the action from $Q^{\pi^{*}}(s,\cdot)$ with the highest value at each state, s. The *action-value function* of such an optimal policy ($Q^{\pi^{*}}$) is called the *optimal action-value function* and is commonly denoted by Q^{*}. In summary, the knowledge of the optimal action-value function alone suffices to know how to act optimally.

Assuming full knowledge of the MDP, the two basic approaches to compute the optimal action-value function are value iteration and policy iteration. Both algorithms compute a sequence of functions Q_k ($k = 0, 1, 2, \ldots$) that converge to Q^{*}. Computing these functions involves computing expectations over the whole state-space, which is impractical for all but the smallest (finite) MDPs. In reinforcement learning methods, expectations are approximated by averaging over samples and using function approximation techniques to cope with the need to represent value functions over large state-action spaces.

Monte Carlo Methods

Monte Carlo methods can be used in an algorithm that mimics policy iteration. Policy iteration consists of two steps: *policy evaluation* and *policy improvement.*

Monte Carlo is used in the policy evaluation step. In this step, given a stationary, deterministic policy π, the goal is to compute the function values $Q^{\pi}(s,a)$ (or a good approximation to them) for all state-action pairs (s,a). Assuming (for simplicity) that the MDP is finite, that sufficient memory is available to accommodate the action-values and that the problem is episodic and after each episode a new one starts from some random initial state. Then, the estimate of the value of a given state-action pair (s,a) can be computed by averaging the sampled returns that originated from (s,a) over time. Given sufficient time, this procedure can thus construct a precise estimate Q of the action-value function Q^{π}. This finishes the description of the policy evaluation step.

In the policy improvement step, the next policy is obtained by computing a *greedy* policy with respect to Q: Given a state s, this new policy returns an action that maximizes $Q(s,\cdot)$. In practice lazy evaluation can defer the computation of the maximizing actions to when they are needed.

Problems with this procedure include:

- The procedure may spend too much time evaluating a suboptimal policy.
- It uses samples inefficiently in that a long trajectory improves the estimate only of the *single* state-action pair that started the trajectory.
- When the returns along the trajectories have *high variance*, convergence is slow.
- It works in episodic problems only.
- It works in small, finite MDPs only.

Temporal Difference Methods

The first problem is corrected by allowing the procedure to change the policy (at some or all states) before the values settle. This too may be problematic as it might prevent convergence. Most current algorithms do this, giving rise to the class of *generalized policy iteration* algorithms. Many *actor critic* methods belong to this category.

The second issue can be corrected by allowing trajectories to contribute to any state-action pair in them. This may also help to some extent with the third problem, although a better solution when returns have high variance is Sutton's temporal difference (TD) methods that are based on the recursive Bellman equation. Note that the computation in TD methods can be incremental (when after each transition the memory is changed and the transition is thrown away), or batch (when the transitions are batched and the estimates are computed once based on the batch). Batch methods, such as the least-squares temporal difference method, may use the information in the samples better, while incremental methods are the only choice when batch methods are infeasible due to their high computational or memory complexity. Some methods try to combine the two approaches. Methods based on temporal differences also overcome the fourth issue.

In order to address the fifth issue, *function approximation methods* are used. *Linear function approximation* starts with a mapping ϕ that assigns a finite-dimensional vector to each state-action pair. Then, the action values of a state-action pair (s,a) are obtained by linearly combining the components of $\phi(s,a)$ with some *weights* θ:

$$Q(s,a) = \sum_{i=1}^{d} \theta_i \phi_i (s,a).$$

The algorithms then adjust the weights, instead of adjusting the values associated with the individual state-action pairs. Methods based on ideas from nonparametric statistics (which can be seen to construct their own features) have been explored.

Value iteration can also be used as a starting point, giving rise to the Q-Learning algorithm and its many variants.

The problem with using action-values is that they may need highly precise estimates of the competing action values that can be hard to obtain when the returns are noisy. Though this problem is mitigated to some extent by temporal difference methods. Using the so-called compatible function approximation method compromises generality and efficiency. Another problem specific to TD comes from their reliance on the recursive Bellman equation. Most TD methods have a so-called λ parameter $(0 \le \lambda \le 1)$ that can continuously interpolate between Monte Carlo methods that do not rely on the Bellman equations and the basic TD methods that rely entirely on the Bellman equations. This can be effective in palliating this issue.

Direct Policy Search

An alternative method is to search directly in (some subset of) the policy space, in which case the problem becomes a case of stochastic optimization. The two approaches available are gradient-based and gradient-free methods.

Gradient-based methods (*policy gradient methods*) start with a mapping from a finite-dimensional (parameter) space to the space of policies: given the parameter vector θ, let π_θ denote the policy associated to θ. Defining the performance function by:

$$\rho(\theta) = \rho^{\pi_\theta}.,$$

under mild conditions this function will be differentiable as a function of the parameter vector θ. If the gradient of ρ was known, one could use gradient ascent. Since an analytic expression for the gradient is not available, only a noisy estimate is available. Such an estimate can be constructed in many ways, giving rise to algorithms such as

Williams' REINFORCE method (which is known as the likelihood ratio method in the simulation-based optimization literature). Policy search methods have been used in the robotics context. Many policy search methods may get stuck in local optima (as they are based on local search).

A large class of methods avoids relying on gradient information.These include simulated annealing, cross-entropy search or methods of evolutionary computation. Many gradient-free methods can achieve (in theory and in the limit) a global optimum. In multiple domains they have demonstrated performance.

Policy search methods may converge slowly given noisy data. For example, this happens in episodic problems when the trajectories are long and the variance of the returns is large. Value-function based methods that rely on temporal differences might help in this case. In recent years, *actor–critic methods* have been proposed and performed well on various problems.

Theory

Both the asymptotic and finite-sample behavior of most algorithms is well understood. Algorithms with provably good online performance (addressing the exploration issue) are known.

Efficient exploration of large MDPs is largely unexplored (except for the case of bandit problems). Although finite-time performance bounds appeared for many algorithms, these bounds are expected to be rather loose and thus more work is needed to better understand the relative advantages and limitations.

For incremental algorithms, asymptotic convergence issues have been settled. Temporal-difference-based algorithms converge under a wider set of conditions than was previously possible (for example, when used with arbitrary, smooth function approximation).

Research

Research topics include

- Adaptive methods that work with fewer (or no) parameters under a large number of condition.
- Addressing the exploration problem in large MDPs.
- Large-scale empirical evaluations.
- Learning and acting under partial information (e.g., using Predictive State Representation).
- Modular and hierarchical reinforcement learning.
- Improving existing value-function and policy search methods.

- Algorithms that work well with large (or continuous) action spaces.
- Transfer learning.
- Lifelong learning.
- Efficient sample-based planning (e.g., based on Monte Carlo tree search).

Multiagent or distributed reinforcement learning is a topic of interest. Applications are expanding.

Reinforcement learning algorithms such as TD learning are under investigation as a model for dopamine-based learning in the brain. In this model, the dopaminergic projections from the substantia nigra to the basal ganglia function as the prediction error. Reinforcement learning has been used as a part of the model for human skill learning, especially in relation to the interaction between implicit and explicit learning in skill acquisition.

End-to-end Reinforcement Learning

The work on learning ATARI TV games by Google DeepMind increased attention to end-to-end reinforcement learning or deep reinforcement learning. This approach extends reinforcement learning to the entire process from observation to action (sensors to motors or end to end) by forming it using a deep network and without explicitly designing state space or action space.

Inverse Reinforcement Learning

In inverse reinforcement learning (IRL), no reward function is given. Instead, the reward function is inferred given an observed behavior from an expert. The idea is to mimic observed behavior, which is often optimal or close to optimal.

Apprenticeship Learning

In apprenticeship learning, an expert demonstrates the target behavior. The system tries to recover the policy via observation.

Recent Advancements in Reinforcement Learning

With the recent success in Deep Learning, now the focus is slowly shifting to applying deep learning to solve reinforcement learning problems. The news recently has been flooded with the defeat of Lee Sedol by a deep reinforcement learning algorithm developed by Google DeepMind. Similar breakthroughs are being seen in video games, where the algorithms developed are achieving human-level accuracy and beyond. Research is still at par, with both industrial and academic masterminds working together to accomplish the goal of building better self-learning robots.

Some major domains where RL has been applied are as follows:

- Game Theory and Multi-Agent Interaction.
- Robotics.
- Computer Networking.
- Vehicular Navigation.
- Medicine.
- Industrial Logistic.

References

- Mehryar Mohri, Afshin Rostamizadeh, Ameet Talwalkar (2012) Foundations of Machine Learning, The MIT Press ISBN 9780262018258
- Settles, Burr (2010), "Active Learning Literature Survey" (PDF), Computer Sciences Technical Report 1648. University of Wisconsin–Madison, retrieved 2014-11-18
- Cornell University Library. "Breiman: Statistical Modeling: The Two Cultures (with comments and a rejoinder by the author)". Retrieved 8 August 2015
- Char, D. S.; Shah, N. H.; Magnus, D. (2018). "Implementing Machine Learning in Health Care – Addressing Ethical Challenges". New England Journal of Medicine. 378 (11): 981–983. doi:10.1056/nejmp1714229. PMID 29539284
- M. Belkin; P. Niyogi (2004). "Semi-supervised Learning on Riemannian Manifolds". Machine Learning. 56 (Special Issue on Clustering): 209–239. doi:10.1023/b:mach.0000033120.25363.1e
- Mohri, Mehryar; Rostamizadeh, Afshin; Talwalkar, Ameet (2012). Foundations of Machine Learning. USA, Massachusetts: MIT Press. ISBN 9780262018258

4

Tools and Techniques of Natural Language Processing

Natural language processing is a component of artificial intelligence that helps computer understand, interpret and manipulate human language in either a speech or text form. Born out of the necessity to fill the gap between human communication and computer understanding, natural language processing employs various methods like parsing and machine translation. The topics elaborated in this chapter will help the reader gain a better perspective of natural language processing and its techniques.

Natural Language Processing

Natural language processing (NLP) is a field of computer science, artificial intelligence and computational linguistics concerned with the interactions between computers and human (natural) languages, and, in particular, concerned with programming computers to fruitfully process large natural language corpora. Challenges in natural language processing frequently involve natural language understanding, natural language generation (frequently from formal, machine-readable logical forms), connecting language and machine perception, managing human-computer dialog systems, or some combination thereof.

History

The history of NLP generally started in the 1950s, although work can be found from earlier periods. In 1950, Alan Turing published an article titled "Computing Machinery and Intelligence" which proposed what is now called the Turing test as a criterion of intelligence.

The Georgetown experiment in 1954 involved fully automatic translation of more than sixty Russian sentences into English. The authors claimed that within three or five years, machine translation would be a solved problem. However, real progress was much slower, and after the ALPAC report in 1966, which found that ten-year-long research had failed to fulfill the expectations, funding for machine translation was dramatically reduced. Little further research in machine translation was conducted until the late 1980s, when the first statistical machine translation systems were developed.

Some notably successful NLP systems developed in the 1960s were SHRDLU, a natural language system working in restricted "blocks worlds" with restricted vocabularies, and ELIZA, a simulation of a Rogerian psychotherapist, written by Joseph Weizenbaum between 1964 and 1966. Using almost no information about human thought or emotion, ELIZA sometimes provided a startlingly human-like interaction. When the "patient" exceeded the very small knowledge base, ELIZA might provide a generic response, for example, responding to "My head hurts" with "Why do you say your head hurts?".

During the 1970s, many programmers began to write "conceptual ontologies", which structured real-world information into computer-understandable data. Examples are MARGIE (Schank, 1975), SAM (Cullingford, 1978), PAM (Wilensky, 1978), TaleSpin (Meehan, 1976), QUALM (Lehnert, 1977), Politics (Carbonell, 1979), and Plot Units (Lehnert 1981). During this time, many chatterbots were written including PARRY, Racter, and Jabberwacky.

Up to the 1980s, most NLP systems were based on complex sets of hand-written rules. Starting in the late 1980s, however, there was a revolution in NLP with the introduction of machine learning algorithms for language processing. This was due to both the steady increase in computational power and the gradual lessening of the dominance of Chomskyan theories of linguistics (e.g. transformational grammar), whose theoretical underpinnings discouraged the sort of corpus linguistics that underlies the machine-learning approach to language processing. Some of the earliest-used machine learning algorithms, such as decision trees, produced systems of hard if-then rules similar to existing hand-written rules. However, part-of-speech tagging introduced the use of hidden Markov models to NLP, and increasingly, research has focused on statistical models, which make soft, probabilistic decisions based on attaching real-valued weights to the features making up the input data. The cache language models upon which many speech recognition systems now rely are examples of such statistical models. Such models are generally more robust when given unfamiliar input, especially input that contains errors (as is very common for real-world data), and produce more reliable results when integrated into a larger system comprising multiple subtasks.

Many of the notable early successes occurred in the field of machine translation, due especially to work at IBM Research, where successively more complicated statistical models were developed. These systems were able to take advantage of existing multilingual textual corpora that had been produced by the Parliament of Canada and the European Union as a result of laws calling for the translation of all governmental proceedings into all official languages of the corresponding systems of government. However, most other systems depended on corpora specifically developed for the tasks implemented by these systems, which was (and often continues to be) a major limitation in the success of these systems. As a result, a great deal of research has gone into methods of more effectively learning from limited amounts of data.

Recent research has increasingly focused on unsupervised and semi-supervised learning algorithms. Such algorithms are able to learn from data that has not been hand-annotated with the desired answers, or using a combination of annotated and non-annotated data. Generally, this task is much more difficult than supervised learning, and typically produces less accurate results for a given amount of input data. However, there is an enormous amount of non-annotated data available (including, among other things, the entire content of the World Wide Web), which can often make up for the inferior results.

In recent years, there has been a flurry of results showing deep learning techniques achieving state-of-the-art results in many natural language tasks, for example in language modeling, parsing, and many others.

Statistical Natural Language Processing

Since the so-called "statistical revolution" in the late 1980s and mid 1990s, much Natural Language Processing research has relied heavily on machine learning.

Formerly, many language-processing tasks typically involved the direct hand coding of rules, which is not in general robust to natural language variation. The machine-learning paradigm calls instead for using statistical inference to automatically learn such rules through the analysis of large *corpora* of typical real-world examples (a *corpus* (plural, "corpora") is a set of documents, possibly with human or computer annotations).

Many different classes of machine learning algorithms have been applied to NLP tasks. These algorithms take as input a large set of "features" that are generated from the input data. Some of the earliest-used algorithms, such as decision trees, produced systems of hard if-then rules similar to the systems of hand-written rules that were then common. Increasingly, however, research has focused on statistical models, which make soft, probabilistic decisions based on attaching real-valued weights to each input feature. Such models have the advantage that they can express the relative certainty of many different possible answers rather than only one, producing more reliable results when such a model is included as a component of a larger system.

Systems based on machine-learning algorithms have many advantages over hand-produced rules:

- The learning procedures used during machine learning automatically focus on the most common cases, whereas when writing rules by hand it is often not at all obvious where the effort should be directed.
- Automatic learning procedures can make use of statistical inference algorithms to produce models that are robust to unfamiliar input (e.g. containing words or structures that have not been seen before) and to erroneous input (e.g. with misspelled words or words accidentally omitted). Generally, handling such input gracefully with hand-written rules—or more generally, creating systems of hand-written rules that make soft decisions—is extremely difficult, error-prone and time-consuming.
- Systems based on automatically learning the rules can be made more accurate simply by supplying more input data. However, systems based on hand-written rules can only be made more accurate by increasing the complexity of the rules, which is a much more difficult task. In particular, there is a limit to the complexity of systems based on hand-crafted rules, beyond which the systems become more and more unmanageable. However, creating more data to input to machine-learning systems simply requires a corresponding increase in the number of man-hours worked, generally without significant increases in the complexity of the annotation process.

Major Evaluations and Tasks

The following is a list of some of the most commonly researched tasks in NLP. Note that some of these tasks have direct real-world applications, while others more commonly serve as subtasks that are used to aid in solving larger tasks.

Though NLP tasks are obviously very closely intertwined, they are frequently, for convenience, subdivided into categories. A coarse division is given below.

Syntax

Lemmatization.

Morphological segmentation:

> Separate words into individual morphemes and identify the class of the morphemes. The difficulty of this task depends greatly on the complexity of the morphology (i.e. the structure of words) of the language being considered. English has fairly simple morphology, especially inflectional morphology, and thus it is often possible to ignore this task entirely and simply model all possible forms of a word (e.g. "open, opens, opened, opening") as separate words. In languages such as Turkish or Meitei, a highly agglutinated Indian language, however, such an approach is not possible, as each dictionary entry has thousands of possible word forms.

Part-of-speech tagging:

> Given a sentence, determine the part of speech for each word. Many words, especially common ones, can serve as multiple parts of speech. For example, "book" can be a noun ("the book on the table") or verb ("to book a flight"); "set" can be a noun, verb or adjective; and "out" can be any of at least five different parts of speech. Some languages have more such ambiguity than others. Languages with little inflectional morphology, such as English are particularly prone to such ambiguity. Chinese is prone to such ambiguity because it is a tonal language during verbalization. Such inflection is not readily conveyed via the entities employed within the orthography to convey intended meaning.

Parsing:

> Determine the parse tree (grammatical analysis) of a given sentence. The grammar for natural languages is ambiguous and typical sentences have multiple possible analyses. In fact, perhaps surprisingly, for a typical sentence there may be thousands of potential parses (most of which will seem completely nonsensical to a human).

Sentence breaking (also known as sentence boundary disambiguation):

> Given a chunk of text, find the sentence boundaries. Sentence boundaries are often marked by periods or other punctuation marks, but these same characters can serve other purposes (e.g. marking abbreviations).

Stemming.

Word segmentation:

> Separate a chunk of continuous text into separate words. For a language like English, this is fairly trivial, since words are usually separated by spaces. However, some written languages like Chinese, Japanese and Thai do not mark word boundaries in such a fashion, and in those languages text segmentation is a significant task requiring knowledge of the vocabulary and morphology of words in the language.

Semantics

Lexical semantics:

What is the computational meaning of individual words in context?

Machine translation:

Automatically translate text from one human language to another. This is one of the most difficult problems, and is a member of a class of problems colloquially termed "AI-complete", i.e. requiring all of the different types of knowledge that humans possess (grammar, semantics, facts about the real world, etc.) in order to solve properly.

Named entity recognition (NER):

Given a stream of text, determine which items in the text map to proper names, such as people or places, and what the type of each such name is (e.g. person, location, organization). Note that, although capitalization can aid in recognizing named entities in languages such as English, this information cannot aid in determining the type of named entity, and in any case is often inaccurate or insufficient. For example, the first word of a sentence is also capitalized, and named entities often span several words, only some of which are capitalized. Furthermore, many other languages in non-Western scripts (e.g. Chinese or Arabic) do not have any capitalization at all, and even languages with capitalization may not consistently use it to distinguish names. For example, German capitalizes all nouns, regardless of whether they refer to names, and French and Spanish do not capitalize names that serve as adjectives.

Natural language generation:

Convert information from computer databases or semantic intents into readable human language.

Natural language understanding:

Convert chunks of text into more formal representations such as first-order logic structures that are easier for computer programs to manipulate. Natural language understanding involves the identification of the intended semantic from the multiple possible semantics which can be derived from a natural language expression which usually takes the form of organized notations of natural languages concepts. Introduction and creation of language metamodel and ontology are efficient however empirical solutions. An explicit formalization of natural languages semantics without confusions with implicit assumptions such as closed-world assumption (CWA) vs. open-world assumption, or subjective Yes/No vs. objective True/False is expected for the construction of a basis of semantics formalization.

Optical character recognition (OCR):

Given an image representing printed text, determine the corresponding text.

Question answering:

Given a human-language question, determine its answer. Typical questions have a specific right answer (such as "What is the capital of Canada?"), but sometimes open-ended questions are also considered (such as "What is the meaning of life?"). Recent works have looked at even more complex questions.

Recognizing Textual entailment:

Given two text fragments, determine if one being true entails the other, entails the other's negation, or allows the other to be either true or false.

Relationship extraction:

Given a chunk of text, identify the relationships among named entities (e.g. who is married to whom).

Sentiment analysis:

Extract subjective information usually from a set of documents, often using online reviews to determine "polarity" about specific objects. It is especially useful for identifying trends of public opinion in the social media, for the purpose of marketing.

Topic segmentation and recognition:

Given a chunk of text, separate it into segments each of which is devoted to a topic, and identify the topic of the segment.

Word sense disambiguation:

Many words have more than one meaning; we have to select the meaning which makes the most sense in context. For this problem, we are typically given a list of words and associated word senses, e.g. from a dictionary or from an online resource such as WordNet.

Discourse

Automatic summarization:

Produce a readable summary of a chunk of text. Often used to provide summaries of text of a known type, such as articles in the financial section of a newspaper.

Coreference resolution:

Given a sentence or larger chunk of text, determine which words ("mentions") refer to the same objects ("entities"). Anaphora resolution is a specific example of this task, and is specifically concerned with matching up pronouns with the nouns or names to which they refer. The more general task of coreference resolution also includes identifying so-called "bridging relationships" involving referring expressions. For example, in a sentence such as "He entered John's house through the front door", "the front door" is a referring expression and the bridging relationship to be identified is the fact that the door being referred to is the front door of John's house (rather than of some other structure that might also be referred to).

Discourse analysis:

This rubric includes a number of related tasks. One task is identifying the discourse structure of connected text, i.e. the nature of the discourse relationships between sentences (e.g. elaboration, explanation, contrast). Another possible task is recognizing and classifying the speech acts in a chunk of text (e.g. yes-no question, content question, statement, assertion, etc.).

Speech

Speech recognition:

Given a sound clip of a person or people speaking, determine the textual representation of the speech. This is the opposite of text to speech and is one of the extremely difficult problems colloquially termed "AI-complete". In natural speech there are hardly any pauses between successive words, and thus speech segmentation is a necessary subtask of speech recognition. Note also that in most spoken languages, the sounds representing successive letters blend into each other in a process termed coarticulation, so the conversion of the analog signal to discrete characters can be a very difficult process.

Speech segmentation:

Given a sound clip of a person or people speaking, separate it into words. A subtask of speech recognition and typically grouped with it.

Natural Language Understanding

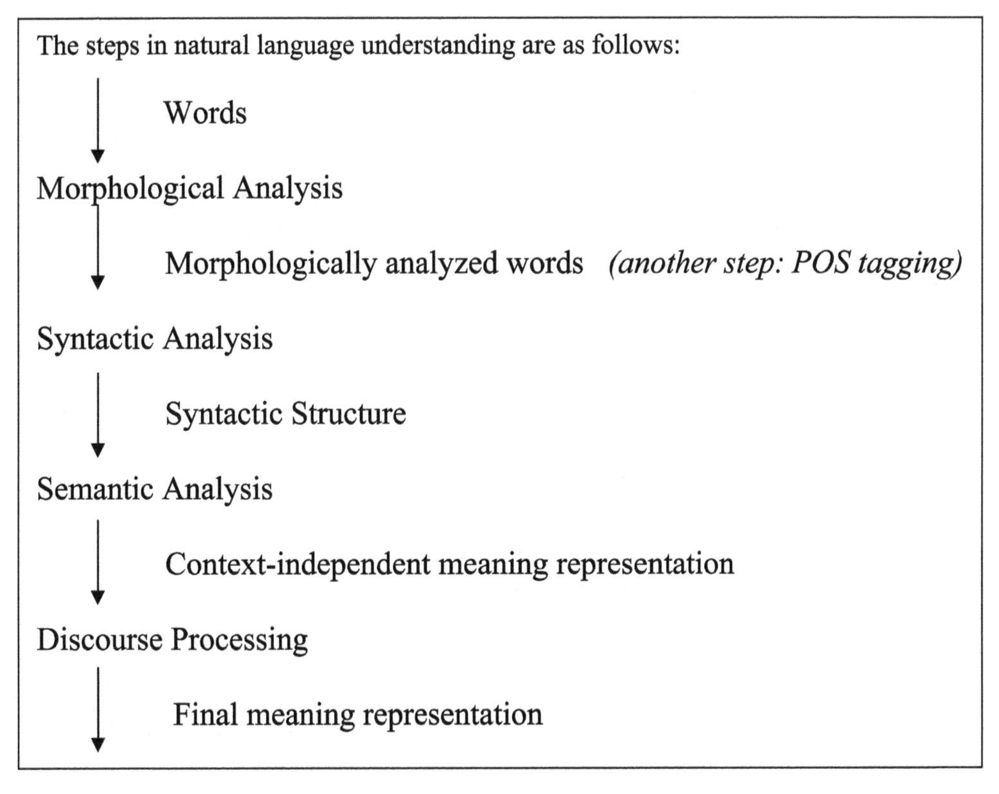

Natural language understanding (NLU) is a subtopic of natural language processing in artificial intelligence that deals with machine reading comprehension. NLU is considered an AI-hard problem.

The process of disassembling and parsing input is more complex than the reverse process of assembling output in natural language generation because of the occurrence of unknown and unexpected features in the input and the need to determine the appropriate syntactic and semantic schemes to apply to it, factors which are pre-determined when outputting language.

There is considerable commercial interest in the field because of its application to news-gathering, text categorization, voice-activation, archiving, and large-scale content-analysis.

History

The program STUDENT, written in 1964 by Daniel Bobrow for his PhD dissertation at MIT is one of the earliest known attempts at natural language understanding by a computer. Eight years after John McCarthy coined the term artificial intelligence, Bobrow's dissertation (titled *Natural Language Input for a Computer Problem Solving System*) showed how a computer can understand simple natural language input to solve algebra word problems.

A year later, in 1965, Joseph Weizenbaum at MIT wrote ELIZA, an interactive program that carried on a dialogue in English on any topic, the most popular being psychotherapy. ELIZA worked by simple parsing and substitution of key words into canned phrases and Weizenbaum sidestepped the problem of giving the program a database of real-world knowledge or a rich lexicon. Yet ELIZA gained surprising popularity as a toy project and can be seen as a very early precursor to current commercial systems such as those used by Ask.com.

In 1969 Roger Schank at Stanford University introduced the conceptual dependency theory for natural language understanding. This model, partially influenced by the work of Sydney Lamb, was extensively used by Schank's students at Yale University, such as Robert Wilensky, Wendy Lehnert, and Janet Kolodner.

In 1970, William A. Woods introduced the augmented transition network (ATN) to represent natural language input. Instead of *phrase structure rules* ATNs used an equivalent set of finite state automata that were called recursively. ATNs and their more general format called "generalized ATNs" continued to be used for a number of years.

In 1971 Terry Winograd finished writing SHRDLU for his PhD thesis at MIT. SHRDLU could understand simple English sentences in a restricted world of children's blocks to direct a robotic arm to move items. The successful demonstration of SHRDLU provided significant momentum for continued research in the field. Winograd continued to be a major influence in the field with the publication of his book *Language as a Cognitive Process*. At Stanford, Winograd would later be the adviser for Larry Page, who co-founded Google.

In the 1970s and 1980s the natural language processing group at SRI International continued research and development in the field. A number of commercial efforts based on the research were undertaken, *e.g.*, in 1982 Gary Hendrix formed Symantec Corporation originally as a company for developing a natural language interface for database queries on personal computers. However, with the advent of mouse driven, graphic user interfaces Symantec changed direction. A number of other commercial efforts were started around the same time, *e.g.*, Larry R. Harris at the Artificial Intelligence Corporation and Roger Schank and his students at Cognitive Systems corp. In 1983, Michael Dyer developed the BORIS system at Yale which bore similarities to the work of Roger Schank and W. G. Lehnart.

The third millennium saw the introduction of systems using machine learning for text classification, such as the IBM Watson. However, this is not NLU. According to John Searle, Watson did not even understand the questions.

John Ball, cognitive scientist and inventor of Patom Theory supports this assessment. NLP has made inroads for applications to support human productivity in service and ecommerce but this has largely been made possible by narrowing the scope of the application. There are thousands of ways to request something in a human language which still defies conventional NLP. "To have a meaningful conversation with machines is only possible when we match every word to the correct meaning based on the meanings of the other words in the sentence – just like a 3-year-old does without guesswork" Patom Theory.

Scope and Context

The umbrella term "natural language understanding" can be applied to a diverse set of computer applications, ranging from small, relatively simple tasks such as short commands issued to robots, to highly complex endeavors such as the full comprehension of newspaper articles or poetry passages. Many real world applications fall between the two extremes, for instance text classification for the automatic analysis of emails and their routing to a suitable department in a corporation does not require in depth understanding of the text, but is far more complex than the management of simple queries to database tables with fixed schemata.

Throughout the years various attempts at processing natural language or *English-like* sentences presented to computers have taken place at varying degrees of complexity. Some attempts have not resulted in systems with deep understanding, but have helped overall system usability. For example, Wayne Ratliff originally developed the *Vulcan* program with an English-like syntax to mimic the English speaking computer in Star Trek. Vulcan later became the dBase system whose easy-to-use syntax effectively launched the personal computer database industry. Systems with an easy to use or *English like* syntax are, however, quite distinct from systems that use a rich lexicon and include an internal representation (often as first order logic) of the semantics of natural language sentences.

Hence the breadth and depth of "understanding" aimed at by a system determine both the complexity of the system (and the implied challenges) and the types of applications it can deal with. The "breadth" of a system is measured by the sizes of its vocabulary and grammar. The "depth" is measured by the degree to which its understanding approximates that of a fluent native speaker. At the narrowest and shallowest, *English-like* command interpreters require minimal complexity, but have a small range of applications. Narrow but deep systems explore and model mechanisms of understanding, but they still have limited application. Systems that attempt to understand the contents of a document such as a news release beyond simple keyword matching and to judge its suitability for a user are broader and require significant complexity, but they are still somewhat shallow. Systems that are both very broad and very deep are beyond the current state of the art.

Components and Architecture

Regardless of the approach used, most natural language understanding systems share some common components. The system needs a lexicon of the language and a parser and grammar rules to break sentences into an internal representation. The construction of a rich lexicon with a suitable ontology requires significant effort, *e.g.*, the Wordnet lexicon required many person-years of effort.

The system also needs a *semantic theory* to guide the comprehension. The interpretation capabilities of a language understanding system depend on the semantic theory it uses. Competing semantic theories of language have specific trade offs in their suitability as the basis of computer-automated semantic interpretation. These range from *naive semantics* or *stochastic semantic analysis* to the use of *pragmatics* to derive meaning from context.

Advanced applications of natural language understanding also attempt to incorporate logical inference within their framework. This is generally achieved by mapping the derived meaning into a set of assertions in predicate logic, then using logical deduction to arrive at conclusions. Therefore, systems based on functional languages such as Lisp need to include a subsystem to represent logical assertions, while logic-oriented systems such as those using the language Prolog generally rely on an extension of the built-in logical representation framework.

The management of context in natural language understanding can present special challenges. A large variety of examples and counter examples have resulted in multiple approaches to the formal modeling of context, each with specific strengths and weaknesses.

Parsing

Parsing syntax analysis or syntactic analysis is the process of analysing a string of symbols, either in natural language or in computer languages, conforming to the rules of a formal grammar. The term *parsing* comes from Latin *pars* (*orationis*), meaning part (of speech).

The term has slightly different meanings in different branches of linguistics and computer science. Traditional sentence parsing is often performed as a method of understanding the exact meaning of a sentence or word, sometimes with the aid of devices such as sentence diagrams. It usually emphasizes the importance of grammatical divisions such as subject and predicate.

Within computational linguistics the term is used to refer to the formal analysis by a computer of a sentence or other string of words into its constituents, resulting in a parse tree showing their syntactic relation to each other, which may also contain semantic and other information.

The term is also used in psycholinguistics when describing language comprehension. In this context, parsing refers to the way that human beings analyze a sentence or phrase (in spoken language or text) "in terms of grammatical constituents, identifying the parts of speech, syntactic relations, etc." This term is especially common when discussing what linguistic cues help speakers to interpret garden-path sentences.

Within computer science, the term is used in the analysis of computer languages, referring to the syntactic analysis of the input code into its component parts in order to facilitate the writing of compilers and interpreters. The term may also be used to describe a split or separation.

Human Languages

Traditional Methods

The traditional grammatical exercise of parsing, sometimes known as *clause analysis*, involves breaking down a text into its component parts of speech with an explanation of the form, function, and syntactic relationship of each part. This is determined in large part from study of the language's conjugations and declensions, which can be quite intricate for heavily inflected languages. To parse a phrase such as 'man bites dog' involves noting that the singular noun 'man' is the subject of the sentence, the verb 'bites' is the third person singular of the present tense of the verb 'to bite', and the singular noun 'dog' is the object of the sentence. Techniques such as sentence diagrams are sometimes used to indicate relation between elements in the sentence.

Parsing was formerly central to the teaching of grammar throughout the English-speaking world, and widely regarded as basic to the use and understanding of written language. However, the general teaching of such techniques is no longer current.

Computational Methods

Normally parsing is defined as separation. To separate the sentence into grammatical meaning or words, phrase, numbers. In some machine translation and natural language processing systems, written texts in human languages are parsed by computer programs. Human sentences are not easily parsed by programs, as there is substantial ambiguity in the structure of human language, whose usage is to convey meaning (or semantics) amongst a potentially unlimited range of possibilities but only some of which are germane to the particular case. So an utterance "Man bites dog" versus "Dog bites man" is definite on one detail but in another language might appear as "Man dog bites" with a reliance on the larger context to distinguish between those two possibilities, if indeed that difference was of concern. It is difficult to prepare formal rules to describe informal behaviour even though it is clear that some rules are being followed.

In order to parse natural language data, researchers must first agree on the grammar to be used. The choice of syntax is affected by both linguistic and computational concerns; for instance some parsing systems use lexical functional grammar, but in general, parsing for grammars of this type is known to be NP-complete. Head-driven phrase structure grammar is another linguistic formalism which has been popular in the parsing community, but other research efforts have focused on less complex formalisms such as the one used in the Penn Treebank. Shallow parsing aims to find only the boundaries of major constituents such as noun phrases. Another popular strategy for avoiding linguistic controversy is dependency grammar parsing.

Most modern parsers are at least partly statistical; that is, they rely on a corpus of training data which has already been annotated (parsed by hand). This approach allows the system to gather information about the frequency with which various constructions occur in specific contexts.

Approaches which have been used include straightforward PCFGs (probabilistic context-free grammars), maximum entropy, and neural nets. Most of the more successful systems use *lexical* statistics (that is, they consider the identities of the words involved, as well as their part of speech). However such systems are vulnerable to overfitting and require some kind of smoothing to be effective.

Parsing algorithms for natural language cannot rely on the grammar having 'nice' properties as with manually designed grammars for programming languages. As mentioned earlier some grammar formalisms are very difficult to parse computationally; in general, even if the desired structure is not context-free, some kind of context-free approximation to the grammar is used to perform a first pass. Algorithms which use context-free grammars often rely on some variant of the CYK algorithm, usually with some heuristic to prune away unlikely analyses to save time. However some systems trade speed for accuracy using, e.g., linear-time versions of the shift-reduce algorithm. A somewhat recent development has been parse reranking in which the parser proposes some large number of analyses, and a more complex system selects the best option.

Psycholinguistics

In psycholinguistics, parsing involves not just the assignment of words to categories, but the evaluation of the meaning of a sentence according to the rules of syntax drawn by inferences made from each word in the sentence. This normally occurs as words are being heard or read. Consequently, psycholinguistic models of parsing are of necessity *incremental*, meaning that they build up an interpretation as the sentence is being processed, which is normally expressed in terms of a partial syntactic structure. Creation of initially wrong structures occurs when interpreting garden path sentences.

Computer Languages

Parser

A parser is a software component that takes input data (frequently text) and builds a data structure – often some kind of parse tree, abstract syntax tree or other hierarchical structure – giving a structural representation of the input, checking for correct syntax in the process. The parsing may be preceded or followed by other steps, or these may be combined into a single step. The parser is often preceded by a separate lexical analyser, which creates tokens from the sequence of input characters; alternatively, these can be combined in scannerless parsing. Parsers may be programmed by hand or may be automatically or semi-automatically generated by a parser generator. Parsing is complementary to templating, which produces formatted *output*. These may be applied to different domains, but often appear together, such as the scanf/printf pair, or the input (front end parsing) and output (back end code generation) stages of a compiler.

The input to a parser is often text in some computer language, but may also be text in a natural language or less structured textual data, in which case generally only certain parts of the text are extracted, rather than a parse tree being constructed. Parsers range from very simple functions such as scanf, to complex programs such as the frontend of a C++ compiler or the HTML parser of a web browser. An important class of simple parsing is done using regular expressions, in which a group of regular expressions defines a regular language and a regular expression engine automatically generating a parser for that language, allowing pattern matching and extraction of text. In other contexts regular expressions are instead used prior to parsing, as the lexing step whose output is then used by the parser.

The use of parsers varies by input. In the case of data languages, a parser is often found as the file reading facility of a program, such as reading in HTML or XML text; these examples are markup languages. In the case of programming languages, a parser is a component of a compiler or interpreter, which parses the source code of a computer programming language to create some form of internal representation; the parser is a key step in the compiler frontend. Programming languages tend to be specified in terms of a deterministic context-free grammar because fast and efficient parsers can be written for them. For compilers, the parsing itself can be done in one pass or multiple passes.

The implied disadvantages of a one-pass compiler can largely be overcome by adding fix-ups, where provision is made for fix-ups during the forward pass, and the fix-ups are applied backwards when the current program segment has been recognized as having been completed. An example where such a fix-up mechanism would be useful would be a forward GOTO statement, where the target of the GOTO is unknown until the program segment is completed. In this case, the application of the fix-up would be delayed until the target of the GOTO was recognized. Obviously, a backward GOTO does not require a fix-up.

Context-free grammars are limited in the extent to which they can express all of the requirements of a language. Informally, the reason is that the memory of such a language is limited. The grammar cannot remember the presence of a construct over an arbitrarily long input; this is necessary for a language in which, for example, a name must be declared before it may be referenced. More powerful grammars that can express this constraint, however, cannot be parsed efficiently. Thus, it is a common strategy to create a relaxed parser for a context-free grammar which accepts a superset of the desired language constructs (that is, it accepts some invalid constructs); later, the unwanted constructs can be filtered out at the semantic analysis (contextual analysis) step.

For example, in Python the following is syntactically valid code:

```
x = 1

print(x)
```

The following code, however, is syntactically valid in terms of the context-free grammar, yielding a syntax tree with the same structure as the previous, but is syntactically invalid in terms of the context-sensitive grammar, which requires that variables be initialized before use:

```
x = 1

print(y)
```

Rather than being analyzed at the parsing stage, this is caught by checking the *values* in the syntax tree, hence as part of *semantic* analysis: context-sensitive syntax is in practice often more easily analyzed as semantics.

Overview of Process

The first stage is the token generation, or lexical analysis, by which the input character stream is split into meaningful symbols defined by a grammar of regular expressions. For example, a calculator program would look at an input such as "12*(3+4)^2" and split it into the tokens 12, *, (, 3, +, 4,), ^, 2, each of which is a meaningful symbol in the context of an arithmetic expression. The lexer would contain rules to tell it that the characters *, +, ^, (and) mark the start of a new token, so meaningless tokens like "12*" or "(3" will not be generated.

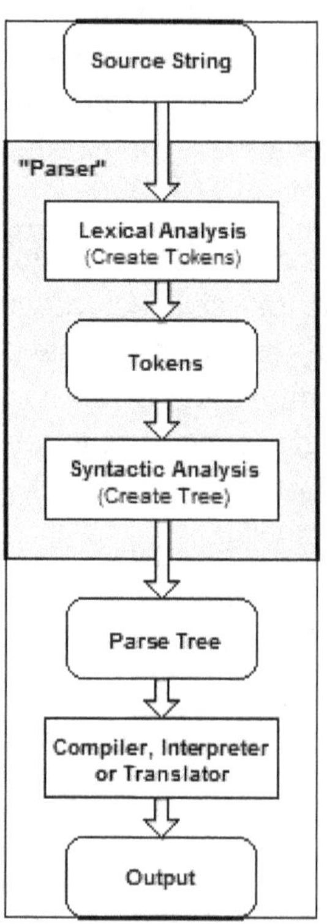

The following example demonstrates the common case of parsing a computer language with two levels of grammar: lexical and syntactic.

The next stage is parsing or syntactic analysis, which is checking that the tokens form an allowable expression. This is usually done with reference to a context-free grammar which recursively defines components that can make up an expression and the order in which they must appear. However, not all rules defining programming languages can be expressed by context-free grammars alone, for example type validity and proper declaration of identifiers. These rules can be formally expressed with attribute grammars.

The final phase is semantic parsing or analysis, which is working out the implications of the expression just validated and taking the appropriate action. In the case of a calculator or interpreter, the action is to evaluate the expression or program, a compiler, on the other hand, would generate some kind of code. Attribute grammars can also be used to define these actions.

Types of Parsers

The *task* of the parser is essentially to determine if and how the input can be derived from the start symbol of the grammar. This can be done in essentially two ways:

- Top-down parsing - Top-down parsing can be viewed as an attempt to find left-most derivations of an input-stream by searching for parse trees using a top-down expansion of the given formal grammar rules. Tokens are consumed from left to right. Inclusive choice is used to accommodate ambiguity by expanding all alternative right-hand-sides of grammar rules.
- Bottom-up parsing - A parser can start with the input and attempt to rewrite it to the start symbol. Intuitively, the parser attempts to locate the most basic elements, then the elements containing these, and so on. LR parsers are examples of bottom-up parsers. Another term used for this type of parser is Shift-Reduce parsing.

LL parsers and recursive-descent parser are examples of top-down parsers which cannot accommodate left recursive production rules. Although it has been believed that simple implementations of top-down parsing cannot accommodate direct and indirect left-recursion and may require exponential time and space complexity while parsing ambiguous context-free grammars, more sophisticated algorithms for top-down parsing have been created by Frost, Hafiz, and Callaghan which accommodate ambiguity and left recursion in polynomial time and which generate polynomial-size representations of the potentially exponential number of parse trees. Their algorithm is able to produce both left-most and right-most derivations of an input with regard to a given context-free grammar.

An important distinction with regard to parsers is whether a parser generates a *leftmost derivation* or a *rightmost derivation*. LL parsers will generate a leftmost derivation and LR parsers will generate a rightmost derivation (although usually in reverse).

Parser Development Software

Some of the well known parser development tools include the following.

- ANTLR,
- Bison,
- Coco/R,
- GOLD,
- JavaCC,
- Lemon,
- Lex,
- LuZc,
- Parboiled,
- Parsec,
- Ragel,

- Spirit Parser Framework,
- Syntax Definition Formalism,
- SYNTAX,
- XPL,
- Yacc,
- PackCC.

Lookahead

Lookahead establishes the maximum incoming tokens that a parser can use to decide which rule it should use. Lookahead is especially relevant to LL, LR, and LALR parsers, where it is often explicitly indicated by affixing the lookahead to the algorithm name in parentheses, such as LALR(1).

Most programming languages, the primary target of parsers, are carefully defined in such a way that a parser with limited lookahead, typically one, can parse them, because parsers with limited lookahead are often more efficient. One important change to this trend came in 1990 when Terence Parr created ANTLR for his Ph.D. thesis, a parser generator for efficient LL(k) parsers, where k is any fixed value.

Parsers typically have only a few actions after seeing each token. They are shift (add this token to the stack for later reduction), reduce (pop tokens from the stack and form a syntactic construct), end, error (no known rule applies) or conflict (does not know whether to shift or reduce).

Lookahead has two advantages.

- It helps the parser take the correct action in case of conflicts. For example, parsing the if statement in the case of an else clause.
- It eliminates many duplicate states and eases the burden of an extra stack. A C language non-lookahead parser will have around 10,000 states. A lookahead parser will have around 300 states.

Example: Parsing the Expression 1 + 2 * 3.

Set of expression parsing rules (called grammar) is as follows,

Rule1:	$E \rightarrow E + E$	Expression is the sum of two expressions.
Rule2:	$E \rightarrow E * E$	Expression is the product of two expressions.
Rule3:	$E \rightarrow$ number	Expression is a simple number
Rule4:	+ has less precedence than *	

Most programming languages (except for a few such as APL and Smalltalk) and algebraic formulas give higher precedence to multiplication than addition, in which case the correct interpretation of the example above is (1 + (2*3)). Note that Rule4 above is a semantic rule. It is possible to rewrite the grammar to incorporate this into the syntax. However, not all such rules can be translated into syntax.

Simple non-lookahead parser actions.

Initially Input = [1,+,2,*,3]:

1. Shift "1" onto stack from input (in anticipation of rule3). Input = [+,2,*,3] Stack = [1].
2. Reduces "1" to expression "E" based on rule3. Stack = [E].
3. Shift "+" onto stack from input (in anticipation of rule1). Input = [2,*,3] Stack = [E,+].
4. Shift "2" onto stack from input (in anticipation of rule3). Input = [*,3] Stack = [E,+,2].
5. Reduce stack element "2" to Expression "E" based on rule3. Stack = [E,+,E].
6. Reduce stack items [E,+] and new input "E" to "E" based on rule1. Stack = [E].
7. Shift "*" onto stack from input (in anticipation of rule2). Input = Stack = [E,*].
8. Shift "3" onto stack from input (in anticipation of rule3). Input = [] (empty) Stack = [E,*,3].
9. Reduce stack element "3" to expression "E" based on rule3. Stack = [E,*,E].
10. Reduce stack items [E,*] and new input "E" to "E" based on rule2. Stack = [E].

The parse tree and resulting code from it is not correct according to language semantics.

To correctly parse without lookahead, there are three solutions:

1. The user has to enclose expressions within parentheses. This often is not a viable solution.
2. The parser needs to have more logic to backtrack and retry whenever a rule is violated or not complete. The similar method is followed in LL parsers.
3. Alternatively, the parser or grammar needs to have extra logic to delay reduction and reduce only when it is absolutely sure which rule to reduce first. This method is used in LR parsers. This correctly parses the expression but with many more states and increased stack depth.

Lookahead parser actions:

1. Shift 1 onto stack on input 1 in anticipation of rule3. It does not reduce immediately.
2. Reduce stack item 1 to simple Expression on input + based on rule3. The lookahead is +, so we are on path to E +, so we can reduce the stack to E.
3. Shift + onto stack on input + in anticipation of rule1.
4. Shift 2 onto stack on input 2 in anticipation of rule3.
5. Reduce stack item 2 to Expression on input * based on rule3. The lookahead * expects only

E before it.

6. Now stack has E + E and still the input is *. It has two choices now, either to shift based on rule2 or reduction based on rule1. Since * has higher precedence than + based on rule4, we shift * onto stack in anticipation of rule2.

7. Shift 3 onto stack on input 3 in anticipation of rule3.

8. Reduce stack item 3 to Expression after seeing end of input based on rule3.

9. Reduce stack items E * E to E based on rule2.

10. Reduce stack items E + E to E based on rule1.

The parse tree generated is correct and simply more efficient than non-lookahead parsers. This is the strategy followed in LALR parsers.

Natural Language Generation

Natural language generation (NLG) is the natural language processing task of generating natural language from a machine representation system such as a knowledge base or a logical form. Psycholinguists prefer the term language production when such formal representations are interpreted as models for mental representations.

It could be said an NLG system is like a translator that converts data into a natural language representation. However, the methods to produce the final language are different from those of a compiler due to the inherent expressivity of natural languages. NLG has existed for a long time but commercial NLG technology has only recently become widely available.

NLG may be viewed as the opposite of natural language understanding: whereas in natural language understanding the system needs to disambiguate the input sentence to produce the machine representation language, in NLG the system needs to make decisions about how to put a concept into words.

A simple example is systems that generate form letters. These do not typically involve grammar rules, but may generate a letter to a consumer, e.g. stating that a credit card spending limit was reached. To put it another way, simple systems use a template not unlike a Word document mail merge, but more complex NLG systems dynamically create text. As in other areas of natural language processing, this can be done using either explicit models of language (e.g., grammars) and the domain, or using statistical models derived by analysing human-written texts.

Example

The *Pollen Forecast for Scotland* system is a simple example of a simple NLG system that could essentially be a template. This system takes as input six numbers, which give predicted pollen levels in different parts of Scotland. From these numbers, the system generates a short textual summary of pollen levels as its output.

For example, using the historical data for 1-July-2005, the software produces.

Grass pollen levels for Friday have increased from the moderate to high levels of yesterday with values of around 6 to 7 across most parts of the country. However, in Northern areas, pollen levels will be moderate with values of 4.

In contrast, the actual forecast (written by a human meteorologist) from this data was

Pollen counts are expected to remain high at level 6 over most of Scotland, and even level 7 in the south east. The only relief is in the Northern Isles and far northeast of mainland Scotland with medium levels of pollen count.

Comparing these two illustrates some of the choices that NLG systems must make; these are further discussed below.

Stages

The process to generate text can be as simple as keeping a list of canned text that is copied and pasted, possibly linked with some glue text. The results may be satisfactory in simple domains such as horoscope machines or generators of personalised business letters. However, a sophisticated NLG system needs to include stages of planning and merging of information to enable the generation of text that looks natural and does not become repetitive. The typical stages of natural language generation, as proposed by Dale and Reiter, are:

Content determination: Deciding what information to mention in the text. For instance, in the pollen example above, deciding whether to explicitly mention that pollen level is 7 in the south east.

Document structuring: Overall organisation of the information to convey. For example, deciding to describe the areas with high pollen levels first, instead of the areas with low pollen levels.

Aggregation: Merging of similar sentences to improve readability and naturalness. For instance, merging the two sentences *Grass pollen levels for Friday have increased from the moderate to high levels of yesterday* and *Grass pollen levels will be around 6 to 7 across most parts of the country* into the single sentence *Grass pollen levels for Friday have increased from the moderate to high levels of yesterday with values of around 6 to 7 across most parts of the country.*

Lexical choice: Putting words to the concepts. For example, deciding whether *medium* or *moderate* should be used when describing a pollen level of 4.

Referring expression generation: Creating referring expressions that identify objects and regions. For example, deciding to use *in the Northern Isles and far northeast of mainland Scotland* to refer to a certain region in Scotland. This task also includes making decisions about pronouns and other types of anaphora.

Realisation: Creating the actual text, which should be correct according to the rules of syntax, morphology, and orthography. For example, using *will be* for the future tense of *to be.*

Applications

The popular media has paid the most attention to NLG systems which generate jokes, but from a commercial perspective, the most successful NLG applications have been *data-to-text* systems which generate textual summaries of databases and data sets; these systems usually perform data analysis as well as text generation. In particular, several systems have been built that produce textual weather forecasts from weather data. The earliest such system to be deployed was FoG, which was used by Environment Canada to generate weather forecasts in French and English in the early 1990s. The success of FoG triggered other work, both research and commercial. Recent research in this area include an experiment which showed that users sometimes preferred computer-generated weather forecasts to human-written ones, in part because the computer forecasts used more consistent terminology, and a demonstration that statistical techniques could be used to generate high-quality weather forecasts. Recent applications include the UK Met Office's text-enhanced forecast.

The use of NLG in financial services is growing as well. In 2016, FactSet discussed with Forbes how they use NLG to automatically write thousands of reports.The use case in financial services seems to be growing solutions like Yseop Compose offer use cases on their website for finance.

This all began in the 1990s when there was interest in using NLG to summarise financial and business data. For example, the SPOTLIGHT system developed at A.C. Nielsen automatically generated readable English text based on the analysis of large amounts of retail sales data. More recently there is interest in using NLG to summarise electronic medical records. Commercial applications in this area are appearing, and researchers have shown that NLG summaries of medical data can be effective decision-support aids for medical professionals. There is also growing interest in using NLG to enhance accessibility, for example by describing graphs and data sets to blind people.

An example of an interactive use of NLG is the WYSIWYM framework. It stands for *What you see is what you meant* and allows users to see and manipulate the continuously rendered view (NLG output) of an underlying formal language document (NLG input), thereby editing the formal language without learning it.

Content generation systems assist human writers and makes writing process more efficient and effective. A content generation tool based on web mining using search engines APIs has been built. The tool imitates the cut-and-paste writing scenario where a writer forms its content from various search results. Relevance verification is essential to filter out irrelevant search results; it is based on matching the parse tree of a query with the parse trees of candidate answers. In an alternative approach, a high-level structure of human-authored text is used to automatically build a template for a new topic for automatically written Wikipedia article.

Several companies have been started since 2009 which build systems that transform data into narrative using NLG and AI techniques. These include Arria NLG, Automated Insights, Narrative Science, Narrativa and Yseop.

Evaluation

As in other scientific fields, NLG researchers need to test how well their systems, modules, and algorithms work. This is called *evaluation*. There are three basic techniques for evaluating NLG systems:

- *Task-based (extrinsic) evaluation*: give the generated text to a person, and assess how well it helps him perform a task (or otherwise achieves its communicative goal). For example, a system which generates summaries of medical data can be evaluated by giving these summaries to doctors, and assessing whether the summaries helps doctors make better decisions.

- *Human ratings*: give the generated text to a person, and ask him or her to rate the quality and usefulness of the text.
- *Metrics*: compare generated texts to texts written by people from the same input data, using an automatic metric such as BLEU.

An ultimate goal is how useful NLG systems are at helping people, which is the first of the above techniques. However, task-based evaluations are time-consuming and expensive, and can be difficult to carry out (especially if they require subjects with specialised expertise, such as doctors). Hence (as in other areas of NLP) task-based evaluations are the exception, not the norm.

Recently researchers are assessing how well human-ratings and metrics correlate with (predict) task-based evaluations. Work is being conducted in the context of Generation Challenges shared-task events. Initial results suggest that human ratings are much better than metrics in this regard. In other words, human ratings usually do predict task-effectiveness at least to some degree (although there are exceptions), while ratings produced by metrics often do not predict task-effectiveness well. These results are preliminary. In any case, human ratings are the most popular evaluation technique in NLG; this is contrast to machine translation, where metrics are widely used.

Natural Language Generation

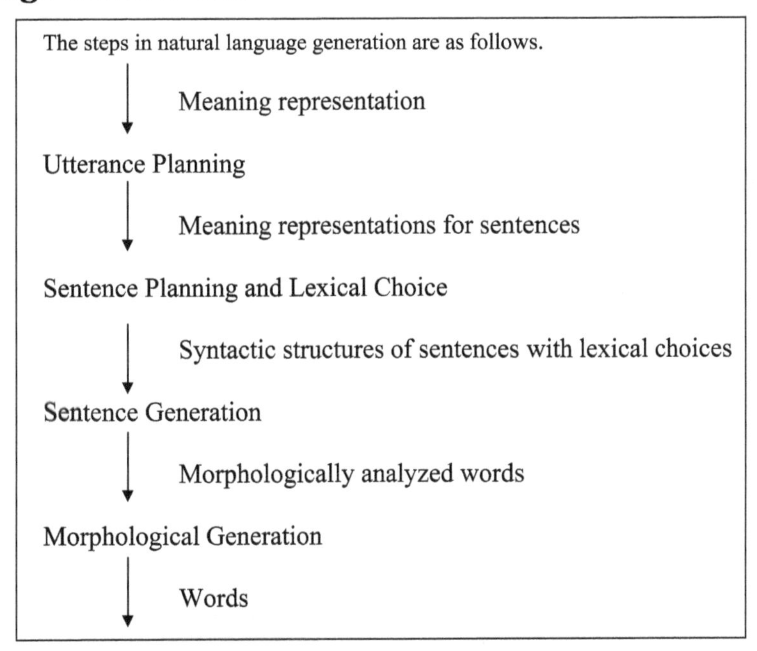

Steps in Language Understanding and Generation

Morphological Analysis

- Analyzing words into their linguistic components (morphemes).

- Morphemes are the smallest meaningful units of language.

cars	car+PLU	
giving	give+PROG	
geliyordum	gel+PROG+PAST+1SG	- I was coming

- Ambiguity: More than one alternatives.

flies	flyVERB+PROG	
fly	NOUN+PLU	
adam	adam+ACC	- the man (accusative)
	adam +P1SG	- my man
	ada+P1SG+ACC - my island (accusative)	

Parts-of-Speech (POS) Tagging

- Each word has a part-of-speech tag to describe its category.
- Part-of-speech tag of a word is one of major word groups (or its subgroups):
  - open classes -- noun, verb, adjective, adverb.
  - Closed classes -- prepositions, determiners, conjuctions, pronouns, particples.
- POS Taggers try to find POS tags for the words.
- duck is a verb or noun? (morphological analyzer cannot make decision).
- A POS tagger may make that decision by looking the surrounding words:
  - Duck! (verb).
  - Duck is delicious for dinner. (noun).

Lexical Processing

- The purpose of lexical processing is to determine meanings of individual words.
- Basic methods is to lookup in a database of meanings – lexicon.
- We should also identify non-words such as punctuation marks.
- Word-level ambiguity -- words may have several meanings, and the correct one cannot be chosen based solely on the word itself:
  - Bank in English.
- Solution -- resolve the ambiguity on the spot by POS tagging (if possible) or pass-on the ambiguity to the other levels.

Syntactic Processing

- Parsing -- converting a flat input sentence into a hierarchical structure that corresponds to the units of meaning in the sentence.
- There are different parsing formalisms and algorithms.
- Most formalisms have two main components:
  - Grammar -- a declarative representation describing the syntactic structure of sentences in the language.
  - parser -- an algorithm that analyzes the input and outputs its structural representation (its parse) consistent with the grammar specification.
- CFGs are in the center of many of the parsing mechanisms. But they are complemented by some additional features that make the formalism more suitable to handle natural languages.

Semantic Analysis

- Assigning meanings to the structures created by syntactic analysis.
- Mapping words and structures to particular domain objects in way consistent with our knowledge of the world.
- Semantic can play an import role in selecting among competing syntactic analyses and discarding illogical analyses:
  - I robbed the bank -- bank is a river bank or a financial institution.
- We have to decide the formalisms which will be used in the meaning representation.

Knowledge Representation for NLP

- Which knowledge representation will be used depends on the application -- Machine Translation, Database Query System.
- Requires the choice of representational framework, as well as the specific meaning vocabulary (what are concepts and relationship between these concepts -- ontology).
- Must be computationally effective.
- Common representational formalisms:
  - First order predicate logic.
  - Conceptual dependency graphs.
  - Semantic networks.
  - Frame-based representations.

Discourse

- Discourses are collection of coherent sentences (not arbitrary set of sentences).
- Discourses have also hierarchical structures (similar to sentences).
- Anaphora resolution -- to resolve referring expression:
  - Mary bought a book for Kelly. She didn't like it:
    - She refers to Mary or Kelly. -- possibly Kelly.
    - It refers to what -- book.
  - Mary had to lie for Kelly. She didn't like it.
- Discourse structure may depend on application:
  - Monologue.
  - Dialogue.
  - Human-Computer Interaction.

Applications of Natural Language Processing

- Machine Translation – Translation between two natural languages:
  - The Babel Fish translations system on Alta Vista.
- Information Retrieval – Web search (uni-lingual or multi-lingual).
- Query Answering/Dialogue – Natural language interface with a database system, or a dialogue system.
- Report Generation – Generation of reports such as weather reports.
- Some Small Applications:
  - Grammar Checking, Spell Checking, Spell Corrector.

Machine Translation

Machine translation, sometimes referred to by the abbreviation MT, is a sub-field of computational linguistics that investigates the use of software to translate text or speech from one language to another.

On a basic level, MT performs simple substitution of words in one language for words in another, but that alone usually cannot produce a good translation of a text because recognition of whole phrases and their closest counterparts in the target language is needed. Solving this problem with corpus statistical, and neural techniques is a rapidly growing field that is leading to better translations, handling differences in linguistic typology, translation of idioms, and the isolation of anomalies.

Current machine translation software often allows for customization by domain or profession (such as weather reports), improving output by limiting the scope of allowable substitutions. This technique is particularly effective in domains where formal or formulaic language is used. It follows that machine translation of government and legal documents more readily produces usable output than conversation or less standardised text.

Improved output quality can also be achieved by human intervention: for example, some systems are able to translate more accurately if the user has unambiguously identified which words in the text are proper names. With the assistance of these techniques, MT has proven useful as a tool to assist human translators and, in a very limited number of cases, can even produce output that can be used as is (e.g., weather reports).

The progress and potential of machine translation have been debated much through its history. Since the 1950s, a number of scholars have questioned the possibility of achieving fully automatic machine translation of high quality. Some critics claim that there are in-principle obstacles to automating the translation process.

History

The idea of machine translation may be traced back to the 17th century. In 1629, René Descartes proposed a universal language, with equivalent ideas in different tongues sharing one symbol. The field of "machine translation" appeared in Warren Weaver's Memorandum on Translation (1949). The first researcher in the field, Yehosha Bar-Hillel, began his research at MIT (1951). A Georgetown University MT research team followed (1951) with a public demonstration of its Georgetown-IBM experiment system in 1954. MT research programs popped up in Japan and Russia (1955), and the first MT conference was held in London (1956). Researchers continued to join the field as the Association for Machine Translation and Computational Linguistics was formed in the U.S. (1962) and the National Academy of Sciences formed the Automatic Language Processing Advisory Committee (ALPAC) to study MT (1964). Real progress was much slower, however, and after the ALPAC report (1966), which found that the ten-year-long research had failed to fulfill expectations, funding was greatly reduced. According to a 1972 report by the Director of Defense Research and Engineering (DDR&E), the feasibility of large-scale MT was reestablished by the success of the Logos MT system in translating military manuals into Vietnamese during that conflict.

The French Textile Institute also used MT to translate abstracts from and into French, English, German and Spanish (1970); Brigham Young University started a project to translate Mormon texts by automated translation (1971); and Xerox used SYSTRAN to translate technical manuals (1978). Beginning in the late 1980s, as computational power increased and became less expensive, more interest was shown in statistical models for machine translation. Various MT companies were launched, including Trados (1984), which was the first to develop and market translation memory technology (1989). The first commercial MT system for Russian / English / German-Ukrainian was developed at Kharkov State University (1991).

MT on the web started with SYSTRAN Offering free translation of small texts (1996), followed by AltaVista Babelfish, which racked up 500,000 requests a day (1997). Franz-Josef Och (the future head of Translation Development AT Google) won DARPA's speed MT competition (2003). More innovations during this time included MOSES, the open-source statistical MT engine (2007), a text/SMS translation service for mobiles in Japan (2008), and a mobile phone with built-in speech-to-speech translation functionality for English, Japanese and Chinese (2009). Recently, Google announced that Google Translate translates roughly enough text to fill 1 million books in one day (2012).

The idea of using digital computers for translation of natural languages was proposed as early as 1946 by A. D. Booth and possibly others. Warren Weaver wrote an important memorandum "Translation" in 1949. The Georgetown experiment was by no means the first such application, and a demonstration was made in 1954 on the APEXC machine at Birkbeck College (University of London) of a rudimentary translation of English into French. Several papers on the topic were published at the time, and even articles in popular journals (for example *Wireless World*, Sept. 1955, Cleave and Zacharov). A similar application, also pioneered at Birkbeck College at the time, was reading and composing Braille texts by computer.

Translation Process

The human translation process may be described as:

1. Decoding the meaning of the source text;
2. Re-encoding this meaning in the target language.

Behind this ostensibly simple procedure lies a complex cognitive operation. To decode the meaning of the source text in its entirety, the translator must interpret and analyse all the features of the text, a process that requires in-depth knowledge of the grammar, semantics, syntax, idioms, etc., of the source language, as well as the culture of its speakers. The translator needs the same in-depth knowledge to re-encode the meaning in the target language.

Therein lies the challenge in machine translation: how to program a computer that will "understand" a text as a person does, and that will "create" a new text in the target language that "sounds" as if it has been written by a person.

In its most general application, this is beyond current technology. Though it works much faster, no automated translation program or procedure, with no human participation, can produce output even close to the quality a human translator can produce. What it can do, however, is provide a general, though imperfect, approximation of the original text, getting the "gist" of it (a process called "gisting"). This is sufficient for many purposes, including making best use of the finite and expensive time of a human translator, reserved for those cases in which total accuracy is indispensable.

This problem may be approached in a number of ways, through the evolution of which accuracy has improved.

Approaches

Machine translation can use a method based on linguistic rules, which means that words will be translated in a linguistic way – the most suitable (orally speaking) words of the target language will replace the ones in the source language.

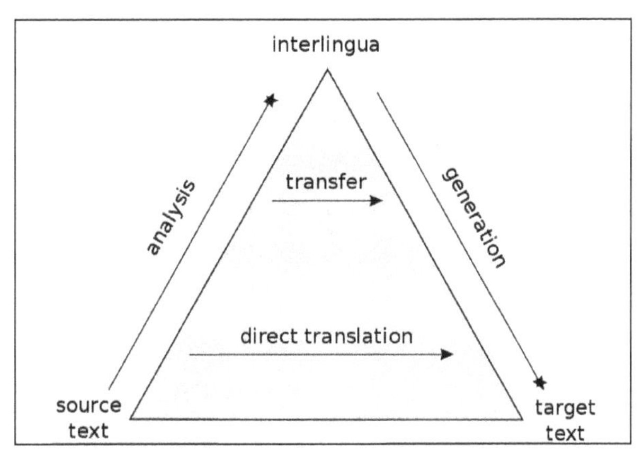

Bernard Vauquois' pyramid showing comparative depths of intermediary representation, interlingual machine translation at the peak, followed by transfer-based, then direct translation.

It is often argued that the success of machine translation requires the problem of natural language understanding to be solved first.

Generally, rule-based methods parse a text, usually creating an intermediary, symbolic representation, from which the text in the target language is generated. According to the nature of the intermediary representation, an approach is described as interlingual machine translation or transfer-based machine translation. These methods require extensive lexicons with morphological, syntactic, and semantic information, and large sets of rules.

Given enough data, machine translation programs often work well enough for a native speaker of one language to get the approximate meaning of what is written by the other native speaker. The difficulty is getting enough data of the right kind to support the particular method. For example, the large multilingual corpus of data needed for statistical methods to work is not necessary for the grammar-based methods. But then, the grammar methods need a skilled linguist to carefully design the grammar that they use.

To translate between closely related languages, the technique referred to as rule-based machine translation may be used.

Rule-based

The rule-based machine translation paradigm includes transfer-based machine translation, interlingual machine translation and dictionary-based machine translation paradigms. This type of translation is used mostly in the creation of dictionaries and grammar programs. Unlike other methods, RBMT involves more information about the linguistics of the source and target languages, using the morphological and syntactic rules and semantic analysis of both languages. The basic approach involves linking the structure of the input sentence with the structure of the output sentence using a parser and an analyzer for the source language, a generator for the target language, and a transfer lexicon for the actual translation. RBMT's biggest downfall is that everything must be made explicit: orthographical variation and erroneous input must be made part of the source language analyser in order to cope with it, and lexical selection rules must be written for all instances of ambiguity. Adapting to new domains in itself is not that hard, as the core grammar is the same across domains, and the domain-specific adjustment is limited to lexical selection adjustment.

Transfer-based Machine Translation

Transfer-based machine translation is similar to interlingual machine translation in that it creates a translation from an intermediate representation that simulates the meaning of the original sentence. Unlike interlingual MT, it depends partially on the language pair involved in the translation.

Interlingual

Interlingual machine translation is one instance of rule-based machine-translation approaches. In this approach, the source language, i.e. the text to be translated, is transformed into an interlingual language, i.e. a "language neutral" representation that is independent of any language. The target language is then generated out of the interlingua. One of the major advantages of this system is that the interlingua becomes more valuable as the number of target languages it can be turned into increases. However, the only interlingual machine translation system that has been made operational at the commercial level is the KANT system (Nyberg and Mitamura, 1992), which is designed to translate Caterpillar Technical English (CTE) into other languages.

Dictionary-based

Machine translation can use a method based on dictionary entries, which means that the words will be translated as they are by a dictionary.

Statistical

Statistical machine translation tries to generate translations using statistical methods based on bilingual text corpora, such as the Canadian Hansard corpus, the English-French record of the Canadian parliament and EUROPARL, the record of the European Parliament. Where such corpora are available, good results can be achieved translating similar texts, but such corpora are still rare for many language pairs. The first statistical machine translation software was CANDIDE from IBM. Google used SYSTRAN for several years, but switched to a statistical translation method in October 2007. In 2005, Google improved its internal translation capabilities by using approximately 200 billion words from United Nations materials to train their system; translation accuracy improved. Google Translate and similar statistical translation programs work by detecting patterns in hundreds of millions of documents that have previously been translated by humans and making intelligent guesses based on the findings. Generally, the more human-translated documents available in a given language, the more likely it is that the translation will be of good quality. Newer approaches into Statistical Machine translation such as METIS II and PRESEMT use minimal corpus size and instead focus on derivation of syntactic structure through pattern recognition. With further development, this may allow statistical machine translation to operate off of a monolingual text corpus. SMT's biggest downfall includes it being dependent upon huge amounts of parallel texts, its problems with morphology-rich languages (especially with translating *into* such languages), and its inability to correct singleton errors.

Example-based

Example-based machine translation (EBMT) approach was proposed by Makoto Nagao in 1984. Example-based machine translation is based on the idea of analogy. In this approach, the corpus that is used is one that contains texts that have already been translated. Given a sentence that is to be translated, sentences from this corpus are selected that contain similar sub-sentential components. The similar sentences are then used to translate the sub-sentential components of the original sentence into the target language, and these phrases are put together to form a complete translation.

Hybrid MT

Hybrid machine translation (HMT) leverages the strengths of statistical and rule-based translation methodologies. Several MT organizations (such as Omniscien Technologies (formerly Asia Online), LinguaSys, Systran, and Polytechnic University of Valencia) claim a hybrid approach that uses both rules and statistics. The approaches differ in a number of ways:

- Rules post-processed by statistics: Translations are performed using a rules based engine. Statistics are then used in an attempt to adjust/correct the output from the rules engine.
- Statistics guided by rules: Rules are used to pre-process data in an attempt to better guide the statistical engine. Rules are also used to post-process the statistical output to perform functions such as normalization. This approach has a lot more power, flexibility and control when translating.

Neural MT

A deep learning based approach to MT, neural machine translation has made rapid progress in recent years, and Google has announced its translation services are now using this technology in preference to its previous statistical methods.

Major Issues

Disambiguation

Word-sense disambiguation concerns finding a suitable translation when a word can have more than one meaning. The problem was first raised in the 1950s by Yehoshua Bar-Hillel. He pointed out that without a "universal encyclopedia", a machine would never be able to distinguish between the two meanings of a word. Today there are numerous approaches designed to overcome this problem. They can be approximately divided into "shallow" approaches and "deep" approaches.

Shallow approaches assume no knowledge of the text. They simply apply statistical methods to the words surrounding the ambiguous word. Deep approaches presume a comprehensive knowledge of the word. So far, shallow approaches have been more successful.

Claude Piron, a long-time translator for the United Nations and the World Health Organization, wrote that machine translation, at its best, automates the easier part of a translator's job; the harder and more time-consuming part usually involves doing extensive research to resolve ambiguities in the source text, which the grammatical and lexical exigencies of the target language require to be resolved:

> Why does a translator need a whole workday to translate five pages, and not an hour or two? ..... About 90% of an average text corresponds to these simple conditions. But unfortunately, there's the other 10%. It's that part that requires six [more] hours of work. There are ambiguities one has to resolve. For instance, the author of the source text, an Australian physician, cited the example of an epidemic which was declared during World War II in a "Japanese prisoner of war camp". Was he talking about an American camp with Japanese prisoners or a Japanese camp with American prisoners? The English has two senses. It's necessary therefore to do research, maybe to the extent of a phone call to Australia.

The ideal deep approach would require the translation software to do all the research necessary for this kind of disambiguation on its own; but this would require a higher degree of AI than has yet been attained. A shallow approach which simply guessed at the sense of the ambiguous English phrase that Piron mentions (based, perhaps, on which kind of prisoner-of-war camp is more often mentioned in a given corpus) would have a reasonable chance of guessing wrong fairly often. A shallow approach that involves "ask the user about each ambiguity" would, by Piron's estimate, only automate about 25% of a professional translator's job, leaving the harder 75% still to be done by a human.

Non-standard Speech

One of the major pitfalls of MT is its inability to translate non-standard language with the same accuracy as standard language. Heuristic or statistical based MT takes input from various sources in standard form of a language. Rule-based translation, by nature, does not include common non-standard usages. This causes errors in translation from a vernacular source or into colloquial language. Limitations on translation from casual speech present issues in the use of machine translation in mobile devices.

Named Entities

Name entities, in narrow sense, refer to concrete or abstract entities in the real world including people, organizations, companies, places etc. It also refers to expressing of time, space, quantity such as 1 July 2011, $79.99 and so on.

Named entities occur in the text being analyzed in statistical machine translation. The initial difficulty that arises in dealing with named entities is simply identifying them in the text. Consider the list of names common in a particular language to illustrate this – the most common names are different for each language and also are constantly changing. If named entities cannot be recognized by the machine translator, they may be erroneously translated as common nouns, which would most likely not affect the BLEU rating of the translation but would change the text's human readability. It is also possible that, when not identified, named entities will be omitted from the output translation, which would also have implications for the text's readability and message.

Another way to deal with named entities is to use transliteration instead of translation, meaning that you find the letters in the target language that most closely correspond to the name in the source language. There have been attempts to incorporate this into machine translation by adding a transliteration step into the translation procedure. However, these attempts still have their problems and have even been cited as worsening the quality of translation. Named entities were still identified incorrectly, with words not being transliterated when they should or being transliterated when they shouldn't. For example, for "Southern California" the first word should be translated directly, while the second word should be transliterated. However, machines would often transliterate both because they treated them as one entity. Words like these are hard for machine translators, even those with a transliteration component, to process.

The lack of attention to the issue of named entity translation has been recognized as potentially stemming from a lack of resources to devote to the task in addition to the complexity of creating a good system for named entity translation. One approach to named entity translation has been to transliterate, and not translate, those words. A second is to create a "do-not-translate" list, which has the same end goal – transliteration as opposed to translation. Both of these approaches still rely on the correct identification of named entities, however.

A third approach to successful named entity translation is a class-based model. In this method, named entities are replaced with a token to represent the class they belong to. For example, "Ted" and "Erica" would both be replaced with "person" class token. In this way the statistical distribution and use of person names in general can be analyzed instead of looking at the distributions of "Ted" and "Erica" individually. A problem that the class based model solves is that the probability of a given name in a specific language will not affect the assigned probability of a translation. A study by Stanford on improving this area of translation gives the examples that different probabilities will be assigned to "David is going for a walk" and "Ankit is going for a walk" for English as a target language due to the different number of occurrences for each name in the training data. A frustrating outcome of the same study by Stanford (and other attempts to improve named recognition translation) is that many times, a decrease in the BLEU scores for translation will result from the inclusion of methods for named entity translation.

Translation from Multiparallel Sources

Some work has been done in the utilization of multiparallel corpora, that is a body of text that has been translated into 3 or more languages. Using these methods, a text that has been translated into 2 or more languages may be utilized in combination to provide a more accurate translation into a third language compared with if just one of those source languages were used alone.

Ontologies in MT

An ontology is a formal representation of knowledge which includes the concepts (such as objects, processes etc.) in a domain and some relations between them. If the stored information is of linguistic nature, one can speak of a lexicon. In NLP, ontologies can be used as a source of knowledge for machine translation systems. With access to a large knowledge base, systems can be enabled to resolve many (especially lexical) ambiguities on their own. In the following classic examples, as humans, we are able to interpret the prepositional phrase according to the context because we use our world knowledge, stored in our lexicons:

"I saw a man/star/molecule with a microscope/telescope/binoculars."

A machine translation system initially would not be able to differentiate between the meanings because syntax does not change. With a large enough ontology as a source of knowledge however, the possible interpretations of ambiguous words in a specific context can be reduced. Other areas of usage for ontologies within NLP include information retrieval, information extraction and text summarization.

Building Ontologies

The ontology generated for the PANGLOSS knowledge-based machine translation system in 1993 may serve as an example of how an ontology for NLP purposes can be compiled:

- A large-scale ontology is necessary to help parsing in the active modules of the machine translation system.
- In the PANGLOSS example, about 50.000 nodes were intended to be subsumed under the smaller, manually-built *upper* (abstract) *region* of the ontology. Because of its size, it had to be created automatically.
- The goal was to merge the two resources LDOCE online and WordNet to combine the benefits of both: concise definitions from Longman, and semantic relations allowing for semi-automatic taxonomization to the ontology from WordNet:
    - A *definition match* algorithm was created to automatically merge the correct meanings of ambiguous words between the two online resources, based on the words that the definitions of those meanings have in common in LDOCE and WordNet. Using a similarity matrix, the algorithm delivered matches between meanings including a confidence factor. This algorithm alone, however, did not match all meanings correctly on its own.
    - A second *hierarchy match* algorithm was therefore created which uses the taxonomic hierarchies found in WordNet (deep hierarchies) and partially in LDOCE (flat hierarchies). This works by first matching unambiguous meanings, then limiting the search space to only the respective ancestors and descendants of those matched meanings. Thus, the algorithm matched locally unambiguous meanings (for instance, while the word *seal* as such is ambiguous, there is only one meaning of "seal" in the *animal* subhierarchy).
- Both algorithms complemented each other and helped constructing a large-scale ontology for the machine translation system. The WordNet hierarchies, coupled with the matching definitions of LDOCE, were subordinated to the ontology's *upper region*. As a result, the PANGLOSS MT system was able to make use of this knowledge base, mainly in its generation element.

Applications

While no system provides the holy grail of fully automatic high-quality machine translation of unrestricted text, many fully automated systems produce reasonable output. The quality of machine translation is substantially improved if the domain is restricted and controlled.

Despite their inherent limitations, MT programs are used around the world. Probably the largest institutional user is the European Commission. The MOLTO project, for example, coordinated by the University of Gothenburg, received more than 2.375 million euros project support from the EU to create a reliable translation tool that covers a majority of the EU languages. The further development of MT systems comes at a time when budget cuts in human translation may increase the EU's dependency on reliable MT programs. The European Commission contributed 3.072 million euros (via its ISA programme) for the creation of MT@EC, a statistical machine translation program tailored to the administrative needs of the EU, to replace a previous rule-based machine translation system.

Google has claimed that promising results were obtained using a proprietary statistical machine translation engine. The statistical translation engine used in the Google language tools for Arabic <-> English and Chinese <-> English had an overall score of 0.4281 over the runner-up IBM's BLEU-4 score of 0.3954 (Summer 2006) in tests conducted by the National Institute for Standards and Technology.

With the recent focus on terrorism, the military sources in the United States have been investing significant amounts of money in natural language engineering. *In-Q-Tel* (a venture capital fund, largely funded by the US Intelligence Community, to stimulate new technologies through private sector entrepreneurs) brought up companies like Language Weaver. Currently the military community is interested in translation and processing of languages like Arabic, Pashto, and Dari. Within these languages, the focus is on key phrases and quick communication between military members and civilians through the use of mobile phone apps. The Information Processing Technology Office in DARPA hosts programs like TIDES and Babylon translator. US Air Force has awarded a $1 million contract to develop a language translation technology.

The notable rise of social networking on the web in recent years has created yet another niche for the application of machine translation software – in utilities such as Facebook, or instant messaging clients such as Skype, GoogleTalk, MSN Messenger, etc. – allowing users speaking different languages to communicate with each other. Machine translation applications have also been released for most mobile devices, including mobile telephones, pocket PCs, PDAs, etc. Due to their portability, such instruments have come to be designated as mobile translation tools enabling mobile business networking between partners speaking different languages, or facilitating both foreign language learning and unaccompanied traveling to foreign countries without the need of the intermediation of a human translator.

Despite being labelled as an unworthy competitor to human translation in 1966 by the Automated Language Processing Advisory Committee put together by the United States government, the quality of machine translation has now been improved to such levels that its application in online collaboration and in the medical field are being investigated. In the Ishida and Matsubara lab of Kyoto University, methods of improving the accuracy of machine translation as a support tool for inter-cultural collaboration in today's globalized society are being studied. The application of this technology in medical settings where human translators are absent is another topic of research however difficulties arise due to the importance of accurate translations in medical diagnoses.

Evaluation

There are many factors that affect how machine translation systems are evaluated. These factors include the intended use of the translation, the nature of the machine translation software, and the nature of the translation process.

Different programs may work well for different purposes. For example, statistical machine translation (SMT) typically outperforms example-based machine translation (EBMT), but researchers found that when evaluating English to French translation, EBMT performs better. The same concept applies for technical documents, which can be more easily translated by SMT because of their formal language.

In certain applications, however, e.g., product descriptions written in a controlled language, a dictionary-based machine-translation system has produced satisfactory translations that require no human intervention save for quality inspection.

There are various means for evaluating the output quality of machine translation systems. The oldest is the use of human judges to assess a translation's quality. Even though human evaluation is time-consuming, it is still the most reliable method to compare different systems such as rule-based and statistical systems. Automated means of evaluation include BLEU, NIST, METEOR, and LEPOR.

Relying exclusively on unedited machine translation ignores the fact that communication in human language is context-embedded and that it takes a person to comprehend the context of the original text with a reasonable degree of probability. It is certainly true that even purely human-generated translations are prone to error. Therefore, to ensure that a machine-generated translation will be useful to a human being and that publishable-quality translation is achieved, such translations must be reviewed and edited by a human. The late Claude Piron wrote that machine translation, at its best, automates the easier part of a translator's job; the harder and more time-consuming part usually involves doing extensive research to resolve ambiguities in the source text, which the grammatical and lexical exigencies of the target language require to be resolved. Such research is a necessary prelude to the pre-editing necessary in order to provide input for machine-translation software such that the output will not be meaningless.

In addition to disambiguation problems, decreased accuracy can occur due to varying levels of training data for machine translating programs. Both example-based and statistical machine translation rely on a vast array of real example sentences as a base for translation, and when too many or too few sentences are analyzed accuracy is jeopardized. Researchers found that when a program is trained on 203,529 sentence pairings, accuracy actually decreases. The optimal level of training data seems to be just over 100,000 sentences, possibly because as training data increasing, the number of possible sentences increases, making it harder to find an exact translation match.

Using Machine Translation as a Teaching Tool

Although there have been concerns about machine translation's accuracy, Dr. Ana Nino of the University of Manchester has researched some of the advantages in utilizing machine translation in the classroom. One such pedagogical method is called using "MT as a Bad Model." MT as a Bad Model forces the language learner to identify inconsistencies or incorrect aspects of a translation; in turn, the individual will (hopefully) possess a better grasp of the language. Dr. Nino cites that this teaching tool was implemented in the late 1980s. At the end of various semesters, Dr. Nino was able to obtain survey results from students who had used MT as a Bad Model (as well as other models.) Overwhelmingly, students felt that they had observed improved comprehension, lexical retrieval, and increased confidence in their target language.

Machine Translation and Signed Languages

In the early 2000s, options for machine translation between spoken and signed languages were severely limited. It was a common belief that deaf individuals could use traditional translators. However, stress, intonation, pitch, and timing are conveyed much differently in spoken languages compared to signed languages. Therefore, a deaf individual may misinterpret or become confused about the meaning of written text that is based on a spoken language.

Researchers Zhao, et al. (2000), developed a prototype called TEAM (translation from English to ASL by machine) that completed English to American Sign Language (ASL) translations. The program would first analyze the syntactic, grammatical, and morphological aspects of the English text. Following this step, the program accessed a sign synthesizer, which acted as a dictionary for ASL. This synthesizer housed the process one must follow to complete ASL signs, as well as the meanings of these signs. Once the entire text is analyzed and the signs necessary to complete the translation are located in the synthesizer, a computer generated human appeared and would use ASL to sign the English text to the user.

Copyright

Only works that are original are subject to copyright protection, so some scholars claim that machine translation results are not entitled to copyright protection because MT does not involve creativity. The copyright at issue is for a derivative work; the author of the original work in the original language does not lose his rights when a work is translated: a translator must have permission to publish a translation.

References

- Goldberg, Yoav (2016) A Primer on Neural Network Models for Natural Language Processing. Journal of Artificial Intelligence Research 57 (2016) 345–420
- Galitsky, Boris (2013). “A Web Mining Tool for Assistance with Creative Writing”. Advances in Information Retrieval. Lecture Notes in Computer Science. 7814: 828–831. doi:10.1007/978-3-642-36973-5_95
- Law A, Freer Y, Hunter J, Logie R, McIntosh N, Quinn J (2005). “A Comparison of Graphical and Textual Presentations of Time Series Data to Support Medical Decision Making in the Neonatal Intensive Care Unit”. Journal of Clinical Monitoring and Computing. 19 (3): 183–94
- Dale, Robert; Reiter, Ehud (2000). Building natural language generation systems. Cambridge, U.K.: Cambridge University Press. ISBN 0-521-02451-X

- Yucong Duan, Christophe Cruz (2011), Formalizing Semantic of Natural Language through Conceptualization from Existence. International Journal of Innovation, Management and Technology(2011) 2 (1), pp. 37-42
- Alisa Kongthon, Chatchawal Sangkeettrakarn, Sarawoot Kongyoung and Choochart Haruechaiyasak. Published by ACM 2009 Article, Bibliometrics Data Bibliometrics. Published in: Proceeding, MEDES '09 Proceedings of the International Conference on Management of Emergent Digital EcoSystems, ACM New York, NY, USA. ISBN 978-1-60558-829-2

5

Artificial Intelligence: Industrial Applications

Artificial intelligence finds diverse applications in the present world. The healthcare sector is a major beneficiary of the user of artificial intelligence. Even in other fields like robotics, virtual reality, optical character recognition or game theory, artificial intelligence is being employed for the benefit of mankind. This chapter delves into the applications of artificial intelligence to provide a better understanding.

Applications of Artificial Intelligence

Artificial intelligence has been used in a wide range of fields including medical diagnosis, stock trading, robot control, law, remote sensing, scientific discovery and toys. However, due to the AI effect, many AI applications are not perceived as AI: "A lot of cutting edge AI has filtered into general applications, often without being called AI because once something becomes useful enough and common enough it's not labeled AI anymore," Nick Bostrom reports. "Many thousands of AI applications are deeply embedded in the infrastructure of every industry." In the late 90s and early 21st century, AI technology became widely used as elements of larger systems, but the field is rarely credited for these successes.

Computer Science

AI researchers have created many tools to solve the most difficult problems in computer science. Many of their inventions have been adopted by mainstream computer science and are no longer considered a part of AI. (See AI effect). According to Russell & Norvig (2003, p. 15), all of the following were originally developed in AI laboratories: time sharing, interactive interpreters, graphical user interfaces and the computer mouse, rapid development environments, the linked list data structure, automatic storage management, symbolic programming, functional programming, dynamic programming and object-oriented programming.

Finance

Financial institutions have long used artificial neural network systems to detect charges or claims outside of the norm, flagging these for human investigation.

Use of AI in banking can be tracked back to 1987 when Security Pacific National Bank in USA set-up a Fraud Prevention Task force to counter the unauthorised use of debit cards. Apps like Kasisito and Moneystream are using AI in financial services.

Banks use artificial intelligence systems to organize operations, invest in stocks, and manage properties. In August 2001, robots beat humans in a simulated financial trading competition.

Hospitals and Medicine

Artificial neural networks are used as clinical decision support systems for medical diagnosis, such as in Concept Processing technology in EMR software.

Other tasks in medicine that can potentially be performed by artificial intelligence include:

- Computer-aided interpretation of medical images. Such systems help scan digital images, *e.g.* from computed tomography, for typical appearances and to highlight conspicuous sections, such as possible diseases. A typical application is the detection of a tumor.
- Heart sound analysis.
- Watson project is another use of AI in this field,a Q/A program that suggest for doctor's of cancer patients.
- Companion robots for the care of the elderly.

Heavy Industry

Robots have become common in many industries and are often given jobs that are considered dangerous to humans. Robots have proven effective in jobs that are very repetitive which may lead to mistakes or accidents due to a lapse in concentration and other jobs which humans may find degrading.

In 2014, China, Japan, the United States, the Republic of Korea and Germany together amounted to 70% of the total sales volume of robots. In the automotive industry, a sector with particularly high degree of automation, Japan had the highest density of industrial robots in the world: 1,414 per 10,000 employees.

Online and Telephone Customer Service

Artificial intelligence is implemented in automated online assistants that can be seen as avatars on web pages. It can avail for enterprises to reduce their operation and training cost. A major underlying technology to such systems is natural language processing. Pypestream uses automated customer service for its mobile application designed to streamline communication with customers.

An automated online assistant providing customer service on a web page.

Transportation

Fuzzy logic controllers have been developed for automatic gearboxes in automobiles. For example, the 2006 Audi TT, VW Touareg and VW Caravell feature the DSP transmission which utilizes Fuzzy Logic. A number of Škoda variants (Škoda Fabia) also currently include a Fuzzy Logic-based controller.

Telecommunications Maintenance

Many telecommunications companies make use of heuristic search in the management of their workforces, for example BT Group has deployed heuristic search in a scheduling application that provides the work schedules of 20,000 engineers.

Toys and Games

The 1990s saw some of the first attempts to mass-produce domestically aimed types of basic Artificial Intelligence for education, or leisure. This prospered greatly with the Digital Revolution, and helped introduce people, especially children, to a life of dealing with various types of Artificial Intelligence, specifically in the form of Tamagotchis and Giga Pets, iPod Touch, the Internet (example: basic search engine interfaces are one simple form), and the first widely released robot, Furby. A mere year later an improved type of domestic robot was released in the form of Aibo, a robotic dog with intelligent features and autonomy.

AI has also been applied to video games, for example video game bots, which are designed to stand in as opponents where humans aren't available or desired; or the AI Director from Left 4 Dead, which decides where enemies spawn and how maps are laid out to be more or less challenging at various points of play.

Music

The evolution of music has always been affected by technology. With AI, scientists are trying to make the computer emulate the activities of the skillful musician. Composition, performance, music theory, sound processing are some of the major areas on which research in Music and Artificial Intelligence are focusing. Among these efforts, Melomics seems to be ahead by powering computer-composers that learn to compose the way humans do.

Aviation

The Air Operations Division (AOD) uses AI for the rule based expert systems. The AOD has use for artificial intelligence for surrogate operators for combat and training simulators, mission management aids, support systems for tactical decision making, and post processing of the simulator data into symbolic summaries.

The use of artificial intelligence in simulators is proving to be very useful for the AOD. Airplane simulators are using artificial intelligence in order to process the data taken from simulated flights. Other than simulated flying, there is also simulated aircraft warfare. The computers are able to come up with the best success scenarios in these situations. The computers can also create strategies based on the placement, size, speed and strength of the forces and counter forces. Pilots may be given assistance in the air during combat by computers. The artificial intelligent programs can sort the information and provide the pilot with the best possible maneuvers, not to mention getting rid of certain maneuvers that would be impossible for a human being to perform. Multiple aircraft are needed to get good approximations for some calculations so computer simulated pilots are used to gather data. These computer simulated pilots are also used to train future air traffic controllers.

The system used by the AOD in order to measure performance was the Interactive Fault Diagnosis and Isolation System, or IFDIS. It is a rule based expert system put together by collecting information from TF-30 documents and the expert advice from mechanics that work on the TF-30. This system was designed to be used for the development of the TF-30 for the RAAF F-111C. The performance system was also used to replace specialized workers. The system allowed the regular workers to communicate with the system and avoid mistakes, miscalculations, or having to speak to one of the specialized workers.

The AOD also uses artificial intelligence in speech recognition software. The air traffic controllers are giving directions to the artificial pilots and the AOD wants to the pilots to respond to the ATC's with simple responses. The programs that incorporate the speech software must be trained, which means they use neural networks. The program used, the Verbex 7000, is still a very early program that has plenty of room for improvement. The improvements are imperative because ATCs use very specific dialog and the software needs to be able to communicate correctly and promptly every time.

The Artificial Intelligence supported Design of Aircraft, or AIDA, is used to help designers in the process of creating conceptual designs of aircraft. This program allows the designers to focus more on the design itself and less on the design process. The software also allows the user to focus less on the software tools. The AIDA uses rule based systems to compute its data. This is a diagram of the arrangement of the AIDA modules. Although simple, the program is proving effective.

In 2003, NASA's Dryden Flight Research Center, and many other companies, created software that could enable a damaged aircraft to continue flight until a safe landing zone can be reached. The software compensates for all the damaged components by relying on the undamaged components. The neural network used in the software proved to be effective and marked a triumph for artificial intelligence.

The Integrated Vehicle Health Management system, also used by NASA, on board an aircraft must process and interpret data taken from the various sensors on the aircraft. The system needs to be able to determine the structural integrity of the aircraft. The system also needs to implement protocols in case of any damage taken the vehicle.

News, Publishing and Writing

The company Narrative Science makes computer generated news and reports commercially available, including summarizing team sporting events based on statistical data from the game in English. It also creates financial reports and real estate analyses.

The company Automated Insights generates personalized recaps and previews for Yahoo Sports Fantasy Football. The company is projected to generate one billion stories in 2014, up from 350 million in 2013.

Another company, called Yseop, uses artificial intelligence to turn structured data into intelligent comments and recommendations in natural language. Yseop is able to write financial reports, executive summaries, personalized sales or marketing documents and more at a speed of thousands of pages per second and in multiple languages including English, Spanish, French & German.

Other

Various tools of artificial intelligence are also being widely deployed in homeland security, speech and text recognition, data mining, and e-mail spam filtering. Applications are also being developed for gesture recognition (understanding of sign language by machines), individual voice recognition, global voice recognition (from a variety of people in a noisy room), facial expression recognition for interpretation of emotion and non verbal cues. Other applications are robot navigation, obstacle avoidance, and object recognition.

List of Applications

Typical problems to which AI methods are applied.

• Artificial creativity. o Optical character recognition. o Handwriting recognition. o Speech recognition. o Face recognition.	• Computer vision, Virtual reality and Image processing. • Diagnosis (artificial intelligence). • Game theory and Strategic planning. • Game artificial intelligence and Computer game bot. • Natural language processing, Translation and Chatterbots. • Nonlinear control and Robotics.

Other fields in which AI methods are implemented.

Robotics

Robotics is the branch of mechanical engineering, electrical engineering and computer science that deals with the design, construction, operation, and application of robots, as well as computer systems for their control, sensory feedback, and information processing.

These technologies deal with automated machines that can take the place of humans in dangerous environments or manufacturing processes, or resemble humans in appearance, behavior, and or cognition. Many of today's robots are inspired by nature, contributing to the field of bio-inspired robotics.

The Shadow robot hand system.

The concept of creating machines that can operate autonomously dates back to classical times, but research into the functionality and potential uses of robots did not grow substantially until the 20th century. Throughout history, it has been frequently assumed that robots will one day be able to mimic human behavior and manage tasks in a human-like fashion. Today, robotics is a rapidly growing field, as technological advances continue; researching, designing, and building new robots serve various practical purposes, whether domestically, commercially, or militarily. Many robots are built to do jobs that are hazardous to people such as defusing bombs, finding survivors in unstable ruins, and exploring mines and shipwrecks. Robotics is also used in STEM (Science, Technology, Engineering, and Mathematics) as a teaching aid.

Etymology

The word *robotics* was derived from the word *robot*, which was introduced to the public by Czech writer Karel Čapek in his play *R.U.R. (Rossum's Universal Robots)*, which was published in 1920. The word *robot* comes from the Slavic word *robota*, which means labour. The play begins in a factory that makes artificial people called *robots*, creatures who can be mistaken for humans – very similar to the modern ideas of androids. Karel Čapek himself did not coin the word. He wrote a short letter in reference to an etymology in the *Oxford English Dictionary* in which he named his brother Josef Čapek as its actual originator.

According to the *Oxford English Dictionary*, the word *robotics* was first used in print by Isaac Asimov, in his science fiction short story "Liar!", published in May 1941 in *Astounding Science Fiction*. Asimov was unaware that he was coining the term; since the science and technology of electrical devices is *electronics*, he assumed *robotics* already referred to the science and technology of robots. In some of Asimov's other works, he states that the first use of the word *robotics* was in his short story *Runaround* (Astounding Science Fiction, March 1942). However, the original publication of "Liar!" predates that of "Runaround" by ten months, so the former is generally cited as the word's origin.

History of Robotics

In 1942 the science fiction writer Isaac Asimov created his Three Laws of Robotics.

In 1948 Norbert Wiener formulated the principles of cybernetics, the basis of practical robotics.

Fully autonomouss only appeared in the second half of the 20th century. The first digitally operated and programmable robot, the Unimate, was installed in 1961 to lift hot pieces of metal from a die casting machine and stack them. Commercial and industrial robots are widespread today and used to perform jobs more cheaply, more accurately and more reliably, than humans. They are also employed in some jobs which are too dirty, dangerous, or dull to be suitable for humans. Robots are widely used in manufacturing, assembly, packing and packaging, transport, earth and space exploration, surgery, weaponry, laboratory research, safety, and the mass production of consumer and industrial goods.

Date	Significance	Robot Name	Inventor
Third century B.C. and earlier	One of the earliest descriptions of automata appears in the *Lie Zi* text, on a much earlier encounter between King Mu of Zhou (1023–957 BC) and a mechanical engineer known as Yan Shi, an 'artificer'. The latter allegedly presented the king with a life-size, human-shaped figure of his mechanical handiwork.		Yan Shi (Chinese: 偃师)
First century A.D. and earlier	Descriptions of more than 100 machines and automata, including a fire engine, a wind organ, a coin-operated machine, and a steam-powered engine, in *Pneumatica* and *Automata* by Heron of Alexandria		Ctesibius, Philo of Byzantium, Heron of Alexandria, and others
c. 420 B.C.E	A wooden, steam propelled bird, which was able to fly		Archytas of Tarentum
1206	Created early humanoid automata, programmable automaton band	Robot band, hand-washing automaton, automated moving peacocks	Al-Jazari
1495	Designs for a humanoid robot	Mechanical Knight	Leonardo da Vinci
1738	Mechanical duck that was able to eat, flap its wings, and excrete	Digesting Duck	Jacques de Vaucanson
1898	Nikola Tesla demonstrates first radio-controlled vessel.	Teleautomaton	Nikola Tesla
1921	First fictional automatons called "robots" appear in the play *R.U.R.*	Rossum's Universal Robots	Karel Čapek
1930s	Humanoid robot exhibited at the 1939 and 1940 World's Fairs	Elektro	Westinghouse Electric Corporation
1946	First general-purpose digital computer	Whirlwind	Multiple people
1948	Simple robots exhibiting biological behaviors	Elsie and Elmer	William Grey Walter
1956	First commercial robot, from the Unimation company founded by George Devol and Joseph Engelberger, based on Devol's patents	Unimate	George Devol
1961	First installed industrial robot.	Unimate	George Devol
1973	First industrial robot with six electromechanically driven axes	Famulus	KUKA Robot Group
1974	The world's first microcomputer controlled electric industrial robot, IRB 6 from ASEA, was delivered to a small mechanical engineering company in southern Sweden. The design of this robot had been patented already 1972.	IRB 6	ABB Robot Group
1975	Programmable universal manipulation arm, a Unimation product	PUMA	Victor Scheinman

Robotic Aspects

There are many types of robots; they are used in many different environments and for many different uses, although being very diverse in application and form they all share three basic similarities when it comes to their construction:

Robotic construction.

Electrical aspect.

```
// Dev-C++ 4.9.9.2
// Project Type: Win32 GUI
// Window: Window Header
#include <Windows.h>
#include "resource.h"
// Window: Window Name
#ifdef NULL
#undef NULL
#define NULL 0
#endif
#define Wnd_Class "WIN_CHK"
#define Wnd_Title "預設視窗"
// Window: Window Parameters
static UINT WndPos_X = 0, WndPos_Y = 0;
// 400 x 300
static UINT WndPos_Width = 400, WndPos_Height = 300;
static HWND hwndWnd = 0;
static HINSTANCE hinstWnd = 0;
LRESULT CALLBACK WndProc(HWND, UINT, WPARAM, LPARAM);
BOOL ProcMsg(void);
BOOL BuildWnd( const char*, const char*);
void InitWindow_PositionCenter( UINT&, UINT&, UINT, UINT, BOOL);
// Window: Window Entry
int WINAPI WinMain(HINSTANCE hInstance, HINSTANCE hPrevInstance,
                   LPSTR lpCmdLine, int nShowCmd)
{
    //==START of WinMain==//
    if ( (hwndWnd = ::FindWindow( Wnd_Class, Wnd_Title)) != NULL )
    {
        ::SetForegroundWindow(hwndWnd);
        return NULL;
    }
    if ( BuildWnd( Wnd_Class, Wnd_Title) == TRUE )
    {
        while ( ProcMsg() == TRUE );
    }
    //==END of WinMain==//
    return NULL;
}
```

A level of programming.

- Robots all have some kind of mechanical construction, a frame, form or shape designed to achieve a particular task. For example, a robot designed to travel across heavy dirt or mud, might use caterpillar tracks. The mechanical aspect is mostly the creator's solution to completing the assigned task and dealing with the physics of the environment around it. Form follows function.
- Robots have electrical components which power and control the machinery. For example,

the robot with caterpillar tracks would need some kind of power to move the tracker treads. That power comes in the form of electricity, which will have to travel through a wire and originate from a battery, a basic electrical circuit. Even petrol powered machines that get their power mainly from petrol still require an electric current to start the combustion process which is why most petrol powered machines like cars, have batteries. The electrical aspect of robots is used for movement (through motors), sensing (where electrical signals are used to measure things like heat, sound, position, and energy status) and operation (robots need some level of electrical energy supplied to their motors and sensors in order to activate and perform basic operations).

- All robots contain some level of computer programming code. A program is how a robot decides when or how to do something. In the caterpillar track example, a robot that needs to move across a muddy road may have the correct mechanical construction, and receive the correct amount of power from its battery, but would not go anywhere without a program telling it to move. Programs are the core essence of a robot, it could have excellent mechanical and electrical construction, but if its program is poorly constructed its performance will be very poor (or it may not perform at all). There are three different types of robotic programs: remote control, artificial intelligence and hybrid. A robot with remote control programing has a preexisting set of commands that it will only perform if and when it receives a signal from a control source, typically a human being with a remote control. It is perhaps more appropriate to view devices controlled primarily by human commands as falling in the discipline of automation rather than robotics. Robots that use artificial intelligence interact with their environment on their own without a control source, and can determine reactions to objects and problems they encounter using their preexisting programming. Hybrid is a form of programming that incorporates both AI and RC functions.

Applications

As more and more robots are designed for specific tasks this method of classification becomes more relevant. For example, many robots are designed for assembly work, which may not be readily adaptable for other applications. They are termed as "assembly robots". For seam welding, some suppliers provide complete welding systems with the robot i.e. the welding equipment along with other material handling facilities like turntables etc. as an integrated unit. Such an integrated robotic system is called a "welding robot" even though its discrete manipulator unit could be adapted to a variety of tasks. Some robots are specifically designed for heavy load manipulation, and are labelled as "heavy duty robots."

Current and potential applications include:

- Military robots.
- Caterpillar plans to develop remote controlled machines and expects to develop fully autonomous heavy robots by 2021. Some cranes already are remote controlled.
- It was demonstrated that a robot can perform a herding task.
- Robots are increasingly used in manufacturing (since the 1960s). In the auto industry they can amount for more than half of the "labor". There are even "lights off" factories such as

an IBM keyboard manufacturing factory in Texas that is 100% automated.

- Robots such as HOSPI are used as couriers in hospitals (hospital robot). Other hospital tasks performed by robots are receptionists, guides and porters helpers.
- Robots can serve as waiters and cooks., also at home. Boris is a robot that can load a dish-washer.
- Robot combat for sport – hobby or sport event where two or more robots fight in an arena to disable each other. This has developed from a hobby in the 1990s to several TV series worldwide.
- Cleanup of contaminated areas, such as toxic waste or nuclear facilities.
- Agricultural robots (AgRobots,).
- Domestic robots, cleaning and caring for the elderly.
- Medical robots performing low-invasive surgery.
- Household robots with full use.
- Nanorobots.

Components

Power Source

At present mostly (lead–acid) batteries are used as a power source. Many different types of batteries can be used as a power source for robots. They range from lead–acid batteries, which are safe and have relatively long shelf lives but are rather heavy compared to silver–cadmium batteries that are much smaller in volume and are currently much more expensive. Designing a battery-powered robot needs to take into account factors such as safety, cycle lifetime and weight. Generators, often some type of internal combustion engine, can also be used. However, such designs are often mechanically complex and need fuel, require heat dissipation and are relatively heavy. A tether connecting the robot to a power supply would remove the power supply from the robot entirely. This has the advantage of saving weight and space by moving all power generation and storage components elsewhere. However, this design does come with the drawback of constantly having a cable connected to the robot, which can be difficult to manage. Potential power sources could be:

- pneumatic (compressed gases).
- Solar power (using the sun's energy and converting it into electrical power).
- Hydraulics (liquids).
- Flywheel energy storage.
- Organic garbage (through anaerobic digestion).
- Nuclear.

Actuation

Actuators are the "muscles" of a robot, the parts which convert stored energy into movement. By far the most popular actuators are electric motors that rotate a wheel or gear, and linear actuators that control industrial robots in factories. There are some recent advances in alternative types of actuators, powered by electricity, chemicals, or compressed air.

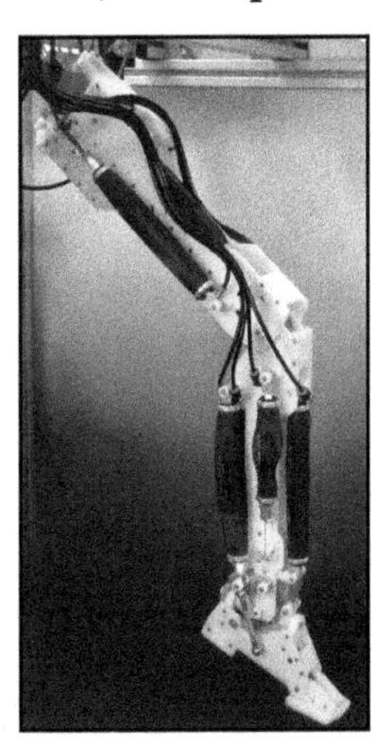

A robotic leg powered by air muscles.

Electric Motors

The vast majority of robots use electric motors, often brushed and brushless DC motors in portable robots or AC motors in industrial robots and CNC machines. These motors are often preferred in systems with lighter loads, and where the predominant form of motion is rotational.

Linear Actuators

Various types of linear actuators move in and out instead of by spinning, and often have quicker direction changes, particularly when very large forces are needed such as with industrial robotics. They are typically powered by compressed air (pneumatic actuator) or an oil (hydraulic actuator).

Series Elastic Actuators

A spring can be designed as part of the motor actuator, to allow improved force control. It has been used in various robots, particularly walking humanoid robots.

Air Muscles

Pneumatic artificial muscles, also known as air muscles, are special tubes that expand(typically up to 40%) when air is forced inside them. They are used in some robot applications.

Muscle Wire

Muscle wire, also known as shape memory alloy, Nitinol® or Flexinol® wire, is a material which contracts (under 5%) when electricity is applied. They have been used for some small robot applications.

Electroactive Polymers

EAPs or EPAMs are a new plastic material that can contract substantially (up to 380% activation strain) from electricity, and have been used in facial muscles and arms of humanoid robots, and to enable new robots to float, fly, swim or walk.

Piezo Motors

Recent alternatives to DC motors are piezo motors or ultrasonic motors. These work on a fundamentally different principle, whereby tiny piezoceramic elements, vibrating many thousands of times per second, cause linear or rotary motion. There are different mechanisms of operation; one type uses the vibration of the piezo elements to step the motor in a circle or a straight line. Another type uses the piezo elements to cause a nut to vibrate or to drive a screw. The advantages of these motors are nanometer resolution, speed, and available force for their size. These motors are already available commercially, and being used on some robots.

Elastic Nanotubes

Elastic nanotubes are a promising artificial muscle technology in early-stage experimental development. The absence of defects in carbon nanotubes enables these filaments to deform elastically by several percent, with energy storage levels of perhaps 10 J/cm^3 for metal nanotubes. Human biceps could be replaced with an 8 mm diameter wire of this material. Such compact "muscle" might allow future robots to outrun and outjump humans.

Sensing

Sensors allow robots to receive information about a certain measurement of the environment, or internal components. This is essential for robots to perform their tasks, and act upon any changes in the environment to calculate the appropriate response. They are used for various forms of measurements, to give the robots warnings about safety or malfunctions, and to provide real time information of the task it is performing.

Touch

Current robotic and prosthetic hands receive far less tactile information than the human hand. Recent research has developed a tactile sensor array that mimics the mechanical properties and touch receptors of human fingertips. The sensor array is constructed as a rigid core surrounded by conductive fluid contained by an elastomeric skin. Electrodes are mounted on the surface of the rigid core and are connected to an impedance-measuring device within the core. When the artificial skin touches an object the fluid path around the electrodes is deformed, producing impedance changes that map the forces received from the object. The researchers expect that an important function of such artificial fingertips will be adjusting robotic grip on held objects.

Scientists from several European countries and Israel developed a prosthetic hand in 2009, called SmartHand, which functions like a real one—allowing patients to write with it, type on a keyboard, play piano and perform other fine movements. The prosthesis has sensors which enable the patient to sense real feeling in its fingertips.

Vision

Computer vision is the science and technology of machines that see. As a scientific discipline, computer vision is concerned with the theory behind artificial systems that extract information from images. The image data can take many forms, such as video sequences and views from cameras.

In most practical computer vision applications, the computers are pre-programmed to solve a particular task, but methods based on learning are now becoming increasingly common.

Computer vision systems rely on image sensors which detect electromagnetic radiation which is typically in the form of either visible light or infra-red light. The sensors are designed using solid-state physics. The process by which light propagates and reflects off surfaces is explained using optics. Sophisticated image sensors even require quantum mechanics to provide a complete understanding of the image formation process. Robots can also be equipped with multiple vision sensors to be better able to compute the sense of depth in the environment. Like human eyes, robots' "eyes" must also be able to focus on a particular area of interest, and also adjust to variations in light intensities.

There is a subfield within computer vision where artificial systems are designed to mimic the processing and behavior of biological system, at different levels of complexity. Also, some of the learning-based methods developed within computer vision have their background in biology.

Other

Other common forms of sensing in robotics use lidar, radar and sonar.

Manipulation

Robots need to manipulate objects; pick up, modify, destroy, or otherwise have an effect. Thus the "hands" of a robot are often referred to as *end effectors*, while the "arm" is referred to as a *manipulator*. Most robot arms have replaceable effectors, each allowing them to perform some small range of tasks. Some have a fixed manipulator which cannot be replaced, while a few have one very general purpose manipulator, for example a humanoid hand. Learning how to manipulate a robot often requires a close feedback between human to the robot, although there are several methods for remote manipulation of robots.

KUKA industrial robot operating in a foundry.

Puma, one of the first industrial robots.

Baxter, a modern and versatile industrial robot developed by Rodney Brooks.

Mechanical Grippers

One of the most common effectors is the gripper. In its simplest manifestation it consists of just two fingers which can open and close to pick up and let go of a range of small objects. Fingers can for example be made of a chain with a metal wire run through it. Hands that resemble and work more like a human hand include the Shadow Hand and the Robonaut hand. Hands that are of a mid-level complexity include the Delft hand. Mechanical grippers can come in various types, including friction and encompassing jaws. Friction jaws use all the force of the gripper to hold the object in place using friction. Encompassing jaws cradle the object in place, using less friction.

Vacuum Grippers

Vacuum grippers are very simple astrictive devices, but can hold very large loads provided the prehension surface is smooth enough to ensure suction.

Pick and place robots for electronic components and for large objects like car windscreens, often use very simple vacuum grippers.

General Purpose Effectors

Some advanced robots are beginning to use fully humanoid hands, like the Shadow Hand, MANUS, and the Schunk hand. These are highly dexterous manipulators, with as many as 20 degrees of freedom and hundreds of tactile sensors.

Locomotion

Rolling Robots

For simplicity most mobile robots have four wheels or a number of continuous tracks. Some researchers have tried to create more complex wheeled robots with only one or two wheels. These can have certain advantages such as greater efficiency and reduced parts, as well as allowing a robot to navigate in confined places that a four-wheeled robot would not be able to.

oSegway in the Robot museum in Nagoya.

Two-wheeled Balancing Robots

Balancing robots generally use a gyroscope to detect how much a robot is falling and then drive the wheels proportionally in the same direction, to counterbalance the fall at hundreds of times per second, based on the dynamics of an inverted pendulum. Many different balancing robots have been designed. While the Segway is not commonly thought of as a robot, it can be thought of as a component of a robot, when used as such Segway refer to them as RMP (Robotic Mobility Platform). An example of this use has been as NASA's Robonaut that has been mounted on a Segway.

One-wheeled Balancing Robots

A one-wheeled balancing robot is an extension of a two-wheeled balancing robot so that it can move in any 2D direction using a round ball as its only wheel. Several one-wheeled balancing robots have been designed recently, such as Carnegie Mellon University's "Ballbot" that is the approximate height and width of a person, and Tohoku Gakuin University's "BallIP". Because of the long, thin shape and ability to maneuver in tight spaces, they have the potential to function better than other robots in environments with people.

Spherical Orb Robots

Several attempts have been made in robots that are completely inside a spherical ball, either by spinning a weight inside the ball, or by rotating the outer shells of the sphere. These have also been referred to as an orb bot or a ball bot.

Six-wheeled Robots

Using six wheels instead of four wheels can give better traction or grip in outdoor terrain such as on rocky dirt or grass.

Tracked Robots

Tank tracks provide even more traction than a six-wheeled robot. Tracked wheels behave as if they were made of hundreds of wheels, therefore are very common for outdoor and military robots, where the robot must drive on very rough terrain. However, they are difficult to use indoors such as on carpets and smooth floors. Examples include NASA's Urban Robot "Urbie".

TALON military robots used by the United States Army.

Walking Applied to Robots

Walking is a difficult and dynamic problem to solve. Several robots have been made which can walk reliably on two legs, however none have yet been made which are as robust as a human. There has been much study on human inspired walking, such as AMBER lab which was established in 2008 by the Mechanical Engineering Department at Texas A&M University. Many other robots have been built that walk on more than two legs, due to these robots being significantly easier to construct. Walking robots can be used for uneven terrains, which would provide better mobility and energy efficiency than other locomotion methods. Hybrids too have been proposed in movies such as I, Robot, where they walk on 2 legs and switch to 4 (arms+legs) when going to a sprint. Typically, robots on 2 legs can walk well on flat floors and can occasionally walk up stairs. None can walk over rocky, uneven terrain. Some of the methods which have been tried are:

ZMP Technique

The Zero Moment Point (ZMP) is the algorithm used by robots such as Honda's ASIMO. The robot's onboard computer tries to keep the total inertial forces (the combination of Earth's gravity and the acceleration and deceleration of walking), exactly opposed by the floor reaction force (the force of the floor pushing back on the robot's foot). In this way, the two forces cancel out, leaving no moment (force causing the robot to rotate and fall over). However, this is not exactly how a human walks, and the difference is obvious to human observers, some of whom have pointed out that ASIMO walks as if it needs the lavatory. ASIMO's walking algorithm is not static, and some dynamic balancing is used (see below). However, it still requires a smooth surface to walk on.

Hopping

Several robots, built in the 1980s by Marc Raibert at the MIT Leg Laboratory, successfully demonstrated very dynamic walking. Initially, a robot with only one leg, and a very small foot, could stay upright simply by hopping. The movement is the same as that of a person on a pogo stick. As the robot falls to one side, it would jump slightly in that direction, in order to catch itself. Soon, the algorithm was generalised to two and four legs. A bipedal robot was demonstrated running and even performing somersaults. A quadruped was also demonstrated which could trot, run, pace, and bound. For a full list of these robots, see the MIT Leg Lab Robots page.

Dynamic Balancing (Controlled Falling)

A more advanced way for a robot to walk is by using a dynamic balancing algorithm, which is potentially more robust than the Zero Moment Point technique, as it constantly monitors the robot's motion, and places the feet in order to maintain stability. This technique was recently demonstrated by Anybots' Dexter Robot, which is so stable, it can even jump. Another example is the TU Delft Flame.

Passive Dynamics

Perhaps the most promising approach utilizes passive dynamics where the momentum of swinging limbs is used for greater efficiency. It has been shown that totally unpowered humanoid mechanisms can walk down a gentle slope, using only gravity to propel themselves. Using this technique, a robot need only supply a small amount of motor power to walk along a flat surface or a little more to walk up a hill. This technique promises to make walking robots at least ten times more efficient than ZMP walkers, like ASIMO.

Other Methods of Locomotion

Flying

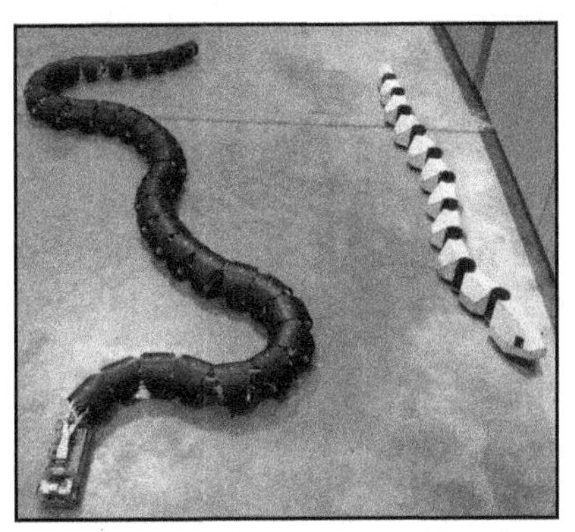

Two robot snakes. Left one has 64 motors (with 2 degrees of freedom per segment), the right one 10.

A modern passenger airliner is essentially a flying robot, with two humans to manage it. The autopilot can control the plane for each stage of the journey, including takeoff, normal flight, and even landing. Other flying robots are uninhabited, and are known as unmanned aerial vehicles (UAVs). They can be smaller and lighter without a human pilot on board, and fly into dangerous territory for military surveillance missions. Some can even fire on targets under command. UAVs are also being developed which can fire on targets automatically, without the need for a command from a human. Other flying robots include cruise missiles, the Entomopter, and the Epson micro helicopter robot. Robots such as the Air Penguin, Air Ray, and Air Jelly have lighter-than-air bodies, propelled by paddles, and guided by sonar.

Snaking

Several snake robots have been successfully developed. Mimicking the way real snakes move, these robots can navigate very confined spaces, meaning they may one day be used to search for people trapped in collapsed buildings. The Japanese ACM-R5 snake robot can even navigate both on land and in water.

Skating

A small number of skating robots have been developed, one of which is a multi-mode walking and skating device. It has four legs, with unpowered wheels, which can either step or roll. Another robot, Plen, can use a miniature skateboard or roller-skates, and skate across a desktop.

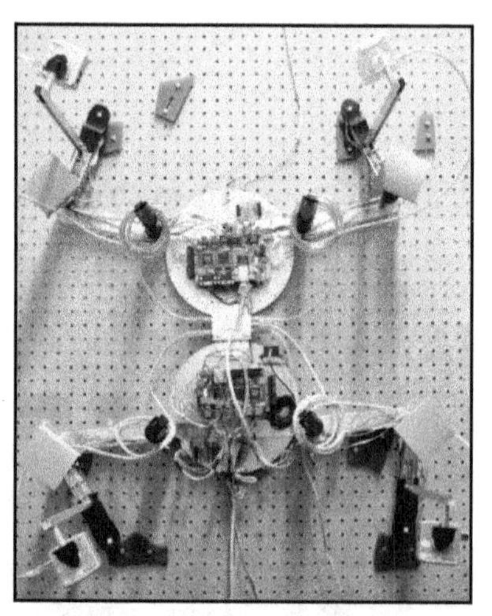

Capuchin, a climbing robot.

Climbing

Several different approaches have been used to develop robots that have the ability to climb vertical surfaces. One approach mimics the movements of a human climber on a wall with protrusions; adjusting the center of mass and moving each limb in turn to gain leverage. An example of this is Capuchin, built by Dr. Ruixiang Zhang at Stanford University, California. Another approach uses the specialized toe pad method of wall-climbing geckoes, which can run on smooth surfaces such as vertical glass. Examples of this approach include Wallbot and Stickybot. China's *Technology Daily* reported on November 15, 2008 that Dr. Li Hiu Yeung and his research group of New Concept Aircraft (Zhuhai) Co., Ltd. had successfully developed a bionic gecko robot named "Speedy Freelander". According to Dr. Li, the gecko robot could rapidly climb up and down a variety of building walls, navigate through ground and wall fissures, and walk upside-down on the ceiling. It was also able to adapt to the surfaces of smooth glass, rough, sticky or dusty walls as well as various types of metallic materials. It could also identify and circumvent obstacles automatically. Its flexibility and speed were comparable to a natural gecko. A third approach is to mimic the motion of a snake climbing a pole.. Lastely one may mimic the movements of a human climber on a wall with protrusions; adjusting the center of mass and moving each limb in turn to gain leverage.

Swimming (Piscine)

It is calculated that when swimming some fish can achieve a propulsive efficiency greater than 90%. Furthermore, they can accelerate and maneuver far better than any man-made boat or submarine, and produce less noise and water disturbance. Therefore, many researchers studying underwater robots would like to copy this type of locomotion. Notable examples are the Essex University Computer Science Robotic Fish G9, and the Robot Tuna built by the Institute of Field Robotics, to analyze and mathematically model thunniform motion. The Aqua Penguin, designed and built by Festo of Germany, copies the streamlined shape and propulsion by front "flippers" of penguins. Festo have also built the Aqua Ray and Aqua Jelly, which emulate the locomotion of manta ray, and jellyfish, respectively.

Robotic Fish: *iSplash*-II.

In 2014 *iSplash*-II was developed by R.J Clapham PhD at Essex University. It was the first robotic fish capable of outperforming real carangiform fish in terms of average maximum velocity (measured in body lengths/ second) and endurance, the duration that top speed is maintained. This build attained swimming speeds of 11.6BL/s (i.e. 3.7 m/s). The first build, *iSplash*-I (2014) was the first robotic platform to apply a full-body length carangiform swimming motion which was found to increase swimming speed by 27% over the traditional approach of a posterior confined wave form.

Sailing

Sailboat robots have also been developed in order to make measurements at the surface of the ocean. A typical sailboat robot is *Vaimos* built by IFREMER and ENSTA-Bretagne. Since the propulsion of sailboat robots uses the wind, the energy of the batteries is only used for the computer, for the communication and for the actuators (to tune the rudder and the sail). If the robot is equipped with solar panels, the robot could theoretically navigate forever. The two main competitions of sailboat robots are WRSC, which takes place every year in Europe, and Sailbot.

The autonomous sailboat robot *Vaimos.*

Environmental Interaction and Navigation

Though a significant percentage of robots in commission today are either human controlled, or operate in a static environment, there is an increasing interest in robots that can operate autonomously in a dynamic environment. These robots require some combination of navigation hardware and software in order to traverse their environment. In particular unforeseen events (e.g. people and other obstacles that are not stationary) can cause problems or collisions. Some highly advanced robots such as ASIMO, and Meinü robot have particularly good robot navigation hardware and software. Also, self-controlled cars, Ernst Dickmanns' driverless car, and the entries in the DARPA Grand Challenge, are capable of sensing the environment well and subsequently making navigational decisions based on this information. Most of these robots employ a GPS navigation device with waypoints, along with radar, sometimes combined with other sensory data such as lidar, video cameras, and inertial guidance systems for better navigation between waypoints.

Radar, GPS, and lidar, are all combined to provide proper navigation and obstacle avoidance (vehicle developed for 2007 DARPA Urban Challenge).

Human-robot Interaction

The state of the art in sensory intelligence for robots will have to progress through several orders of magnitude if we want the robots working in our homes to go beyond vacuum-cleaning the floors. If robots are to work effectively in homes and other non-industrial environments, the way they are instructed to perform their jobs, and especially how they will be told to stop will be of critical importance. The people who interact with them may have little or no training in robotics, and so any interface will need to be extremely intuitive. Science fiction authors also typically assume that robots will eventually be capable of communicating with humans through speech, gestures, and facial expressions, rather than a command-line interface. Although speech would be the most natural way for the human to communicate, it is unnatural for the robot. It will probably be a long time before robots interact as naturally as the fictional C-3PO, or Data of Star Trek, Next Generation.

Kismet can produce a range of facial expressions.

Speech Recognition

Interpreting the continuous flow of sounds coming from a human, in real time, is a difficult task for a computer, mostly because of the great variability of speech. The same word, spoken by the same person may sound different depending on local acoustics, volume, the previous word, whether or not the speaker has a cold, etc.. It becomes even harder when the speaker has a different accent. Nevertheless, great strides have been made in the field since Davis, Biddulph, and Balashek designed the first "voice input system" which recognized "ten digits spoken by a single user with 100% accuracy" in 1952. Currently, the best systems can recognize continuous, natural speech, up to 160 words per minute, with an accuracy of 95%.

Robotic Voice

Other hurdles exist when allowing the robot to use voice for interacting with humans. For social reasons, synthetic voice proves suboptimal as a communication medium, making it necessary to develop the emotional component of robotic voice through various techniques.

Gestures

One can imagine, in the future, explaining to a robot chef how to make a pastry, or asking directions from a robot police officer. In both of these cases, making hand gestures would aid the verbal descriptions. In the first case, the robot would be recognizing gestures made by the human, and perhaps repeating them for confirmation. In the second case, the robot police officer would gesture to indicate "down the road, then turn right". It is likely that gestures will make up a part of the interaction between humans and robots. A great many systems have been developed to recognize human hand gestures.

Facial Expression

Facial expressions can provide rapid feedback on the progress of a dialog between two humans, and soon may be able to do the same for humans and robots. Robotic faces have been constructed by Hanson Robotics using their elastic polymer called Frubber, allowing a large number of facial expressions due to the elasticity of the rubber facial coating and embedded subsurface motors (servos). The coating and servos are built on a metal skull. A robot should know how to approach a human, judging by their facial expression and body language. Whether the person is happy, frightened, or crazy-looking affects the type of interaction expected of the robot. Likewise, robots like Kismet and the more recent addition, Nexi can produce a range of facial expressions, allowing it to have meaningful social exchanges with humans.

Artificial Emotions

Artificial emotions can also be generated, composed of a sequence of facial expressions and/or gestures. As can be seen from the movie Final Fantasy: The Spirits Within, the programming of these artificial emotions is complex and requires a large amount of human observation. To simplify this programming in the movie, presets were created together with a special software program. This decreased the amount of time needed to make the film. These presets could possibly be transferred for use in real-life robots.

Personality

Many of the robots of science fiction have a personality, something which may or may not be desirable in the commercial robots of the future. Nevertheless, researchers are trying to create robots which appear to have a personality: i.e. they use sounds, facial expressions, and body language to try to convey an internal state, which may be joy, sadness, or fear. One commercial example is Pleo, a toy robot dinosaur, which can exhibit several apparent emotions.

Social Intelligence

The Socially Intelligent Machines Lab of the Georgia Institute of Technology researches new concepts of guided teaching interaction with robots. Aim of the projects is a social robot learns task goals from human demonstrations without prior knowledge of high-level concepts. These new concepts are grounded from low-level continuous sensor data through unsupervised learning, and task goals are subsequently learned using a Bayesian approach. These concepts can be used to transfer knowledge to future tasks, resulting in faster learning of those tasks. The results are demonstrated by the robot *Curi* who can scoop some pasta from a pot onto a plate and serve the sauce on top.

Control

The mechanical structure of a robot must be controlled to perform tasks. The control of a robot involves three distinct phases – perception, processing, and action (robotic paradigms). Sensors give information about the environment or the robot itself (e.g. the position of its joints or its end effector). This information is then processed to be stored or transmitted, and to calculate the appropriate signals to the actuators (motors) which move the mechanical.

RuBot II can resolve manually Rubik cubes.

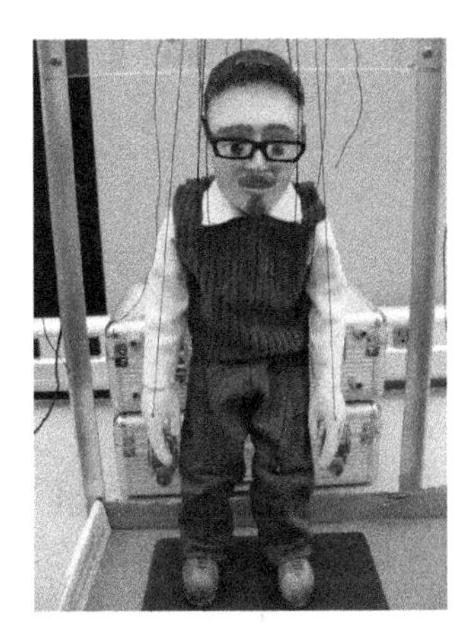

Puppet Magnus, a robot-manipulated marionette with complex control systems.

The processing phase can range in complexity. At a reactive level, it may translate raw sensor information directly into actuator commands. Sensor fusion may first be used to estimate parameters of interest (e.g. the position of the robot's gripper) from noisy sensor data. An immediate task (such as moving the gripper in a certain direction) is inferred from these estimates. Techniques from control theory convert the task into commands that drive the actuators.

At longer time scales or with more sophisticated tasks, the robot may need to build and reason with a "cognitive" model. Cognitive models try to represent the robot, the world, and how they interact. Pattern recognition and computer vision can be used to track objects. Mapping techniques can be used to build maps of the world. Finally, motion planning and other artificial intelligence techniques may be used to figure out how to act. For example, a planner may figure out how to achieve a task without hitting obstacles, falling over, etc.

Autonomy Levels

TOPIO, a humanoid robot, played ping pong at Tokyo IREX 2009.

Control systems may also have varying levels of autonomy:

1. Direct interaction is used for haptic or tele-operated devices, and the human has nearly complete control over the robot's motion.

2. Operator-assist modes have the operator commanding medium-to-high-level tasks, with the robot automatically figuring out how to achieve them.

3. An autonomous robot may go for extended periods of time without human interaction. Higher levels of autonomy do not necessarily require more complex cognitive capabilities. For example, robots in assembly plants are completely autonomous, but operate in a fixed pattern.

Another classification takes into account the interaction between human control and the machine motions:

1. Teleoperation. A human controls each movement, each machine actuator change is specified by the operator.
2. Supervisory. A human specifies general moves or position changes and the machine decides specific movements of its actuators.
3. Task-level autonomy. The operator specifies only the task and the robot manages itself to complete it.
4. Full autonomy. The machine will create and complete all its tasks without human interaction.

Robotics Research

Much of the research in robotics focuses not on specific industrial tasks, but on investigations into new types of robots, alternative ways to think about or design robots, and new ways to manufacture them but other investigations, such as MIT's cyberflora project, are almost wholly academic.

A first particular new innovation in robot design is the opensourcing of robot-projects. To describe the level of advancement of a robot, the term "Generation Robots" can be used. This term is coined by Professor Hans Moravec, Principal Research Scientist at the Carnegie Mellon University Robotics Institute in describing the near future evolution of robot technology. *First generation* robots, Moravec predicted in 1997, should have an intellectual capacity comparable to perhaps a lizard and should become available by 2010. Because the *first generation* robot would be incapable of learning, however, Moravec predicts that the *second generation* robot would be an improvement over the *first* and become available by 2020, with the intelligence maybe comparable to that of a mouse. The *third generation* robot should have the intelligence comparable to that of a monkey. Though *fourth generation* robots, robots with human intelligence, professor Moravec predicts, would become possible, he does not predict this happening before around 2040 or 2050.

The second is evolutionary robots. This is a methodology that uses evolutionary computation to help design robots, especially the body form, or motion and behavior controllers. In a similar way to natural evolution, a large population of robots is allowed to compete in some way, or their ability to perform a task is measured using a fitness function. Those that perform worst are removed from the population, and replaced by a new set, which have new behaviors based on those of the winners. Over time the population improves, and eventually a satisfactory robot may appear. This happens without any direct programming of the robots by the researchers. Researchers use this method both to create better robots, and to explore the nature of evolution. Because the process often requires many generations of robots to be simulated, this technique may be run entirely or mostly in simulation, then tested on real robots once the evolved algorithms are good enough.

Currently, there are about 10 million industrial robots toiling around the world, and Japan is the top country having high density of utilizing robots in its manufacturing industry.

Dynamics and Kinematics

The study of motion can be divided into kinematics and dynamics. Direct kinematics refers to the calculation of end effector position, orientation, velocity, and acceleration when the corresponding joint values are known. Inverse kinematics refers to the opposite case in which required joint values are calculated for given end effector values, as done in path planning. Some special aspects of kinematics include handling of redundancy (different possibilities of performing the same movement), collision avoidance, and singularity avoidance. Once all relevant positions, velocities, and accelerations have been calculated using kinematics, methods from the field of dynamics are used to study the effect of forces upon these movements. Direct dynamics refers to the calculation of accelerations in the robot once the applied forces are known. Direct dynamics is used in computer simulations of the robot. Inverse dynamics refers to the calculation of the actuator forces necessary to create a prescribed end effector acceleration. This information can be used to improve the control algorithms of a robot.

In each area mentioned above, researchers strive to develop new concepts and strategies, improve existing ones, and improve the interaction between these areas. To do this, criteria for "optimal" performance and ways to optimize design, structure, and control of robots must be developed and implemented.

Bionics and Biomimetics

Bionics and biomimetics apply the physiology and methods of locomotion of animals to the design of robots. For example, the design of BionicKangaroo was based on the way kangaroos jump.

Education and Training

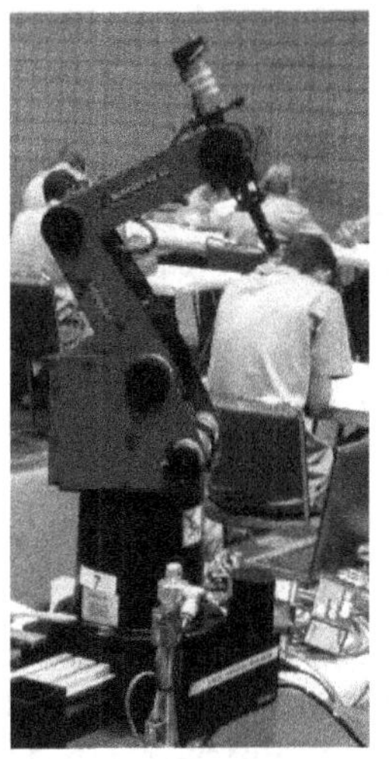

The SCORBOT-ER 4u educational robot.

Robotics engineers design robots, maintain them, develop new applications for them, and conduct research to expand the potential of robotics. Robots have become a popular educational tool in some middle and high schools, particularly in parts of the USA, as well as in numerous youth summer camps, raising interest in programming, artificial intelligence and robotics among students. First-year computer science courses at some universities now include programming of a robot in addition to traditional software engineering-based coursework.

Career Training

Universities offer bachelors, masters, and doctoral degrees in the field of robotics. Vocational schools offer robotics training aimed at careers in robotics.

Certification

The Robotics Certification Standards Alliance (RCSA) is an international robotics certification authority that confers various industry- and educational-related robotics certifications.

Summer Robotics Camp

Several national summer camp programs include robotics as part of their core curriculum. In addition, youth summer robotics programs are frequently offered by celebrated museums such as the American Museum of Natural History and The Tech Museum of Innovation in Silicon Valley, CA, just to name a few.

Robotics Competitions

There are lots of competitions all around the globe. One of the most important competitions is the FLL or FIRST Lego League. The idea of this specific competition is that kids start developing knowledge and getting into robotics while playing with Legos since they are 9 years old. This competition is associated with Ni or National Instruments.

Robotics Afterschool Programs

Many schools across the country are beginning to add robotics programs to their after school curriculum. Some major programs for afterschool robotics include FIRST Robotics Competition, Botball and B.E.S.T. Robotics. Robotics competitions often include aspects of business and marketing as well as engineering and design.

The Lego company began a program for children to learn and get excited about robotics at a young age.

Employment

Robotics is an essential component in many modern manufacturing environments. As factories increase their use of robots, the number of robotics–related jobs grow and have been observed to be steadily rising. The employment of robots in industries has increased productivity and efficiency savings and is typically seen as a long term investment for benefactors.

A robot technician builds small all-terrain robots. (Courtesy: MobileRobots Inc).

Occupational Safety and Health Implications of Robotics

A discussion paper drawn up by EU-OSHA highlights how the spread of robotics presents both opportunities and challenges for occupational safety and health (OSH).

The greatest OSH benefits stemming from the wider use of robotics should be substitution for people working in unhealthy or dangerous environments. In space, defence, security, or the nuclear industry, but also in logistics, maintenance and inspection, autonomous robots are particularly useful in replacing human workers performing dirty, dull or unsafe tasks, thus avoiding workers' exposures to hazardous agents and conditions and reducing physical, ergonomic and psychosocial risks. For example, robots are already used to perform repetitive and monotonous tasks, to handle radioactive material or to work in explosive atmospheres. In the future, many other highly repetitive, risky or unpleasant tasks will be performed by robots in a variety of sectors like agriculture, construction, transport, healthcare, firefighting or cleaning services.

Despite these advances, there are certain skills to which humans will be better suited than machines for some time to come and the question is how to achieve the best combination of human and robot skills. The advantages of robotics include heavy-duty jobs with precision and repeatability, whereas the advantages of humans include creativity, decision-making, flexibility and adaptability. This need to combine optimal skills has resulted in collaborative robots and humans sharing a common workspace more closely and led to the development of new approaches and standards to guarantee the safety of the "man-robot merger". Some European countries are including robotics in their national programmes and trying to promote a safe and flexible co-operation between robots and operators to achieve better productivity. For example, the German Federal Institute for Occupational Safety and Health (BAuA) organises annual workshops on the topic "human-robot collaboration".

In future, co-operation between robots and humans will be diversified, with robots increasing their autonomy and human-robot collaboration reaching completely new forms. Current approaches and technical standards aiming to protect employees from the risk of working with collaborative robots will have to be revised.

Virtual Reality

Virtual reality (VR) typically refers to computer technologies that use software to generate realistic images, sounds and other sensations that replicate a real environment (or create an imaginary setting), and simulate a user's physical presence in this environment, by enabling the user to interact with this space and any objects depicted therein using specialized display screens or projectors and other devices. VR has been defined as "...a realistic and immersive simulation of a three-dimensional environment, created using interactive software and hardware, and experienced or controlled by movement of the body" or as an "immersive, interactive experience generated by a computer". A person using virtual reality equipment is typically able to "look around" the artificial world, move about in it and interact with features or items that are depicted on a screen or in goggles. Virtual realities artificially create sensory experiences, which can include sight, touch, hearing, and, less commonly, smell. Most 2016-era virtual realities are displayed either on a computer monitor, a projector screen, or with a virtual reality headset (also called head-mounted display or HMD). HMDs typically take the form of head-mounted goggles with a screen in front of the eyes. Some simulations include additional sensory information and provide sounds through speakers or headphones. Virtual Reality actually brings the user into the digital world by cutting off outside stimuli. In this way user is solely focusing on the digital content.

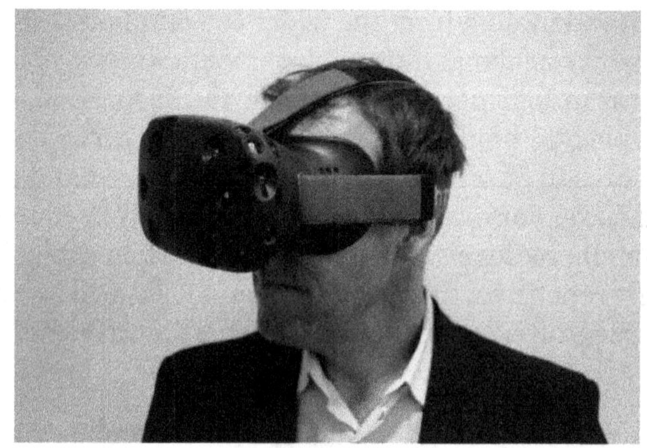

A person wearing a virtual reality headset called the "HTC Vive". It was developed in co-production between HTC and Valve Corporation.

Some advanced haptic systems in the 2010s now include tactile information, generally known as force feedback in medical, video gaming and military training applications. Some VR systems used in video games can transmit vibrations and other sensations to the user via the game controller. Virtual reality also refers to remote communication environments which provide a virtual presence of users with through telepresence and telexistence or the use of a virtual artifact (VA), either through the use of standard input devices such as a keyboard and mouse, or through multimodal devices such as a wired glove or omnidirectional treadmills. The immersive environment can be similar to the real world in order to create a lifelike experience—for example, in simulations for pilot or combat training, which depict realistic images and sounds of the world, where the normal laws of physics apply (e.g., in flight simulators), or it can differ significantly from reality, such as in VR video games that take place in fantasy settings, where gamers can use fictional magic and telekinesis powers.

Etymology and Terminology

In 1938, Antonin Artaud described the illusory nature of characters and objects in the theatre as "la réalité virtuelle" in a collection of essays, *Le Théâtre et son double*. The English translation of this book, published in 1958 as *The Theater and its Double*, is the earliest published use of the term "virtual reality". The term "artificial reality", coined by Myron Krueger, has been in use since the 1970s. The term "virtual reality" was used in *The Judas Mandala*, a 1982 science fiction novel by Damien Broderick. The Oxford English Dictionary cites a 1987 article titled "*Virtual reality*", but the article is not about VR technology. "Virtual" has had the meaning "being something in essence or effect, though not actually or in fact" since the mid-1400s, "... probably via sense of "capable of producing a certain effect" (early 1400s)". The term "virtual" was used in the "[c]omputer sense of "not physically existing but made to appear by software" since 1959. The term "reality" has been used in English since the 1540s, to mean "quality of being real," from "French réalité and directly Medieval Latin realitatem (nominative realitas), from Late Latin realis".

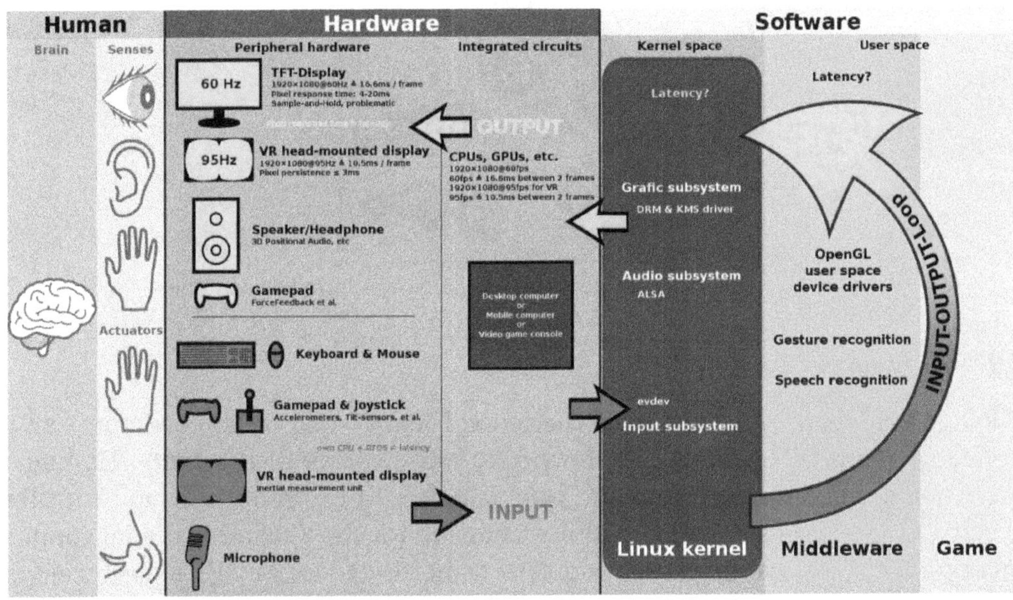

Paramount for the sensation of immersion into virtual reality are a high frame rate (at least 95 fps), as well as a low latency. Furthermore, a pixel persistence lower than 3 ms is required, because if not, users will feel sick when moving their head around.

Virtual reality is also called "virtual realities", "immersive multimedia", "augmented reality" (or AR), "artificial reality" or "computer-simulated reality". A dictionary definition for "cyberspace" states that this word is a synonym for "virtual reality".

History

Before The 1950S

The first references to the concept of virtual reality came from science fiction. Stanley G. Weinbaum's 1935 short story "Pygmalion's Spectacles" describes a goggle-based virtual reality system with holographic recording of fictional experiences, including smell and touch.

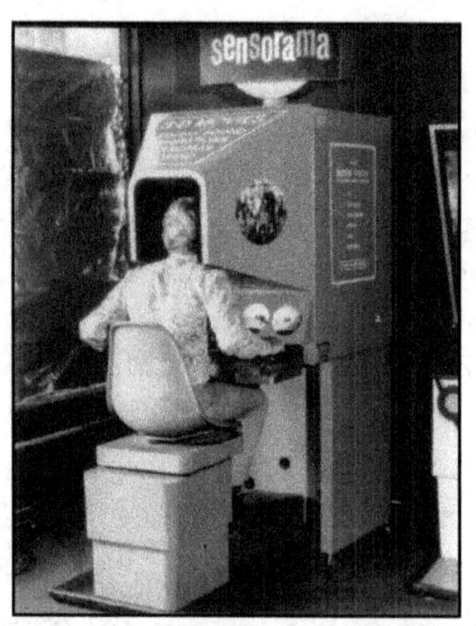

The Sensorama was released in the 1950s.

View-Master, a stereoscopic visual simulator, was introduced in 1939.

1950–1970

Morton Heilig wrote in the 1950s of an "Experience Theatre" that could encompass all the senses in an effective manner, thus drawing the viewer into the onscreen activity. He built a prototype of his vision dubbed the Sensorama in 1962, along with five short films to be displayed in it while engaging multiple senses (sight, sound, smell, and touch). Predating digital computing, the Sensorama was a mechanical device. Around the same time, Douglas Engelbart used computer screens as both input and output devices. In 1968, Ivan Sutherland, with the help of his student Bob Sproull, created what is widely considered to be the first virtual reality and augmented reality (AR) head-mounted display (HMD) system. It was primitive both in terms of user interface and realism, and the HMD to be worn by the user was so heavy that it had to be suspended from the ceiling. The graphics comprising the virtual environment were simple wire-frame model rooms. The formidable appearance of the device inspired its name, The Sword of Damocles.

1970–1990

Also notable among the earlier hypermedia and virtual reality systems was the Aspen Movie Map, which was created at MIT in 1978. The program was a crude virtual simulation of Aspen, Colorado in which users could wander the streets in one of three modes: summer, winter, and polygons. The first two were based on photographs—the researchers actually photographed every possible movement through the city's street grid in both seasons—and the third was a basic 3-D model of the city. Atari founded a research lab for virtual reality in 1982, but the lab was closed after two years due to Atari Shock (North American video game crash of 1983). However, its hired employees, such as Tom Zimmerman, Scott Fisher, Jaron Lanier and Brenda Laurel, kept their research and development on VR-related technologies. By the 1980s the term "virtual reality" was popularized by Jaron Lanier, one of the modern pioneers of the field. Lanier had founded the company VPL Research in 1985. VPL Research has developed several VR devices like the Data Glove, the Eye Phone, and the Audio Sphere. VPL licensed the Data Glove technology to Mattel, which used it to make an accessory known as the Power Glove. While the Power Glove was hard to use and not popular, at US$75, it was early affordable VR device.

Battlezone, an arcade video game from 1980, used 3D vector graphics to immerse the player in a VR world.(Atari).

During this time, virtual reality was not well known, though it did receive media coverage in the late 1980s. Most of its popularity came from marginal cultures, like cyberpunks, who viewed the technology as a potential means for social change, and the recreational drug subculture, who praised virtual reality not only as a new art form, but as an entirely new frontier. Some drug users consume drugs while using VR technologies. The concept of virtual reality was popularized in mass media by movies such as *Brainstorm* (1983) and *The Lawnmower Man*. The VR research boom of the 1990s was accompanied by the non-fiction book *Virtual Reality* (1991) by Howard Rheingold. The book served to demystify the subject, making it more accessible to researchers outside of the computer sphere and sci-fi enthusiasts.

Once the industry began to attract media coverage, some even compared the innovations in virtual reality to the Wright Brothers' pioneering invention of the airplane. In 1990, Jonathan Waldern, a VR Ph.D, demonstrates "Virtuality" at the Computer Graphics 90 exhibition staged at London's Alexandra Palace. This new system was an arcade machine that would use a virtual reality headset to immerse players. *CyberEdge* and *PCVR*, two VR industry magazines, started to publish in the early 1990s. However, most ideas about VR remained theoretical due to the limited computing power available at the time. The extremely high cost of the technology made it impossible for consumers to adopt. When the Internet became widely available, this became the technology focus for most people. The VR industry mainly provided VR devices for medical, flight simulation, automobile industry design, and military training purposes from 1970 to 1990.

1990–2000

In 1991, Sega announced the Sega VR headset for arcade games and the Mega Drive console. It used LCD screens in the visor, stereo headphones, and inertial sensors that allowed the system to track and react to the movements of the user's head. In the same year, Virtuality launched and went on to become the first mass-produced, networked, multiplayer VR entertainment system. It was released in many countries, including a dedicated VR arcade at Embarcadero Center in San Francisco. Costing up to $73,000 per multi-pod Virtuality system, they featured headsets and exoskeleton gloves that gave one of the first "immersive" VR experiences. Antonio Medina, a MIT graduate and NASA scientist, designed a virtual reality system to "drive" Mars rovers from Earth in apparent real time despite the substantial delay of Mars-Earth-Mars signals. The system, termed "Computer-Simulated Teleoperation" as published by Rand, is an extension of virtual reality.

In 1991, Carolina Cruz-Neira, Daniel J. Sandin and Thomas A. DeFanti from the Electronic Visualization Laboratory created the first cubic immersive room, replacing goggles by a multi-projected environment where people can see their body and other people around. In that same year, *Computer Gaming World* predicted "Affordable VR by 1994". By 1994, Sega released the Sega VR-1 motion simulator arcade attraction, in SegaWorld amusement arcades. It was able to track head movement and featured 3D polygon graphics in stereoscopic 3D, powered by the Sega Model 1 arcade system board. Also in 1994 Apple released QuickTime VR, which, despite using the term "VR", was unable to represent virtual reality, and instead displayed 360 photographic panoramas.

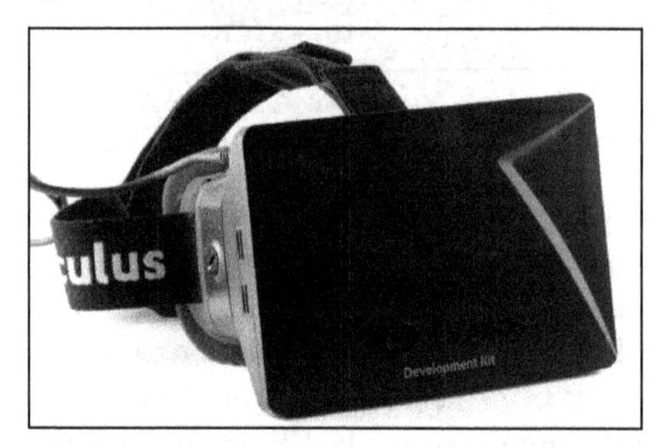

A 2013 developer version of Oculus Rift from Oculus VR, a company Facebook acquired in 2014 for $2 billion.

A year later, the artist Maurice Benayoun created the first VR artwork connecting in real time 2 continents: the "Tunnel under the Atlantic" between the Pompidou Centre in Paris and the Museum of Contemporary Art in Montreal. The installation included dynamic real time 3d modeling, video chat, spatialized sound and AI content management. A non-VR system called the Virtual Boy was created by Nintendo and was released in Japan on July 21, 1995 and in North America on August 15, 1995. Also in 1995, a group in Seattle created public demonstrations of a "CAVE-like" 270 degree immersive projection room called the Virtual Environment Theater, produced by entrepreneurs Chet Dagit and Bob Jacobson. Then in 1996 the same system was shown in tradeshow exhibits sponsored by Netscape Communications, and championed by Jim Barksdale, for the first time showing VR connected to the Internet with World Wide Web content feeds embedded in VRML 3D virtual world models. Forte released the VFX1, a PC-powered virtual reality headset in 1995, which was supported by games including *Descent*, *Star Wars: Dark Forces*, *System Shock* and *Quake*. In 1999, entrepreneur Philip Rosedale formed Linden Lab with an initial focus on the development of hardware that would enable computer users to be fully immersed in a 360 degree virtual reality experience. In its earliest form, the company struggled to produce a commercial version of "The Rig," which was realized in prototype form as a clunky steel contraption with several computer monitors that users could wear on their shoulders. That vision soon morphed into the software-based, 3D virtual world Second Life.

2000–2016

In 2001, SAS3 or SAS Cube became the first PC based cubic room, developed by Z-A Production (Maurice Benayoun, David Nahon), Barco, Clarté, installed in Laval France in April 2001. The SAS library gave birth to Virtools VRPack. By 2007, Google introduced Street View, a service that shows panoramic views of an increasing number of worldwide positions such as roads, indoor buildings and rural areas. It also features a stereoscopic 3D mode, introduced in 2010. In 2010, Palmer Luckey, who later went on to found Oculus VR, designed the first prototype of the Oculus Rift. This prototype, built on a shell of another virtual reality headset, displayed only 2-D images and was noticeably cumbersome to wear. However, it boasted a 90-degree field of vision that was previously unseen anywhere in the market at the time. This initial design would later serve as a basis from which the later designs came.

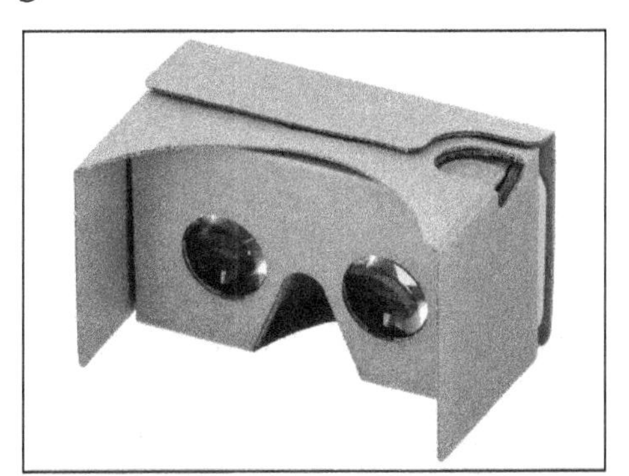

The affordable and accessible Google Cardboard standard.

In 2013, Nintendo filed a patent for the concept of using VR technology to produce a more realistic 3D effect on a 2D television. A camera on the TV tracks the viewer's location relative to the TV, and if the viewer moves, everything on the screen reorients itself appropriately. "For example, if you were looking at a forest, you could shift your head to the right to discover someone standing behind a tree." In July 2013, Guild Software's Vendetta Online was widely reported as the first MMORPG to support the Oculus Rift, making it potentially the first persistent online world with native support for a consumer virtual reality headset. Since 2013, there have been several virtual reality devices that seek to enter the market to complement Oculus Rift to enhance the game experience. One, Virtuix Omni, is based on the ability to move in a three dimensional environment through an omnidirectional treadmill.

On March 25, 2014, Facebook purchased a company that makes virtual reality headsets, Oculus VR, for $2 billion. In that same month, Sony announced Project Morpheus (its code name for PlayStation VR), a virtual reality headset for the PlayStation 4 video game console. Google announces

Cardboard, a do-it-yourself stereoscopic viewer for smartphones. The user places her smartphone in the cardboard holder, which she wears on her head. In 2015, the Kickstarter campaign for Gloveone, a pair of gloves providing motion tracking and haptic feedback, was successfully funded, with over $150,000 in contributions.

In February–March 2015, HTC partnered with Valve Corporation announced their virtual reality headset HTC Vive and controllers, along with their tracking technology called Lighthouse, which utilizes "base stations" mounted to the wall above the user's head in the corners of a room for positional tracking of the Vive headset and its motion controllers using infrared light. The company announced its plans to release the Vive to the public in April 2016 on December 8, 2015. Units began shipping on April 5, 2016.

In July 2015, OnePlus became the first company to launch a product using virtual reality. They used VR as the platform to launch their second flagship device the OnePlus 2, first viewable using an app on the Google Play Store, then on YouTube. The launch was viewable using OnePlus Cardboard, based on the Google's own Cardboard platform. The whole VR launch had a runtime of 33 minutes, and was viewable in all countries. Also in 2015, Jaunt, a startup company developing cameras and a cloud distribution platform, whose content will be accessible using an app, reached $100 million in funding from such sources as Disney and Madison Square Garden. On April 27, 2016, Mojang announced that Minecraft is now playable on the Gear VR. Minecraft is still being developed for the Oculus Rift headset but a separate version was released to the Oculus Store for use with the Gear VR. This version is similar to the Pocket Edition of Minecraft.

Use

Education and Training

Research has been done on learning in virtual reality, as its immersive qualities may enhance learning. VR is used by trainers to provide learners with a virtual environment where they can develop their skills without the real-world consequences of failing. Thomas A. Furness III was one of the first to develop the use of VR for military training when, in 1982, he presented the Air Force with his first working model of a virtual flight simulator he called the Visually Coupled Airborne Systems Simulator (VCASS). By the time he started his work on VCASS, aircraft were becoming increasingly complicated to handle and virtual reality provided a better solution to previous training methods. Furness attempted to incorporate his knowledge of human visual and auditory processing to create a virtual interface that was more intuitive to use. The second phase of his project, which he called the "Super Cockpit," was even more advanced, with high resolution graphics (for the time) and a responsive display. Furness is often credited as a pioneer in virtual reality for this research. VR plays an important role in combat training for the military. It allows the recruits to train under a controlled environment where they are to respond to different types of combat situations. A fully immersive virtual reality that uses head-mounted display (HMD), data suits, data glove, and VR weapon are used to train for combat. This setup allows the training's reset time to be cut down, and allows more repetition in a shorter amount of time. The fully immersive training environment allows the soldiers to train through a wide variety of terrains, situations and scenarios.

VR is also used in flight simulation for the Air Force where people are trained to be pilots. The simulator would sit on top of a hydraulic lift system that reacts to the user inputs and events. When the pilot steer the aircraft, the module would turn and tilt accordingly to provide haptic feedback. The flight simulator can range from a fully enclosed module to a series of computer monitors providing the pilot's point of view. The most important reasons on using simulators over learning with a real aircraft are the reduction of transference time between land training and real flight, the safety, economy and absence of pollution. By the same token, virtual driving simulations are used to train tank drivers on the basics before allowing them to operate the real vehicle. Finally, the same goes for truck driving simulators, in which Belgian firemen are for example trained to drive in a way that prevents as much damage as possible. As these drivers often have less experience than other truck drivers, virtual reality training allows them to compensate this. In the near future, similar projects are expected for all drivers of priority vehicles, including the police.

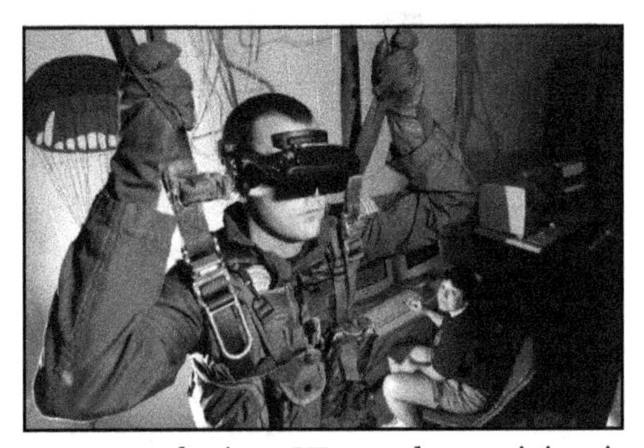

U.S. Navy personnel using a VR parachute training simulator.
A headscreen-wearing soldier sits at a gunner station while learning in a Virtual Training Suite.

Medical personnel are able to train through VR to deal with a wider variety of injuries. An experiment was performed by sixteen surgical residents where eight of them went through laparoscopic cholecystectomy through VR training. They then came out 29% faster at gallbladder dissection than the controlled group. With the increased commercial availability of certified training programs for basic skills training in VR environments, students have the ability to familiarize themselves with necessary skills in a corrective and repetitive environment; VR is also proven to help students familiarize themselves with skills not specific to any particular procedure. VR application was used to train road crossing skills in children. It proved to be rather successful. However some students with autistic spectrum disorders after such training might be unable to distinguish virtual from real. As a result, they may attempt quite dangerous road crossings.

Video Games

Playstation VR headset used in video games.

A person wearing haptic feedback devices, which enable her to feel elements in the virtual world.

The use of graphics, sound and input technology in video games can be incorporated into VR. Several Virtual Reality head mounted displays (HMD) were released for gaming during the early-mid 1990s. These included the Virtual Boy developed by Nintendo, the iGlasses developed by Virtual I-O, the Cybermaxx developed by Victormaxx and the VFX1 Headgear developed by Forte Technologies. Other modern examples of narrow VR for gaming include the Wii Remote, the Kinect, and the PlayStation Move/PlayStation Eye, all of which track and send motion input of the players to the game console somewhat accurately. Several companies were working on a new generation of VR headsets, which were released on March 28, 2016: Oculus Rift is a head-mounted display for gaming purposes developed by Oculus VR, an American technology company that was acquired for US$2 billion by Facebook in 2014. One of its rivals was named by Sony as PlayStation VR (codenamed Morpheus), which requires a PS4 instead of a PC to run. In 2015, Valve Corporation announced their partnership with HTC to make a VR headset capable of tracking the exact position of its user in a 4.5 by 4.5 meters area, the HTC Vive. All these virtual reality headsets are tethered headsets that use special lenses to magnify and stretch a 5.7-inch screen (in the case of Morpheus) across the field of vision. There are more gaming VR headsets in development, each with its own special abilities. StarVR offers a 210° field of view, whereas FOVE tracks the position of your eyes as an input method.

Entertainment

Virtual reality technologies are also widely used in entertainment and have reflected in virtual reality simulators (VR simulators/ VR amusements/ VR game simulators/ vr motion simulators).

Fine Arts

David Em was the first fine artist to create navigable virtual worlds in the 1970s. His early work was done on mainframes at Information International, Inc., Jet Propulsion Laboratory, and California Institute of Technology. Jeffrey Shaw explored the potential of VR in fine arts with early works like *Legible City* (1989), *Virtual Museum* (1991), and *Golden Calf* (1994). Canadian artist Char Davies created immersive VR art pieces *Osmose* (1995) and *Ephémère* (1998). Maurice Benayoun's work introduced metaphorical, philosophical or political content, combining VR, network, generation and intelligent agents, in works like *Is God Flat?* (1994), "Is the Devil Curved?" (1995), *The Tunnel under the Atlantic* (1995), and *World Skin, a Photo Safari in the Land of War* (1997). Other pioneering artists working in VR have include Knowbotic Research, Rebecca Allen and Perry Hoberman.

Engineering

The use of 3D computer-aided design (CAD) data was limited by 2D monitors and paper printouts until the mid-to-late 1990s, when video projectors, 3D tracking, and computer technology enabled a renaissance in the use 3D CAD data in virtual reality environments. With the use of active shutter glasses and multi-surface projection units immersive engineering was made possible by companies like VRcom and IC.IDO. Virtual reality has been used in automotive, aerospace, and ground transportation original equipment manufacturers (OEMs) in their product engineering and manufacturing engineering . Virtual reality adds more dimensions to virtual prototyping, product building, assembly, service, performance use-cases. This enables engineers from different disciplines to view their design as its final product. Engineers can view the virtual bridge, building or other structure from any angle. As well, some computer models allow engineers to test their structure's resistance to winds, weight, and other elements. Immersive VR engineering systems enable engineers, management and investors to see virtual prototypes prior to the availability of any physical prototypes.

Heritage and Archaeology

The first use of a VR presentation in a heritage application was in 1994, when a museum visitor interpretation provided an interactive "walk-through" of a 3D reconstruction of Dudley Castle in England as it was in 1550. This consisted of a computer controlled laserdisc-based system designed by British-based engineer Colin Johnson. The system was featured in a conference held by the British Museum in November 1994, and in the subsequent technical paper, *Imaging the Past – Electronic Imaging and Computer Graphics in Museums and Archaeology*. Virtual reality enables heritage sites to be recreated extremely accurately, so that the recreations can be published in various media. The original sites are often inaccessible to the public or, due to the poor state of their preservation, hard to picture. This technology can be used to develop virtual replicas of caves, natural environment, old towns, monuments, sculptures and archaeological elements.

Architectural Design

A visitor at Mozilla Berlin Hackshibition trying Oculus Rift virtual reality experience on Firefox.

One of the first recorded uses of virtual reality in architecture was in the late 1980s when the University of North Carolina modeled its Sitterman Hall, home of its computer science department, in a virtual environment. Several companies, including IrisVR and Floored, Inc., provide software or services that allow architectural design firms and various clients in the real estate industry to tour virtual models of proposed building designs. IrisVR currently provides software that allows users to convert design files created in CAD programs like SketchUp and Revit into files viewable with an Oculus Rift, HTC Vive, or a smartphone "in one click," without the need for complex tiered workflows or knowledge of game engines such as Unity3D. Floored, meanwhile, manually constructs and refines Rift-viewable 3D models in-house from either CAD files for un-built designs or physical scans of already built, brick-and-mortar buildings, and provides clients with access to its own viewing software, which can be used with either an Oculus Rift or a standard 2D web browser, afterward.

VR software products like these can provide a number of benefits to architects and their clients. During the design process, architects can use VR to experience the designs they are working on before they are built. Seeing a design in VR can give architect a correct sense of scale and proportion. Having an interactive VR model also eliminates the need to make physical miniatures to demonstrate a design to clients or the public. Later on, after a building is constructed, developers and owners can create a VR model of a space that allows potential buyers or tenants to tour a space in VR, even if real-life circumstances make a physical tour unfeasible. For instance, if the owner of an apartment building has a VR model of a space while the building is under construction, she can begin showing and renting the units before they are even ready to be occupied. Furthermore, this sort of showing can be conducted over any distance, as long as the potential customer has access to a VR setup (or, even, with the help of Google Cardboard or a similar phone-based VR headset, nothing but a smartphone.)

Urban Design

In 2010, 3D virtual reality was beginning to be used for urban regeneration, planning and transportation projects. In 2007, development began on a virtual reality software which took design coordinate geometry used by land surveyors and civil engineers and incorporated precision spatial information created automatically by the lines and curves typically shown on subdivision plats and land surveying plans. These precise spatial areas cross referenced color and texture to an item list. The item list contained a set of controls for 3D rendering, such as water reflective surfaces or building height. The land surface in software to create a contour map uses a digital terrain model (DTM). By 2010, prototype software was developed for LandMentor, a technology to automate the process leading from design to virtualization. The first beta users in 2011 were able drape the design or survey data over the digital terrain to create data structures that were passed into a video game engine. The engine was able to create a virtual interactive world. The software was improved to implement 3D models from other free or commercially sold software to create a more realistic virtual reality.

A land development plan using Prefurbia, a 4th generation design system.

A streetscape with homes, showing architectural shaping and blending.

Therapy

The primary use of VR in a therapeutic role is its application to various forms of exposure therapy, including phobia treatments.

Theme Parks

Since 2015, virtual reality has been installed onto a number of roller coasters, including Galactica at Alton Towers, The New Revolution at Six Flags Magic Mountain and Alpenexpress at Europa-park, amongst others.

Concerts

In Oslo Spektrum on May the 3rd 2016, Norwegian pop band a-ha cleared away their normal stage-production to give room for a very different concert performance in collaboration with Void, a Norwegian computational design studio working in the intersection between design, architecture, art and technology. The collaboration resulted in a unique one-of-a-kind concert with advanced scenography using 360 virtual reality technology. It used movement sensors that reacted to the band members' movements, voices and instruments. 3D cameras, 20000 lines of codes, 1000 square meters of projection film and massive projectors was set up into a visual show that made the Oslo Spektrum arena in Oslo, Norway into a light installation and visual experience that unfolded live for the audience instead of a pre programmed sequence. The stereoscopic VR-experience was made available for Android users directly through a YouTube app and also made available for iPhone users and other platforms.

Assembled Google Cardboard VR.

Retail

Lowe's, IKEA and Wayfair and other retailers have developed systems that allow their products to be seen in virtual reality, to give consumers a better idea of how the product will fit into their home, or to allow the consumer to get a better look at the product from home. Consumers looking at digital photos of the products can "turn" the product around virtually, and see it from the side or the back. This enables customers to get a better sense of how a product looks and about its features, than with the typical single picture used in traditional paper catalogues. The retail travel industry such as Cruise About and Flight Centre have been adopting VR to enable customer in their stores to view cruise cabins, tourism content, and hotel rooms prior to booking.

Charity

Non-profit organisations such as Amnesty International, UNICEF, and World Wide Fund for Nature (WWF) have started using virtual reality to bring potential supporters closer to their work, effectively bringing distant social, political and environmental issues and projects to members of the public in immersive ways not possible with traditional media. Panoramic 360 views of conflict in Syria and face to face encounters with CGI tigers in Nepal have been used in experiential activations and shared online to both educate and gain financial support for such charitable work.

Exercise and fitness

Certain companies are using VR to target the fitness industry.

Film

Many companies, including GoPro, Nokia, Samsung, Ricoh and Nikon, develop omnidirectional cameras, also known as 360-degree cameras or VR cameras, that have the ability to record in all directions. These cameras are used to create images and videos that can be viewed in VR. (See VR photography.) Films produced for VR permit the audience to view the entire environment in every scene, creating an interactive viewing experience. Production companies, such as Fox Searchlight Pictures and Skybound, utilize VR cameras to produce films that are interactive in VR. Fox Searchlight, Oculus and Samsung Gear VR collaborated on a project titled "Wild – The Experience", starring Reese Witherspoon. The VR film was presented at the Consumer Electronics Show as well as the Sundance Film Festival in January 2015. On December 8, 2015, the production company Skybound announced their VR thriller titled "Gone". In collaboration with the VR production company WEVR, and Samsung Gear VR, the 360-degree video series was released on January 20, 2016.

Media

Media companies such as Paramount Pictures, and Disney have applied VR into marketing campaigns creating interactive forms of media. In October 2014 Paramount Pictures, in collaboration with the media production company Framestore, created a VR experience utilizing the Oculus DK2. The experience was dubbed a "time sensitive adventure in space" that took place in a portion of the Endurance space ship from the film "Interstellar." The experience was available to the public at limited AMC theater locations. In May 2016, Disney released a VR experience titled Disney

Movies VR on Valve Corporation's Steam software, free for download. The experience allows users to interact with the characters and worlds from the Disney, Marvel, and Lucasfilm universes.

Pornography

Pornographic studios such as Naughty America, BaDoinkVR and Kink have applied VR into their products since late 2015 or early 2016. The clips and videos are shot from an angle that resembles POV-style porn.

Marketing

Virtual Reality has the potential to completely replace many forms of digital marketing. Marketing strategies in small and middle sized enterprises, ever more frequently include virtual reality in their ad concepts, POS material and budgets. Virtual Reality presents a unique opportunity for advertisers to reach a completely immersed audience.

Sports Viewing

In September 2016, Agon announced that the upcoming World Chess Championship match between Magnus Carlsen and Sergey Karjakin would be "the first in any sport to be broadcast in 360-degree virtual reality."

In Fiction

Many science fiction books and films have imagined characters being "trapped in virtual reality" or entering into virtual reality. A comprehensive and specific fictional model for virtual reality was published in 1935 in the short story "Pygmalion's Spectacles" by Stanley G. Weinbaum. A more modern work to use this idea was Daniel F. Galouye's novel *Simulacron-3*, which was made into a German teleplay titled *Welt am Draht* ("World on a Wire") in 1973. Other science fiction books have promoted the idea of virtual reality as a partial, but not total, substitution for the misery of reality, or have touted it as a method for creating virtual worlds in which one may escape from Earth. Stanisław Lem's 1961 story "I (Profesor Corcoran)", translated in English as "Further Reminiscences of Ijon Tichy I", dealt with a scientist who created a number of computer-simulated people living in a virtual world. Lem further explored the implications of what he termed "phantomatics" in his nonfictional 1964 treatise *Summa Technologiae*. The Piers Anthony novel *Killobyte* follows the story of a paralyzed cop trapped in a virtual reality game by a hacker, whom he must stop to save a fellow trapped player slowly succumbing to insulin shock.

A number of other popular fictional works use the concept of virtual reality. These include William Gibson's 1984 *Neuromancer*, which defined the concept of cyberspace, and his 1994 *Virtual Light*, where a presentation viewable in VR-like goggles was the MacGuffin. Other examples are Neal Stephenson's *Snow Crash*, in which he made extensive reference to the term avatar to describe one's representation in a virtual world, and Rudy Rucker's *The Hacker and the Ants*, in which programmer Jerzy Rugby uses VR for robot design and testing. The Otherland series of 4 novels by Tad Williams, published from 1996 to 2001 and set in the 2070s, shows a world where the Internet has become accessible via virtual reality. The *Doctor Who* serial "The Deadly Assassin", first broadcast in 1976, introduced a dream-like computer-generated reality, known as the Matrix. British BBC2 sci-fi series *Red Dwarf* featured a virtual reality game titled "Better Than Life", in which the main characters had spent many years connected. Saban's syndicated superhero television series *VR Troopers* also made use of the concept. The holodeck featured in *Star Trek: The Next Generation* is one of the best known examples of virtual reality in popular culture, including the ability for users to interactively modify scenarios in real time with a natural language interface. The depiction differs from others in the use of a physical room rather than a neural interface or headset.

The *.hack* multimedia franchise is based on a virtual reality MMORPG dubbed "The World". The French animated series *Code Lyoko* is based on the virtual world of *Lyoko* and the Internet. In 2009, British digital radio station BBC Radio 7 broadcast *Planet B*, a science-fiction drama set in a virtual world. *Planet B* was the largest ever commission for an original drama programme. The 2012 series *Sword Art Online* involves the concept of a virtual reality MMORPG of the same name, with the possibility of dying in real life when a player dies in the game. Also, in its 2014 sequel, *Sword Art Online II*, the idea of bringing a virtual character into the real world via mobile cameras is posed; this concept is used to allow a bedridden individual to attend public school for the first time.*Accel World* (2012) expands the concept of virtual reality using the game *Brain Burst*, a game which allows players to gain and receive points to keep accelerating; accelerating is when an individual's brain perceives the images around them 1000 times faster, heightening their sense of awareness.

In October 2016, television series *Halcyon* was released as a "virtual reality series", where some episodes are broadcast on conventional television, some as VR content for interfaces like Oculus Rift. The show, itself, is a crime drama following the world's first "VR Crimes Unit" in 2048.

Motion Pictures

World Skin (1997), Maurice Benayoun's virtual reality interactive installation.

- Rainer Werner Fassbinder's 1973 film *Welt am Draht*, based on Daniel F. Galouye's novel Simulacron-3, shows a virtual reality simulation *inside* another virtual reality simulation
- In 1983, the Natalie Wood/Christopher Walken film *Brainstorm* revolved around the production, use, and misuse of a VR device.
- *Total Recall*, directed by Paul Verhoeven and based on the Philip K. Dick story "We Can Remember It for You Wholesale".
- A VR-like system, used to record and play back dreams, figures centrally in Wim Wenders'

1991 film *Until the End of the World.*

- The 1992 film *The Lawnmower Man* tells the tale of a research scientist who uses a VR system to jumpstart the mental and physical development of his mentally handicapped gardener.
- The 1993 film *Arcade* is centered around a new virtual reality game (from which the film gets its name) that actively traps those who play it inside its world.
- The 1995 film *Strange Days* is a science-fiction thriller about a fictional virtual reality trend in which users buy illegal VR recordings of criminal offences recorded from the offender's point of view (POV).
- The 1995 film *Johnny Mnemonic* has the main character Johnny (played by Keanu Reeves) use virtual reality goggles and brain–computer interfaces to access the Internet and extract encrypted information in his own brain.
- The 1995 film *Virtuosity* has Russell Crowe as a virtual reality serial killer name SID 6.7 (Sadistic, Intelligent and Dangerous) who is used in a simulation to train real-world police officer, but manages to escape into the real world.
- The 1999 film *The Thirteenth Floor* is an adaptation of Daniel F. Galouye's novel *Simulacron-3*, and tells about two virtual reality simulations, one in another.
- In 1999, *The Matrix* and later sequels explored the possibility that our world is actually a vast virtual reality (or more precisely, simulated reality) created by artificially intelligent machines.
- *eXistenZ* (1999), by David Cronenberg, in which level switches occur so seamlessly and numerously that at the end of the movie it is difficult to tell whether the main characters are back in "reality".
- In the film *Avatar*, the humans are hooked up via advanced technologies with avatars, enabling the avatars to remotely perform the actions of the humans.
- *Surrogates* (2009) is based on a brain–computer interface that allows people to control realistic humanoid robots, giving them full sensory feedback.
- The 2010 science fiction thriller film *Inception* is about a professional thief who steals information by infiltrating the subconscious. He creates artificial thoughts that are so realistic that once they are implanted in a person's mind, the person thinks these are his own thoughts.

Concerns and challenges

There are certain health and safety considerations of virtual reality. For example, a number of unwanted symptoms have been caused by prolonged use of virtual reality, and these may have slowed proliferation of the technology. Most virtual reality systems come with consumer warnings. Virtual reality sickness (also known as cybersickness) occurs when a person's exposure to a virtual environment causes symptoms that are similar to motion sickness symptoms. The most common symptoms are general discomfort, headache, stomach awareness, nausea, vomiting, pallor, sweating, fatigue, drowsiness, disorientation, and apathy. Other symptoms include postural instability and retching. Virtual reality sickness is different from motion sickness in that it can be caused by the visually-induced perception of self-motion; real self-motion is not needed. It is also different from simulator sickness; non-virtual reality simulator sickness tends to be characterized by oculomotor disturbances, whereas virtual reality sickness tends to be characterized by disorientation.

In addition, there are social, conceptual, and philosophical considerations and implications associated with the use of virtual reality. What the phrase "virtual reality" means or refers to can be ambiguous. In the book *The Metaphysics of Virtual Reality* by Michael R. Heim, seven different concepts of virtual reality are identified: simulation, interaction, artificiality, immersion, telepresence, full-body immersion, and network communication. There has been an increase in interest in the potential social impact of new technologies, such as virtual reality. In the book *Infinite Reality: Avatars, Eternal Life, New Worlds, and the Dawn of the Virtual Revolution,* Blascovich and Bailenson review the literature on the psychology and sociology behind life in virtual reality. Mychilo S. Cline's book *Power, Madness, and Immortality: The Future of Virtual Reality*, argues that virtual reality will lead to a number of important changes in human life and activity. He argues that virtual reality will be integrated into daily life and activity, and will be used in various human ways. Another such speculation has been written up on how to reach ultimate happiness via virtual reality. He also argues that techniques will be developed to influence human behavior, interpersonal communication, and cognition. As we spend more and more time in virtual space, there would be a gradual "migration to virtual space", resulting in important changes in economics, worldview, and culture. Philosophical implications of VR are discussed in books, including Philip Zhai's *Get Real: A Philosophical Adventure in Virtual Reality* (1998) and *Digital Sensations: Space, Identity and Embodiment in Virtual Reality* (1999), written by Ken Hillis.

Virtual reality technology faces a number of challenges, most of which involve motion sickness and technical matters. Users might become disoriented in a purely virtual environment, causing balance issues; computer latency might affect the simulation, providing a less-than-satisfactory end-user experience; the complicated nature of head-mounted displays and input systems such as specialized gloves and boots may require specialized training to operate, and navigating the non-virtual environment (if the user is not confined to a limited area) might prove dangerous without external sensory information. In January 2014, Michael Abrash gave a talk on VR at Steam Dev Days. He listed all the requirements necessary to establish presence and concluded that a great VR system will be available in 2015 or soon after. While the visual aspect of VR is close to being solved, he stated that there are other areas of VR that need solutions, such as 3D audio, haptics, body tracking, and input. However, 3D audio effects exist in games and simulate the head-related transfer function of the listener (especially using headphones). Examples include Environmental Audio Extensions (EAX), DirectSound and OpenAL. VR audio developer Varun Nair points out that from a design perspective, sound for VR is still very much an open book. Many of the game audio design principles, especially those related to FPS games, crumble in virtual reality. He encourages more sound designers to get involved in virtual reality audio to experiment and push VR audio forward. There have been rising concerns that with the advent of virtual reality, some users may experience virtual reality addiction.

Pioneers and Notables

- Thomas A. Furness III,
- Maurice Benayoun,
- Mark Bolas,
- Fred Brooks,
- Anshe Chung,
- Edmond Couchot,
- James H. Clark,
- Doug Church,
- Char Davies,
- Tom DeFanti,
- David Em,
- Scott Fisher,
- William Gibson,
- Morton Heilig,
- Eric Howlett,
- Myron Krueger,
- Knowbotic Research,
- Jaron Lanier,
- Brenda Laurel,
- Palmer Luckey,
- Michael Naimark,
- Randy Pausch,
- Mark Pesce,
- Warren Robinett,
- Philip Rosedale,
- Louis Rosenberg,
- Dan Sandin,
- Susumu Tachi,
- Ivan Sutherland.

Commercial Industries

The companies working in the virtual reality sector fall broadly into three categories of involvement: hardware (making headsets and input devices specific to VR), software (producing software for interfacing with the hardware or for delivering content to users) and content creation (producing content, whether interactive or passive storylines, games, and artificial worlds, for consumption and exploration with VR hardware).

HMD devices:

- Carl Zeiss (Carl Zeiss Cinemizer),
- Facebook (Oculus Rift),
- Google (Google Cardboard),
- HTC (HTC Vive),
- Microsoft (Microsoft HoloLens),
- Razer (OSVR Hacker Dev Kit),
- Samsung (Samsung Gear VR),
- Sony Computer Entertainment (PS VR),
- Starbreeze Studios (StarVR).

See Comparison of retail head-mounted displays.

Input devices:

- Cyberith Virtualizer,
- Intugine,
- Leap Motion,
- Nokia (Nokia OZO camera),
- Sixense,
- uSens,
- Virtuix Omni,
- ZSpace (company).

Software:

- VREAM,
- vorpX,

- Dacuda.

Content:

- Framestore,
- iClone,
- Innervision,
- Moving Picture Company,
- Reel FX,
- xRes.

Emerging technologies:

- 360 degree video,
- Augmented reality,
- HoloLens,
- Intel RealSense,
- Magic Leap,
- Mixed reality.

Companies:

- Google,
- Facebook,
- Apple,
- HTC,
- Valve,
- Samsung,
- Microsoft,
- Intel,
- Campustours,
- Sketchfab.

Artists:

- Rebecca Allen,

- Maurice Benayoun,
- Sheldon Brown,
- Char Davies,
- David Em,
- Myron Krueger,
- Jaron Lanier,
- Brenda Laurel,
- Michael Naimark,
- Jeffrey Shaw,
- Nicole Stenger,
- Tamiko Thiel.

Optical Character Recognition

Optical character recognition (optical character reader, OCR) is the mechanical or electronic conversion of images of typed, handwritten or printed text into machine-encoded text, whether from a scanned document, a photo of a document, a scene-photo (for example the text on signs and billboards in a landscape photo) or from subtitle text superimposed on an image (for example from a television broadcast). It is widely used as a form of information entry from printed paper data records, whether passport documents, invoices, bank statements, computerised receipts, business cards, mail, printouts of static-data, or any suitable documentation. It is a common method of digitising printed texts so that they can be electronically edited, searched, stored more compactly, displayed on-line, and used in machine processes such as cognitive computing, machine translation, (extracted) text-to-speech, key data and text mining. OCR is a field of research in pattern recognition, artificial intelligence and computer vision.

Early versions needed to be trained with images of each character, and worked on one font at a time. Advanced systems capable of producing a high degree of recognition accuracy for most fonts are now common, and with support for a variety of digital image file format inputs. Some systems are capable of reproducing formatted output that closely approximates the original page including images, columns, and other non-textual components.

History

Early optical character recognition may be traced to technologies involving telegraphy and creating reading devices for the blind. In 1914, Emanuel Goldberg developed a machine that read characters and converted them into standard telegraph code. Concurrently, Edmund Fournier d'Albe developed the Optophone, a handheld scanner that when moved across a printed page, produced tones that corresponded to specific letters or characters.

In the late 1920s and into the 1930s Emanuel Goldberg developed what he called a "Statistical Machine" for searching microfilm archives using an optical code recognition system. In 1931 he was granted USA Patent number 1,838,389 for the invention. The patent was acquired by IBM.

With the advent of smart-phones and smartglasses, OCR can be used in internet connected mobile device applications that extract text captured using the device's camera. These devices that do not have OCR functionality built-in to the operating system will typically use an OCR API to extract the text from the image file captured and provided by the device. The OCR API returns the extracted text, along with information about the location of the detected text in the original image back to the device app for further processing (such as text-to-speech) or display.

Blind and Visually Impaired Users

In 1974, Ray Kurzweil started the company Kurzweil Computer Products, Inc. and continued development of omni-font OCR, which could recognise text printed in virtually any font (Kurzweil is often credited with inventing omni-font OCR, but it was in use by companies, including CompuScan, in the late 1960s and 1970s). Kurzweil decided that the best application of this technology would be to create a reading machine for the blind, which would allow blind people to have a computer read text to them out loud. This device required the invention of two enabling technologies – the CCD flatbed scanner and the text-to-speech synthesiser. On January 13, 1976, the successful finished product was unveiled during a widely reported news conference headed by Kurzweil and the leaders of the National Federation of the Blind. In 1978, Kurzweil Computer Products began selling a commercial version of the optical character recognition computer program. LexisNexis was one of the first customers, and bought the program to upload legal paper and news documents onto its nascent online databases. Two years later, Kurzweil sold his company to Xerox, which had an interest in further commercialising paper-to-computer text conversion. Xerox eventually spun it off as Scansoft, which merged with Nuance Communications. The research group headed by A. G. Ramakrishnan at the Medical intelligence and language engineering lab, Indian Institute of Science, has developed PrintToBraille tool, an open source GUI frontend that can be used by any OCR to convert scanned images of printed books to Braille books.

In the 2000s, OCR was made available online as a service (WebOCR), in a cloud computing environment, and in mobile applications like real-time translation of foreign-language signs on a smartphone.

Various commercial and open source OCR systems are available for most common writing systems, including Latin, Cyrillic, Arabic, Hebrew, Indic, Bengali (Bangla), Devanagari, Tamil, Chinese, Japanese, and Korean characters.

Applications

OCR engines have been developed into many kinds of object-oriented OCR applications, such as receipt OCR, invoice OCR, check OCR, legal billing document OCR.

They can be used for:

- Data entry for business documents, e.g. check, passport, invoice, bank statement and receipt.

- Automatic number plate recognition.
- Automatic insurance documents key information extraction.
- Extracting business card information into a contact list.
- More quickly make textual versions of printed documents, e.g. book scanning for Project Gutenberg.
- Make electronic images of printed documents searchable, e.g. Google Books.
- Converting handwriting in real time to control a computer (pen computing).
- Defeating CAPTCHA anti-bot systems, though these are specifically designed to prevent OCR.
- Assistive technology for blind and visually impaired users.

Types

- Optical character recognition (OCR) – targets typewritten text, one glyph or character at a time.
- Optical word recognition – targets typewritten text, one word at a time (for languages that use a space as a word divider). (Usually just called "OCR".)
- Intelligent character recognition (ICR) – also targets handwritten printscript or cursive text one glyph or character at a time, usually involving machine learning.
- Intelligent word recognition (IWR) – also targets handwritten printscript or cursive text, one word at a time. This is especially useful for languages where glyphs are not separated in cursive script.

OCR is generally an "offline" process, which analyses a static document. Handwriting movement analysis can be used as input to handwriting recognition. Instead of merely using the shapes of glyphs and words, this technique is able to capture motions, such as the order in which segments are drawn, the direction, and the pattern of putting the pen down and lifting it. This additional information can make the end-to-end process more accurate. This technology is also known as "online character recognition", "dynamic character recognition", "real-time character recognition", and "intelligent character recognition".

Techniques

Pre-processing

OCR software often "pre-processes" images to improve the chances of successful recognition. Techniques include:

- De-skew – If the document was not aligned properly when scanned, it may need to be tilted a few degrees clockwise or counterclockwise in order to make lines of text perfectly horizontal or vertical.

- Despeckle – remove positive and negative spots, smoothing edges.
- Binarisation – Convert an image from color or greyscale to black-and-white (called a "binary image" because there are two colours). The task of binarisation is performed as a simple way of separating the text (or any other desired image component) from the background. The task of binarisation itself is necessary since most commercial recognition algorithms work only on binary images since it proves to be simpler to do so. In addition, the effectiveness of the binarisation step influences to a significant extent the quality of the character recognition stage and the careful decisions are made in the choice of the binarisation employed for a given input image type; since the quality of the binarisation method employed to obtain the binary result depends on the type of the input image (scanned document, scene text image, historical degraded document etc.).
- Line removal – Cleans up non-glyph boxes and lines.
- Layout analysis or "zoning" – Identifies columns, paragraphs, captions, etc. as distinct blocks. Especially important in multi-column layouts and tables.
- Line and word detection – Establishes baseline for word and character shapes, separates words if necessary.
- Script recognition – In multilingual documents, the script may change at the level of the words and hence, identification of the script is necessary, before the right OCR can be invoked to handle the specific script.
- Character isolation or "segmentation" – For per-character OCR, multiple characters that are connected due to image artifacts must be separated; single characters that are broken into multiple pieces due to artifacts must be connected.
- Normalise aspect ratio and scale.

Segmentation of fixed-pitch fonts is accomplished relatively simply by aligning the image to a uniform grid based on where vertical grid lines will least often intersect black areas. For proportional fonts, more sophisticated techniques are needed because whitespace between letters can sometimes be greater than that between words, and vertical lines can intersect more than one character.

Character Recognition

There are two basic types of core OCR algorithm, which may produce a ranked list of candidate characters.

Matrix matching involves comparing an image to a stored glyph on a pixel-by-pixel basis; it is also known as "pattern matching", "pattern recognition", or "image correlation". This relies on the input glyph being correctly isolated from the rest of the image, and on the stored glyph being in a similar font and at the same scale. This technique works best with typewritten text and does not work well when new fonts are encountered. This is the technique the early physical photocell-based OCR implemented, rather directly.

Feature extraction decomposes glyphs into "features" like lines, closed loops, line direction, and line intersections. These are compared with an abstract vector-like representation of a character, which might reduce to one or more glyph prototypes. General techniques of feature detection in computer vision are applicable to this type of OCR, which is commonly seen in "intelligent" handwriting recognition and indeed most modern OCR software. Nearest neighbour classifiers such as the k-nearest neighbors algorithm are used to compare image features with stored glyph features and choose the nearest match.

Software such as Cuneiform and Tesseract use a two-pass approach to character recognition. The second pass is known as "adaptive recognition" and uses the letter shapes recognised with high confidence on the first pass to recognise better the remaining letters on the second pass. This is advantageous for unusual fonts or low-quality scans where the font is distorted (e.g. blurred or faded).

The OCR result can be stored in the standardised ALTO format, a dedicated XML schema maintained by the United States Library of Congress.

Post-processing

OCR accuracy can be increased if the output is constrained by a lexicon – a list of words that are allowed to occur in a document. This might be, for example, all the words in the English language, or a more technical lexicon for a specific field. This technique can be problematic if the document contains words not in the lexicon, like proper nouns. Tesseract uses its dictionary to influence the character segmentation step, for improved accuracy.

The output stream may be a plain text stream or file of characters, but more sophisticated OCR systems can preserve the original layout of the page and produce, for example, an annotated PDF that includes both the original image of the page and a searchable textual representation.

"Near-neighbor analysis" can make use of co-occurrence frequencies to correct errors, by noting that certain words are often seen together. For example, "Washington, D.C." is generally far more common in English than "Washington DOC".

Knowledge of the grammar of the language being scanned can also help determine if a word is likely to be a verb or a noun, for example, allowing greater accuracy.

The Levenshtein Distance algorithm has also been used in OCR post-processing to further optimize results from an OCR API.

Application-specific Optimisations

In recent years, the major OCR technology providers began to tweak OCR systems to better deal with specific types of input. Beyond an application-specific lexicon, better performance can be had by taking into account business rules, standard expression, or rich information contained in color images. This strategy is called "Application-Oriented OCR" or "Customised OCR", and has been applied to OCR of license plates, business cards, invoices, screenshots, ID cards, driver licenses, and automobile manufacturing.

OCR Tools

Google, ABBYY, Adobe Acrobat, LEAD Technologies, and ScanSnap provide tools that can extract text from images or convert images into text-searchable document formats. For any project related to paperless offices, the use of OCR tools will be required to achieve the objectives of paperless offices and homes.

Workarounds

There are several techniques for solving the problem of character recognition by means other than improved OCR algorithms.

Forcing Better Input

Special fonts like OCR-A, OCR-B, or MICR fonts, with precisely specified sizing, spacing, and distinctive character shapes, allow a higher accuracy rate during transcription. These were often used in early matrix-matching systems.

"Comb fields" are pre-printed boxes that encourage humans to write more legibly – one glyph per box. These are often printed in a "dropout color" which can be easily removed by the OCR system.

Palm OS used a special set of glyphs, known as "Graffiti" which are similar to printed English characters but simplified or modified for easier recognition on the platform's computationally limited hardware. Users would need to learn how to write these special glyphs.

Zone-based OCR restricts the image to a specific part of a document. This is often referred to as "Template OCR".

Crowdsourcing

Crowdsourcing humans to perform the character recognition can quickly process images like computer-driven OCR, but with higher accuracy for recognising images than is obtained with computers. Practical systems include the Amazon Mechanical Turk and reCAPTCHA. The National Library of Finland has developed an online interface for users correct OCRed texts in the standardised ALTO format. Crowdsourcing has also been used not to perform character recognition directly but to invite software developers to develop image processing algorithms, for example, through the use of rank-order tournaments.

Accuracy

Commissioned by the U.S. Department of Energy (DOE), the Information Science Research Institute (ISRI) had the mission to foster the improvement of automated technologies for understanding machine printed documents, and it conducted the most authoritative of the *Annual Test of OCR Accuracy* from 1992 to 1996.

Recognition of Latin-script, typewritten text is still not 100% accurate even where clear imaging is available. One study based on recognition of 19th- and early 20th-century newspaper pages concluded that character-by-character OCR accuracy for commercial OCR software varied from 81% to 99%; total accuracy can be achieved by human review or Data Dictionary Authentication. Other areas—including recognition of hand printing, cursive handwriting, and printed text in other scripts (especially those East Asian language characters which have many strokes for a single character)—are still the subject of active research. The MNIST database is commonly used for testing systems' ability to recognise handwritten digits.

Accuracy rates can be measured in several ways, and how they are measured can greatly affect the reported accuracy rate. For example, if word context (basically a lexicon of words) is not used to correct software finding non-existent words, a character error rate of 1% (99% accuracy) may result in an error rate of 5% (95% accuracy) or worse if the measurement is based on whether each whole word was recognised with no incorrect letters.

Web based OCR systems for recognising hand-printed text on the fly have become well known as commercial products in recent years (see Tablet PC history). Accuracy rates of 80% to 90% on neat, clean hand-printed characters can be achieved by pen computing software, but that accuracy rate still translates to dozens of errors per page, making the technology useful only in very limited applications.

Recognition of cursive text is an active area of research, with recognition rates even lower than that of hand-printed text. Higher rates of recognition of general cursive script will likely not be possible without the use of contextual or grammatical information. For example, recognising entire words from a dictionary is easier than trying to parse individual characters from script. Reading the *Amount* line of a cheque (which is always a written-out number) is an example where using a smaller dictionary can increase recognition rates greatly. The shapes of individual cursive characters themselves simply do not contain enough information to accurately (greater than 98%) recognise all handwritten cursive script.

Unicode

Characters to support OCR were added to the Unicode Standard in June 1993, with the release of version 1.1.

Some of these characters are mapped from fonts specific to MICR, OCR-A or OCR-B.

Optical Character Recognition Official Unicode Consortium code chart (PDF)																
	0	1	2	3	4	5	6	7	8	9	A	B	C	D	E	F
U+244x	⑀	⑁	⑂	⑃	⑄	⑅	⑆	⑇	⑈	⑉	⑊					
U+245x																
Notes																
1. As of Unicode version 9.0 2. Grey areas indicate non-assigned code points																

Game Theory

Game theory is "the study of mathematical models of conflict and cooperation between intelligent rational decision-makers." Game theory is mainly used in economics, political science, and psychology, as well as logic, computer science, biology and poker. Originally, it addressed zero-sum games, in which one person's gains result in losses for the other participants. Today, game theory applies to a wide range of behavioral relations, and is now an umbrella term for the science of logical decision making in humans, animals, and computers.

Modern game theory began with the idea regarding the existence of mixed-strategy equilibria in two-person zero-sum games and its proof by John von Neumann. Von Neumann's original proof used Brouwer fixed-point theorem on continuous mappings into compact convex sets, which became a standard method in game theory and mathematical economics. His paper was followed by the 1944 book *Theory of Games and Economic Behavior*, co-written with Oskar Morgenstern, which considered cooperative games of several players. The second edition of this book provided an axiomatic theory of expected utility, which allowed mathematical statisticians and economists to treat decision-making under uncertainty.

This theory was developed extensively in the 1950s by many scholars. Game theory was later explicitly applied to biology in the 1970s, although similar developments go back at least as far as the 1930s. Game theory has been widely recognized as an important tool in many fields. With the Nobel Memorial Prize in Economic Sciences going to game theorist Jean Tirole in 2014, eleven game-theorists have now won the economics Nobel Prize. John Maynard Smith was awarded the Crafoord Prize for his application of game theory to biology.

History

Early discussions of examples of two-person games occurred long before the rise of modern, mathematical game theory. The first known discussion of game theory occurred in a letter written by Charles Waldegrave, an active Jacobite, and uncle to James Waldegrave, a British diplomat, in 1713. In this letter, Waldegrave provides a minimax mixed strategy solution to a two-person version of the card game le Her, and the problem is now known as Waldegrave problem. James Madison made what we now recognize as a game-theoretic analysis of the ways states can be expected to behave under different systems of taxation. In his 1838 *Recherches sur les principes mathématiques de la théorie des richesses* (*Researches into the Mathematical Principles of the Theory of Wealth*), Antoine Augustin Cournot considered a duopoly and presents a solution that is a restricted version of the Nash equilibrium.

John von Neumann.

In 1913 Ernst Zermelo published *Über eine Anwendung der Mengenlehre auf die Theorie des Schachspiels*. It proved that the optimal chess strategy is strictly determined. This paved the way for more general theorems.

The Danish mathematician Zeuthen proved that the mathematical model had a winning strategy by using Brouwer's fixed point theorem. In his 1938 book *Applications aux Jeux de Hasard* and earlier notes, Émile Borel proved a minimax theorem for two-person zero-sum matrix games only when the pay-off matrix was symmetric. Borel conjectured that non-existence of mixed-strategy equilibria in two-person zero-sum games would occur, a conjecture that was proved false.

Game theory did not really exist as a unique field until John von Neumann published a paper in 1928. Von Neumann's original proof used Brouwer's fixed-point theorem on continuous mappings into compact convex sets, which became a standard method in game theory and mathematical economics. His paper was followed by his 1944 book *Theory of Games and Economic Behavior* co-authored with Oskar Morgenstern. The second edition of this book provided an axiomatic theory of utility, which reincarnated Daniel Bernoulli's old theory of utility (of the money) as an independent discipline. Von Neumann's work in game theory culminated in this 1944 book. This foundational work contains the method for finding mutually consistent solutions for two-person zero-sum games. During the following time period, work on game theory was primarily focused on cooperative game theory, which analyzes optimal strategies for groups of individuals, presuming that they can enforce agreements between them about proper strategies.

In 1950, the first mathematical discussion of the prisoner's dilemma appeared, and an experiment was undertaken by notable mathematicians Merrill M. Flood and Melvin Dresher, as part of the RAND Corporation's investigations into game theory. RAND pursued the studies because of possible applications to global nuclear strategy. Around this same time, John Nash developed a criterion for mutual consistency of players' strategies, known as Nash equilibrium, applicable to a wider variety of games than the criterion proposed by von Neumann and Morgenstern. This equilibrium is sufficiently general to allow for the analysis of non-cooperative games in addition to cooperative ones.

Game theory experienced a flurry of activity in the 1950s, during which time the concepts of the core, the extensive form game, fictitious play, repeated games, and the Shapley value were developed. In addition, the first applications of game theory to philosophy and political science occurred during this time.

Prize-winning Achievements

In 1965, Reinhard Selten introduced his solution concept of subgame perfect equilibria, which further refined the Nash equilibrium (later he would introduce trembling hand perfection as well). In 1967, John Harsanyi developed the concepts of complete information and Bayesian games. Nash, Selten and Harsanyi became Economics Nobel Laureates in 1994 for their contributions to economic game theory.

In the 1970s, game theory was extensively applied in biology, largely as a result of the work of John Maynard Smith and his evolutionarily stable strategy. In addition, the concepts of correlated equilibrium, trembling hand perfection, and common knowledge were introduced and analyzed.

In 2005, game theorists Thomas Schelling and Robert Aumann followed Nash, Selten and Harsanyi as Nobel Laureates. Schelling worked on dynamic models, early examples of evolutionary game theory. Aumann contributed more to the equilibrium school, introducing an equilibrium coarsening, correlated equilibrium, and developing an extensive formal analysis of the assumption of common knowledge and of its consequences.

In 2007, Leonid Hurwicz, together with Eric Maskin and Roger Myerson, was awarded the Nobel Prize in Economics "for having laid the foundations of mechanism design theory." Myerson's contributions include the notion of proper equilibrium, and an important graduate text: *Game Theory, Analysis of Conflict*. Hurwicz introduced and formalized the concept of incentive compatibility.

In 2012, Alvin E. Roth and Lloyd S. Shapley were awarded the Nobel Prize in Economics "for the theory of stable allocations and the practice of market design" and, in 2014, the Nobel went to game theorist Jean Tirole.

Game Types

Cooperative/Non-cooperative

A game is *cooperative* if the players are able to form binding commitments externally enforced (e.g. through contract law). A game is *non-cooperative* if players cannot form alliances or if all agreements need to be self-enforcing (e.g. through credible threats).

Cooperative games are often analysed through the framework of *cooperative game theory*, which focuses on predicting which coalitions will form, the joint actions that groups take and the resulting collective payoffs. It is opposed to the traditional *non-cooperative game theory* which focuses on predicting individual players' actions and payoffs and analyzing Nash equilibria.

Cooperative game theory provides a high-level approach as it only describes the structure, strategies and payoffs of coalitions, whereas non-cooperative game theory also looks at how bargaining procedures will affect the distribution of payoffs within each coalition. As non-cooperative game theory is more general, cooperative games can be analyzed through the approach of non-cooperative game theory (the converse does not hold) provided that sufficient assumptions are made to encompass all the possible strategies available to players due to the possibility of external enforcement of cooperation. While it would thus be optimal to have all games expressed under a non-cooperative framework, in many instances insufficient information is available to accurately model the formal procedures available to the players during the strategic bargaining process, or the resulting model would be of too high complexity to offer a practical tool in the real world. In such cases, cooperative game theory provides a simplified approach that allows to analyze the game at large without having to make any assumption about bargaining powers.

Symmetric/Asymmetric

	E	F
E	1, 2	0, 0
F	0, 0	1, 2
An asymmetric game		

A symmetric game is a game where the payoffs for playing a particular strategy depend only on the other strategies employed, not on who is playing them. If the identities of the players can be changed without changing the payoff to the strategies, then a game is symmetric. Many of the commonly studied 2×2 games are symmetric. The standard representations of chicken, the prisoner's dilemma, and the stag hunt are all symmetric games. Some scholars would consider certain asymmetric games as examples of these games as well. However, the most common payoffs for each of these games are symmetric.

Most commonly studied asymmetric games are games where there are not identical strategy sets for both players. For instance, the ultimatum game and similarly the dictator game have different strategies for each player. It is possible, however, for a game to have identical strategies for both players, yet be asymmetric. For example, the game pictured to the right is asymmetric despite having identical strategy sets for both players.

Zero-sum/Non-zero-sum

Zero-sum games are a special case of constant-sum games, in which choices by players can neither increase nor decrease the available resources. In zero-sum games the total benefit to all players in the game, for every combination of strategies, always adds to zero (more informally, a player benefits only at the equal expense of others). Poker exemplifies a zero-sum game (ignoring the possibility of the house's cut), because one wins exactly the amount one's opponents lose. Other zero-sum games include matching pennies and most classical board games including Go and chess.

	A	B
A	−1, 1	3, −3
B	0, 0	−2, 2

A zero-sum game

Many games studied by game theorists (including the famed prisoner's dilemma) are non-zero-sum games, because the outcome has net results greater or less than zero. Informally, in non-zero-sum games, a gain by one player does not necessarily correspond with a loss by another.

Constant-sum games correspond to activities like theft and gambling, but not to the fundamental economic situation in which there are potential gains from trade. It is possible to transform any game into a (possibly asymmetric) zero-sum game by adding a dummy player (often called "the board") whose losses compensate the players' net winnings.

Simultaneous/Sequential

Simultaneous games are games where both players move simultaneously, or if they do not move simultaneously, the later players are unaware of the earlier players' actions (making them *effectively* simultaneous). Sequential games (or dynamic games) are games where later players have some knowledge about earlier actions. This need not be perfect information about every action of earlier players; it might be very little knowledge. For instance, a player may know that an earlier player did not perform one particular action, while he does not know which of the other available actions the first player actually performed.

The difference between simultaneous and sequential games is captured in the different representations discussed above. Often, normal form is used to represent simultaneous games, while extensive form is used to represent sequential ones. The transformation of extensive to normal form is one way, meaning that multiple extensive form games correspond to the same normal form. Consequently, notions of equilibrium for simultaneous games are insufficient for reasoning about sequential games; see subgame perfection.

In short, the differences between sequential and simultaneous games are as follows:

	Sequential	**Simultaneous**
Normally denoted by	Decision trees	Payoff matrices
Prior knowledge of opponent's move?	Yes	No
Time axis? Yes No		
Also known as	Extensive-form game Extensive game	Strategy game Strategic game

Perfect Information and Imperfect Information

An important subset of sequential games consists of games of perfect information. A game is one of perfect information if, in extensive form, all players know the moves previously made by all other players. Simultaneous games can not be games of perfect information, because the conversion to extensive form converts simultaneous moves into a sequence of moves with earlier moves being unknown. Most games studied in game theory are imperfect-information games. Interesting examples of perfect-information games include the ultimatum game and centipede game. Recreational games of perfect information games include chess and checkers. Many card games are games of imperfect information, such as poker or contract bridge.

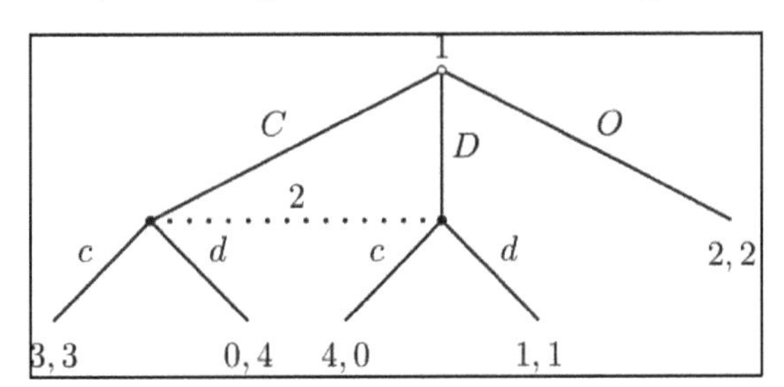

A game of imperfect information (the dotted line represents ignorance on the part of player 2, formally called an information set).

Perfect information is often confused with complete information, which is a similar concept. Complete information requires that every player know the strategies and payoffs available to the other players but not necessarily the actions taken. Games of incomplete information can be reduced, however, to games of imperfect information by introducing "moves by nature".

Combinatorial Games

Games in which the difficulty of finding an optimal strategy stems from the multiplicity of possible moves are called combinatorial games. Examples include chess and go. Games that involve imperfect or incomplete information may also have a strong combinatorial character, for instance backgammon. There is no unified theory addressing combinatorial elements in games. There are, however, mathematical tools that can solve particular problems and answer general questions.

Games of perfect information have been studied in combinatorial game theory, which has developed novel representations, e.g. surreal numbers, as well as combinatorial and algebraic (and sometimes non-constructive) proof methods to solve games of certain types, including "loopy" games that may result in infinitely long sequences of moves. These methods address games with higher combinatorial complexity than those usually considered in traditional (or "economic") game theory. A typical game that has been solved this way is hex. A related field of study, drawing from computational complexity theory, is game complexity, which is concerned with estimating the computational difficulty of finding optimal strategies.

Research in artificial intelligence has addressed both perfect and imperfect (or incomplete) information games that have very complex combinatorial structures (like chess, go, or backgammon) for which no provable optimal strategies have been found. The practical solutions involve computational heuristics, like alpha-beta pruning or use of artificial neural networks trained by reinforcement learning, which make games more tractable in computing practice.

Infinitely Long Games

Games, as studied by economists and real-world game players, are generally finished in finitely many moves. Pure mathematicians are not so constrained, and set theorists in particular study games that last for infinitely many moves, with the winner (or other payoff) not known until *after* all those moves are completed.

The focus of attention is usually not so much on the best way to play such a game, but whether one player has a winning strategy. (It can be proven, using the axiom of choice, that there are games – even with perfect information and where the only outcomes are "win" or "lose" – for which *neither* player has a winning strategy.) The existence of such strategies, for cleverly designed games, has important consequences in descriptive set theory.

Discrete and Continuous Games

Much of game theory is concerned with finite, discrete games, that have a finite number of players, moves, events, outcomes, etc. Many concepts can be extended, however. Continuous games allow players to choose a strategy from a continuous strategy set. For instance, Cournot competition is typically modeled with players' strategies being any non-negative quantities, including fractional quantities.

Differential Games

Differential games such as the continuous pursuit and evasion game are continuous games where the evolution of the players' state variables is governed by differential equations. The problem of finding an optimal strategy in a differential game is closely related to the optimal control theory. In particular, there are two types of strategies: the open-loop strategies are found using the Pontryagin maximum principle while the closed-loop strategies are found using Bellman's Dynamic Programming method.

A particular case of differential games are the games with a random time horizon. In such games, the terminal time is a random variable with a given probability distribution function. Therefore, the players maximize the mathematical expectation of the cost function. It was shown that the modified optimization problem can be reformulated as a discounted differential game over an infinite time interval.

Many-player and Population Games

Games with an arbitrary, but finite, number of players are often called n-person games. Evolutionary game theory considers games involving a population of decision makers, where the frequency with which a particular decision is made can change over time in response to the decisions made by all individuals in the population. In biology, this is intended to model (biological) evolution, where genetically programmed organisms pass along some of their strategy programming to their offspring. In economics, the same theory is intended to capture population changes because people play the game many times within their lifetime, and consciously (and perhaps rationally) switch strategies.

Stochastic Outcomes (and Relation to Other Fields)

Individual decision problems with stochastic outcomes are sometimes considered "one-player games". These situations are not considered game theoretical by some authors.[by whom?] They may be modeled using similar tools within the related disciplines of decision theory, operations research, and areas of artificial intelligence, particularly AI planning (with uncertainty) and multi-agent system. Although these fields may have different motivators, the mathematics involved are substantially the same, e.g. using Markov decision processes (MDP).

Stochastic outcomes can also be modeled in terms of game theory by adding a randomly acting player who makes "chance moves" ("moves by nature"). This player is not typically considered a third player in what is otherwise a two-player game, but merely serves to provide a roll of the dice where required by the game.

For some problems, different approaches to modeling stochastic outcomes may lead to different solutions. For example, the difference in approach between MDPs and the minimax solution is that the latter considers the worst-case over a set of adversarial moves, rather than reasoning in expectation about these moves given a fixed probability distribution. The minimax approach may be advantageous where stochastic models of uncertainty are not available, but may also be overestimating extremely unlikely (but costly) events, dramatically swaying the strategy in such scenarios if it is assumed that an adversary can force such an event to happen. (See Black swan theory for more discussion on this kind of modeling issue, particularly as it relates to predicting and limiting losses in investment banking.)

General models that include all elements of stochastic outcomes, adversaries, and partial or noisy observability (of moves by other players) have also been studied. The "gold standard" is considered to be partially observable stochastic game (POSG), but few realistic problems are computationally feasible in POSG representation.

Metagames

These are games the play of which is the development of the rules for another game, the target or subject game. Metagames seek to maximize the utility value of the rule set developed. The theory of metagames is related to mechanism design theory.

The term metagame analysis is also used to refer to a practical approach developed by Nigel Howard. whereby a situation is framed as a strategic game in which stakeholders try to realise their objectives by means of the options available to them. Subsequent developments have led to the formulation of confrontation analysis.

Pooling Games

These are games prevailing over all forms of society. Pooling games are repeated plays with changing payoff table in general over an experienced path and their equilibrium strategies usually take a form of evolutionary social convention and economic convention. Pooling game theory emerges to formally recognize the interaction between optimal choice in one play and the emergence of forthcoming payoff table update path, identify the invariance existence and robustness, and predict variance over time. The theory is based upon topological transformation classification of payoff table update over time to predict variance and invariance, and is also within the jurisdiction of the computational law of reachable optimality for ordered system.

Representation of Games

The games studied in game theory are well-defined mathematical objects. To be fully defined, a game must specify the following elements: the *players* of the game, the *information* and *actions* available to each player at each decision point, and the *payoffs* for each outcome. (Eric Rasmusen refers to these four "essential elements" by the acronym "PAPI".) A game theorist typically uses these elements, along with a solution concept of their choosing, to deduce a set of equilibrium strategies for each player such that, when these strategies are employed, no player can profit by unilaterally deviating from their strategy. These equilibrium strategies determine an equilibrium to the game—a stable state in which either one outcome occurs or a set of outcomes occur with known probability.

Most cooperative games are presented in the characteristic function form, while the extensive and the normal forms are used to define noncooperative games.

Extensive Form

The extensive form can be used to formalize games with a time sequencing of moves. Games here are played on trees (as pictured here). Here each vertex (or node) represents a point of choice for a player. The player is specified by a number listed by the vertex. The lines out of the vertex represent a possible action for that player. The payoffs are specified at the bottom of the tree. The extensive form can be viewed as a multi-player generalization of a decision tree.

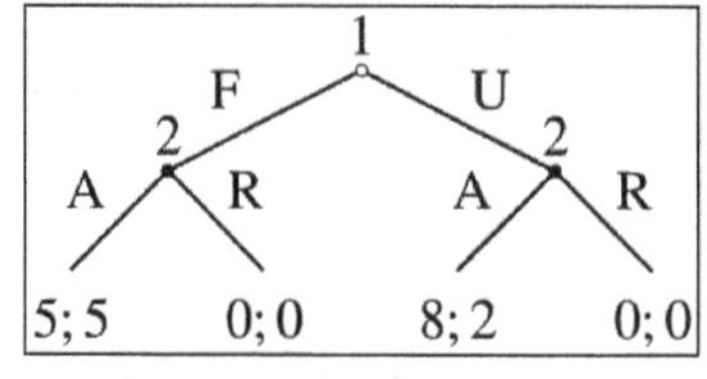

An extensive form game.

The game pictured consists of two players. The way this particular game is structured (i.e., with sequential decision making and perfect information), *Player 1* "moves" first by choosing either *F* or *U* (letters are assigned arbitrarily for mathematical purposes). Next in the sequence, *Player 2*, who has now seen *Player 1's* move, chooses to play either *A* or *R*. Once *Player 2* has made his/ her choice, the game is considered finished and each player gets their respective payoff. Suppose that *Player 1* chooses *U* and then *Player 2* chooses *A*: *Player 1* then gets a payoff of "eight" (which in real-world terms can be interpreted in many ways, the simplest of which is in terms of money but could mean things such as eight days of vacation or eight countries conquered or even eight more opportunities to play the same game against other players) and *Player 2* gets a payoff of "two".

The extensive form can also capture simultaneous-move games and games with imperfect information. To represent it, either a dotted line connects different vertices to represent them as being part of the same information set (i.e. the players do not know at which point they are), or a closed line is drawn around them. (See example in the imperfect information section.)

Normal Form

The normal (or strategic form) game is usually represented by a matrix which shows the players, strategies, and payoffs (see the example to the right). More generally it can be represented by any function that associates a payoff for each player with every possible combination of actions. In the accompanying example there are two players; one chooses the row and the other chooses the column. Each player has two strategies, which are specified by the number of rows and the number of columns. The payoffs are provided in the interior. The first number is the payoff received by the row player (Player 1 in our example); the second is the payoff for the column player (Player 2 in our example). Suppose that Player 1 plays *Up* and that Player 2 plays *Left*. Then Player 1 gets a payoff of 4, and Player 2 gets 3.

	Player 2 chooses *Left*	Player 2 chooses *Right*
Player 1 chooses *Up*	**4, 3**	**−1, −1**
Player 1 chooses *Down*	**0, 0**	**3, 4**
Normal form or payoff matrix of a 2-player, 2-strategy game		

When a game is presented in normal form, it is presumed that each player acts simultaneously or, at least, without knowing the actions of the other. If players have some information about the choices of other players, the game is usually presented in extensive form.

Every extensive-form game has an equivalent normal-form game, however the transformation to normal form may result in an exponential blowup in the size of the representation, making it computationally impractical.

Characteristic Function Form

In games that possess removable utility, separate rewards are not given; rather, the characteristic function decides the payoff of each unity. The idea is that the unity that is 'empty', so to speak, does not receive a reward at all.

The origin of this form is to be found in John von Neumann and Oskar Morgenstern's book; when looking at these instances, they guessed that when a union **C** appears, it works against the fraction $\left(\frac{\mathbf{N}}{\mathbf{C}}\right)$ as if two individuals were playing a normal game. The balanced payoff of C is a basic function. Although there are differing examples that help determine coalitional amounts from normal games, not all appear that in their function form can be derived from such.

Formally, a characteristic function is seen as: (N,v), where N represents the group of people and $v: 2^N \rightarrow \mathbf{R}$ is a normal utility.
Such characteristic functions have expanded to describe games where there is no removable utility.

General and Applied Uses

As a method of applied mathematics, game theory has been used to study a wide variety of human and animal behaviors. It was initially developed in economics to understand a large collection of economic behaviors, including behaviors of firms, markets, and consumers. The first use of game-theoretic analysis was by Antoine Augustin Cournot in 1838 with his solution of the Cournot duopoly. The use of game theory in the social sciences has expanded, and game theory has been applied to political, sociological, and psychological behaviors as well.

Although pre-twentieth century naturalists such as Charles Darwin made game-theoretic kinds of statements, the use of game-theoretic analysis in biology began with Ronald Fisher's studies of animal behavior during the 1930s. This work predates the name "game theory", but it shares many important features with this field. The developments in economics were later applied to biology largely by John Maynard Smith in his book *Evolution and the Theory of Games.*

In addition to being used to describe, predict, and explain behavior, game theory has also been used to develop theories of ethical or normative behavior and to prescribe such behavior. In economics and philosophy, scholars have applied game theory to help in the understanding of good or proper behavior. Game-theoretic arguments of this type can be found as far back as Plato.

Description and Modeling

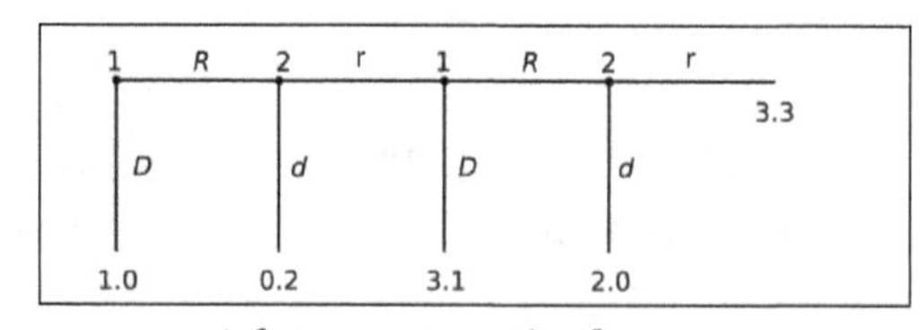

A four-stage centipede game.

The primary use of game theory is to describe and model how human populations behave. Some scholars believe that by finding the equilibria of games they can predict how actual human populations will behave when confronted with situations analogous to the game being studied. This particular view of game theory has been criticized. It is argued that the assumptions made by game theorists are often violated when applied to real world situations. Game theorists usually assume players act rationally, but in practice, human behavior often deviates from this model. Game theorists respond by comparing their assumptions to those used in physics. Thus while their assumptions do not always hold, they can treat game theory as a reasonable scientific ideal akin to the models used by physicists. However, empirical work has shown that in some classic games, such as the centipede game, guess 2/3 of the average game, and the dictator game, people regularly do not play Nash equilibria. There is an ongoing debate regarding the importance of these experiments and whether the analysis of the experiments fully captures all aspects of the relevant situation.

Some game theorists, following the work of John Maynard Smith and George R. Price, have turned to evolutionary game theory in order to resolve these issues. These models presume either no rationality or bounded rationality on the part of players. Despite the name, evolutionary game theory does not necessarily presume natural selection in the biological sense. Evolutionary game theory includes both biological as well as cultural evolution and also models of individual learning (for example, fictitious play dynamics).

Prescriptive or Normative Analysis

Some scholars, like Leonard Savage, see game theory not as a predictive tool for the behavior of human beings, but as a suggestion for how people ought to behave. Since a strategy, corresponding to a Nash equilibrium of a game constitutes one's best response to the actions of the other players – provided they are in (the same) Nash equilibrium – playing a strategy that is part of a Nash equilibrium seems appropriate. This normative use of game theory has also come under criticism.

	Cooperate	Defect
Cooperate	-1, -1	-10, 0
Defect	0, -10	-5, -5

The Prisoner's Dilemma

Economics and Business

Game theory is a major method used in mathematical economics and business for modeling competing behaviors of interacting agents. Applications include a wide array of economic phenomena and approaches, such as auctions, bargaining, mergers & acquisitions pricing, fair division, duopolies, oligopolies, social network formation, agent-based computational economics, general equilibrium, mechanism design, and voting systems; and across such broad areas as experimental economics, behavioral economics, information economics, industrial organization, and political economy.

This research usually focuses on particular sets of strategies known as "solution concepts" or "equilibria". A common assumption is that players act rationally. In non-cooperative games, the most famous of these is the Nash equilibrium. A set of strategies is a Nash equilibrium if each represents a best response to the other strategies. If all the players are playing the strategies in a Nash equilibrium, they have no unilateral incentive to deviate, since their strategy is the best they can do given what others are doing.

The payoffs of the game are generally taken to represent the utility of individual players.

A prototypical paper on game theory in economics begins by presenting a game that is an abstraction of a particular economic situation. One or more solution concepts are chosen, and the author demonstrates which strategy sets in the presented game are equilibria of the appropriate type. Naturally one might wonder to what use this information should be put. Economists and business professors suggest two primary uses (noted above): *descriptive* and *prescriptive*.

Political Science

The application of game theory to political science is focused in the overlapping areas of fair division, political economy, public choice, war bargaining, positive political theory, and social choice theory. In each of these areas, researchers have developed game-theoretic models in which the players are often voters, states, special interest groups, and politicians.

Early examples of game theory applied to political science are provided by Anthony Downs. In his book *An Economic Theory of Democracy*, he applies the Hotelling firm location model to the political process. In the Downsian model, political candidates commit to ideologies on a one-dimensional policy space. Downs first shows how the political candidates will converge to the ideology preferred by the median voter if voters are fully informed, but then argues that voters choose to remain rationally ignorant which allows for candidate divergence. Game Theory was applied in 1962 to the Cuban missile crisis during the presidency of John F. Kennedy.

It has also been proposed that game theory explains the stability of any form of political government. Taking the simplest case of a monarchy, for example, the king, being only one person, does not and cannot maintain his authority by personally exercising physical control over all or even any significant number of his subjects. Sovereign control is instead explained by the recognition by each citizen that all other citizens expect each other to view the king (or other established government) as the person whose orders will be followed. Coordinating communication among citizens to replace the sovereign is effectively barred, since conspiracy to replace the sovereign is generally punishable as a crime. Thus, in a process that can be modeled by variants of the prisoner's dilemma, during periods of stability no citizen will find it rational to move to replace the sovereign, even if all the citizens know they would be better off if they were all to act collectively.

A game-theoretic explanation for democratic peace is that public and open debate in democracies send clear and reliable information regarding their intentions to other states. In contrast, it is difficult to know the intentions of nondemocratic leaders, what effect concessions will have, and if promises will be kept. Thus there will be mistrust and unwillingness to make concessions if at least one of the parties in a dispute is a non-democracy.

Game theory could also help predict a nation's responses when there is a new rule or law to be applied to that nation. One example would be Peter John Wood's (2013) research when he looked into what nations could do to help reduce climate change. Wood thought this could be accomplished by making treaties with other nations to reduce green house gas emissions. However, he concluded that this idea could not work because it would create a prisoner's dilemma to the nations.

Biology

Unlike those in economics, the payoffs for games in biology are often interpreted as corresponding to fitness. In addition, the focus has been less on equilibria that correspond to a notion of rationality and more on ones that would be maintained by evolutionary forces. The best known equilibrium in biology is known as the *evolutionarily stable strategy* (ESS), first introduced in (Smith & Price 1973). Although its initial motivation did not involve any of the mental requirements of the Nash equilibrium, every ESS is a Nash equilibrium.

	Hawk	Dove
Hawk	20, 20	80, 40
Dove	40, 80	60, 60
The hawk-dove game		

In biology, game theory has been used as a model to understand many different phenomena. It was first used to explain the evolution (and stability) of the approximate 1:1 sex ratios. (Fisher 1930) suggested that the 1:1 sex ratios are a result of evolutionary forces acting on individuals who could be seen as trying to maximize their number of grandchildren.

Additionally, biologists have used evolutionary game theory and the ESS to explain the emergence of animal communication. The analysis of signaling games and other communication games has provided insight into the evolution of communication among animals. For example, the mobbing behavior of many species, in which a large number of prey animals attack a larger predator, seems to be an example of spontaneous emergent organization. Ants have also been shown to exhibit feed-forward behavior akin to fashion (see Paul Ormerod's *Butterfly Economics*).

Biologists have used the game of chicken to analyze fighting behavior and territoriality.

According to Maynard Smith, in the preface to *Evolution and the Theory of Games*, "paradoxically, it has turned out that game theory is more readily applied to biology than to the field of economic behaviour for which it was originally designed". Evolutionary game theory has been used to explain many seemingly incongruous phenomena in nature.

One such phenomenon is known as biological altruism. This is a situation in which an organism appears to act in a way that benefits other organisms and is detrimental to itself. This is distinct from traditional notions of altruism because such actions are not conscious, but appear to be evolutionary adaptations to increase overall fitness. Examples can be found in species ranging from vampire bats that regurgitate blood they have obtained from a night's hunting and give it to group members who have failed to feed, to worker bees that care for the queen bee for their entire lives and never mate, to vervet monkeys that warn group members of a predator's approach, even when it endangers that individual's chance of survival. All of these actions increase the overall fitness of a group, but occur at a cost to the individual.

Evolutionary game theory explains this altruism with the idea of kin selection. Altruists discriminate between the individuals they help and favor relatives. Hamilton's rule explains the evolutionary rationale behind this selection with the equation $c<b*r$ where the cost (c) to the altruist must be less than the benefit (b) to the recipient multiplied by the coefficient of relatedness (r). The more closely related two organisms are causes the incidences of altruism to increase because they share many of the same alleles. This means that the altruistic individual, by ensuring that the alleles of its close relative are passed on, (through survival of its offspring) can forgo the option of having offspring itself because the same number of alleles are passed on. Helping a sibling for example (in diploid animals), has a coefficient of ½, because (on average) an individual shares

½ of the alleles in its sibling's offspring. Ensuring that enough of a sibling's offspring survive to adulthood precludes the necessity of the altruistic individual producing offspring. The coefficient values depend heavily on the scope of the playing field; for example if the choice of whom to favor includes all genetic living things, not just all relatives, we assume the discrepancy between all humans only accounts for approximately 1% of the diversity in the playing field, a co-efficient that was ½ in the smaller field becomes 0.995. Similarly if it is considered that information other than that of a genetic nature (e.g. epigenetics, religion, science, etc.) persisted through time the playing field becomes larger still, and the discrepancies smaller.

Computer Science and Logic

Game theory has come to play an increasingly important role in logic and in computer science. Several logical theories have a basis in game semantics. In addition, computer scientists have used games to model interactive computations. Also, game theory provides a theoretical basis to the field of multi-agent systems.

Separately, game theory has played a role in online algorithms; in particular, the k-server problem, which has in the past been referred to as *games with moving costs* and *request-answer games.* Yao's principle is a game-theoretic technique for proving lower bounds on the computational complexity of randomized algorithms, especially online algorithms.

The emergence of the internet has motivated the development of algorithms for finding equilibria in games, markets, computational auctions, peer-to-peer systems, and security and information markets. Algorithmic game theory and within it algorithmic mechanism design combine computational algorithm design and analysis of complex systems with economic theory.

Philosophy

Game theory has been put to several uses in philosophy. Responding to two papers by W.V.O. Quine (1960, 1967), Lewis (1969) used game theory to develop a philosophical account of convention. In so doing, he provided the first analysis of common knowledge and employed it in analyzing play in coordination games. In addition, he first suggested that one can understand meaning in terms of signaling games. This later suggestion has been pursued by several philosophers since Lewis. Following Lewis (1969) game-theoretic account of conventions, Edna Ullmann-Margalit (1977) and Bicchieri (2006) have developed theories of social norms that define them as Nash equilibria that result from transforming a mixed-motive game into a coordination game.

	Stag	Hare
Stag	3, 3	0, 2
Hare	2, 0	2, 2
	Stag hunt	

Game theory has also challenged philosophers to think in terms of interactive epistemology: what it means for a collective to have common beliefs or knowledge, and what are the consequences of this knowledge for the social outcomes resulting from agents' interactions. Philosophers who have worked in this area include Bicchieri (1989, 1993), Skyrms (1990), and Stalnaker (1999).

In ethics, some authors have attempted to pursue Thomas Hobbes' project of deriving morality from self-interest. Since games like the prisoner's dilemma present an apparent conflict between morality and self-interest, explaining why cooperation is required by self-interest is an important component of this project. This general strategy is a component of the general social contract view in political philosophy (for examples, see Gauthier (1986) and Kavka (1986)).

Other authors have attempted to use evolutionary game theory in order to explain the emergence of human attitudes about morality and corresponding animal behaviors. These authors look at several games including the prisoner's dilemma, stag hunt, and the Nash bargaining game as providing an explanation for the emergence of attitudes about morality (see, e.g., Skyrms (1996, 2004) and Sober and Wilson (1999)).

In Popular Culture

Based on the book by Sylvia Nasar, the life story of game theorist and mathematician John Nash was turned into the biopic *A Beautiful Mind* starring Russell Crowe.

"Games theory" and "theory of games" are mentioned in the military science fiction novel *Starship Troopers* by Robert A. Heinlein. In the 1997 film of the same name, the character Carl Jenkins refers to his assignment to military intelligence as to "games and theory."

The film *Dr. Strangelove* satirizes game theoretic ideas about deterrence theory. For example, nuclear deterrence depends on the threat to retaliate catastrophically if a nuclear attack is detected. A game theorist might argue that such threats can fail to be *credible*, in the sense that they can lead to subgame imperfect equilibria. The movie takes this idea one step further, with the Russians irrevocably committing to a catastrophic nuclear response without making the threat public.

Liar Game is a popular Japanese Manga, television program and movie, where each episode presents the main characters with a Game Theory type game. The show's supporting characters reflect and explore game theory's predictions around self-preservation strategies used in each challenge. The main character however, who is portrayed as an innocent, naive and good hearted young lady Kansaki Nao, always attempts to convince the other players to follow a mutually beneficial strategy where everybody wins. Kansaki Nao's seemingly simple strategies that appear to be the product of her innocent good nature actually represent optimal equilibrium solutions which Game Theory attempts to solve. Other players however, usually use her naivety against her to follow strategies that serve self-preservation. The show improvises heavily on Game Theory predictions and strategies to provide each episode's script, the players decisions. In a sense, each episode exhibits a Game Theory game and the strategies/ equilibria/ solutions provide the script which is coloured in by the actors.

References

- Jörg Bewersdorff (2005), Luck, logic, and white lies: the mathematics of games, A K Peters, Ltd., pp. ix–xii and chapter 31, ISBN 978-1-56881-210-6
- Albert, Michael H.; Nowakowski, Richard J.; Wolfe, David (2007), Lessons in Play: In Introduction to Combinatorial Game Theory, A K Peters Ltd, pp. 3–4, ISBN 978-1-56881-277-9
- Bicchieri, C. (2006), The Grammar of Society: the Nature and Dynamics of Social Norms, Cambridge University Press, ISBN 0521573726

- Russell, Stuart J.; Norvig, Peter (2003). Artificial Intelligence: A Modern Approach (2nd ed.). Upper Saddle River, New Jersey: Prentice Hall. ISBN 0-13-790395-2
- National Research Council (1999). "Developments in Artificial Intelligence". Funding a Revolution: Government Support for Computing Research. National Academy Press. ISBN 0-309-06278-0. OCLC 246584055
- Crane, Carl D.; Joseph Duffy (1998). Kinematic Analysis of Robot Manipulators. Cambridge University Press. ISBN 0-521-57063-8. Retrieved 2007-10-16
- "Focal Points Seminar on review articles in the future of work - Safety and health at work - EU-OSHA". osha.europa.eu. Retrieved 2016-04-19

Permissions

All chapters in this book are published with permission under the Creative Commons Attribution Share Alike License or equivalent. Every chapter published in this book has been scrutinized by our experts. Their significance has been extensively debated. The topics covered herein carry significant information for a comprehensive understanding. They may even be implemented as practical applications or may be referred to as a beginning point for further studies.

We would like to thank the editorial team for lending their expertise to make the book truly unique. They have played a crucial role in the development of this book. Without their invaluable contributions this book wouldn't have been possible. They have made vital efforts to compile up to date information on the varied aspects of this subject to make this book a valuable addition to the collection of many professionals and students.

This book was conceptualized with the vision of imparting up-to-date and integrated information in this field. To ensure the same, a matchless editorial board was set up. Every individual on the board went through rigorous rounds of assessment to prove their worth. After which they invested a large part of their time researching and compiling the most relevant data for our readers.

The editorial board has been involved in producing this book since its inception. They have spent rigorous hours researching and exploring the diverse topics which have resulted in the successful publishing of this book. They have passed on their knowledge of decades through this book. To expedite this challenging task, the publisher supported the team at every step. A small team of assistant editors was also appointed to further simplify the editing procedure and attain best results for the readers.

Apart from the editorial board, the designing team has also invested a significant amount of their time in understanding the subject and creating the most relevant covers. They scrutinized every image to scout for the most suitable representation of the subject and create an appropriate cover for the book.

The publishing team has been an ardent support to the editorial, designing and production team. Their endless efforts to recruit the best for this project, has resulted in the accomplishment of this book. They are a veteran in the field of academics and their pool of knowledge is as vast as their experience in printing. Their expertise and guidance has proved useful at every step. Their uncompromising quality standards have made this book an exceptional effort. Their encouragement from time to time has been an inspiration for everyone.

The publisher and the editorial board hope that this book will prove to be a valuable piece of knowledge for students, practitioners and scholars across the globe.

Index

Printed in the USA
CPSIA information can be obtained
at www.ICGtesting.com
JSHW052019301024
72690JS00004B/116

9 781639 890620